VISIONS OF A BETTER WORLD

VISIONS OF A BETTER WORLD

Howard Thurman's Pilgrimage to India
and the Origins of African American Nonviolence

QUINTON H. DIXIE

&

PETER EISENSTADT

DISCARD

BEACON PRESS, BOSTON

Beacon Press

25 Beacon Street

Boston, Massachusetts 02108-2892

www.beacon.org

Beacon Press books
are published under the auspices of
the Unitarian Universalist Association of Congregations.

14 13 12 11   8 7 6 5 4 3 2 1

This book is printed on acid-free paper that meets the uncoated paper
ANSI/NISO specifications for permanence as revised in 1992.

Text design by Wilsted & Taylor Publishing Services

Library of Congress Cataloging-in-Publication Data
Dixie, Quinton Hosford.
Visions of a better world : Howard Thurman's pilgrimage to India and the origins
of African American nonviolence / Quinton Dixie & Peter Eisenstadt.
p. cm.
Includes bibliographical references and index.
ISBN 978-0-8070-0045-8 (hardcover : acid-free paper) 1. Thurman, Howard,
1899–1981—Travel—India. 2. Christian pilgrims and pilgrimages—India—
History—20th century. 3. Thurman, Howard, 1899–1981—Political and social
views. 4. Nonviolence—Political aspects—History—20th century.
5. Nonviolence—Religious aspects—Christianity. 6. African American
theologians—Biography. 7. African American Baptists—Biography. 8. African
American pacifists—Biography. 9. African Americans—Civil rights—History—
20th century. 10. Civil rights—United States—Philosophy—History—
20th century. I. Eisenstadt, Peter R., 1954– II. Title.
BX6495.T53D49 2011
280'.4092—dc22
2010047377

[B]

CONTENTS

Foreword

We need a moral prophetic minority of all colors who muster the courage to question the powers that be, the courage to be impatient with evil and patient with people, and the courage to fight for social justice. Such courage rests on a deep democratic vision of a better world that lures us and a blood-drenched hope that sustains us.

—CORNEL WEST

ONE OF THE MANY challenges of directing a publishing project like the Howard Thurman Papers Project is the problem of too much data. In most respects it is a good problem to have. At the same time, the practical concerns of modern publishing render it impossible to make available to the masses all the information one is able to gather about the subject. Moreover, there are always themes and stories that don't make it into the volumes or portraits of a person that cry out for more light. In *Visions of a Better World*, Quinton Dixie and Peter Eisenstadt shed additional light on a pivotal moment in the life of Howard Thurman—his pilgrimage to India, Burma, and Ceylon in 1935 and 1936. Anyone who knows anything about Thurman is aware of the journey, but few people know the breadth of the trip and the depth of its impact on him. The image of Howard Thurman embedded in the public consciousness is that of a wise, introspective mystic concerned with maximizing his individual spiritual assets. What Dixie and Eisenstadt have been able to show is a courageous and radical Thurman. Indeed, during the 1930s and 1940s he was a radical pacifist, a radical integrationist, and a radical follower of Jesus. All this culminated in his commitment to social justice through nonviolent, noncooperation with evil.

———

Nonviolence, a term popularized and probably coined by Gandhi, has gone by many names: direct action, civil disobedience, passive resistance, satyagraha, ahimsa, and many others in many different lands. Its American history, prior to Gandhi, was already extensive. Perhaps the original pioneers of nonviolent resistance, at least as a conscious political tactic, were American abolitionists such as William Lloyd Garrison and Henry David Thoreau, who (via Tolstoy) were both major influences on Gandhi's early thinking. African Americans, in the abolitionist movement, in bondage, and after emancipation, regularly used civil disobedience as a tactic to make their lives endurable. For Thurman, the Negro spirituals were an unparalleled record of the various ways in which enslaved African Americans used religion to find the courage to resist their masters, knowing that challenges to their dominance could have fatal consequences. "In God's presence," Thurman would write of the message of the spirituals, "there would be freedom; slavery is no part of the purpose or the plan of God." Rosa Parks's challenge to segregated public transportation had many forerunners, among them Frederick Douglass, dating back to the antebellum period. The tactic of challenging segregation in public entertainment by small integrated groups demanding their collective admission dates back to approximately 1910.

But Gandhi's example transformed nonviolence from an occasional tactic into a political philosophy, a religious belief, and a way of life. American admirers of Gandhi, black and white, started to proliferate during the interwar years. Among those who fell within the ambit of Gandhi and his ideals was Howard Thurman. From his undergraduate days at Morehouse College in Atlanta in the early 1920s, he was a member of the premier Christian pacifist organization in the country, the Fellowship of Reconciliation. He soon became its most prominent African American member. If Thurman was opposed to militarism and foreign wars, the core of his pacifism was always an opposition to the violence inherent in racial oppression at home. This was the subject of an important article by Thurman written as early as 1929, one of the first by a black author to explicitly link nonviolent resistance to the struggle against Jim Crow.

Visions of a Better World places Thurman where he properly belongs—at the beginning of the African American conversation about nonviolence and social change. His vision was deeply rooted in his sense of what was possible in a society that chose to live out its democratic ideals. And it was grounded in the hope of a people who had suffered for righteousness' sake. Inspired by what he learned in India, Thurman went on to provide the spiritual blueprint for the civil rights movement.

WALTER EARL FLUKER
Boston, Massachusetts

Introduction

LONG BEFORE THE TWO men met, long before he had any in-
kling that a meeting would ever be possible, Howard Thurman had
been preparing for an encounter with Mohandas K. (Mahatma) Gandhi. When the meeting took place, in early 1936, Thurman and his
colleagues would be the first African Americans to meet with the famous leader of the Indian independence movement. Thurman's time
in India was less a transformation than a confirmation of what had
long been his core belief: Christianity, as it had been traditionally
practiced, was incapable of taking on the greatest challenge of the
day, social and racial inequality. Howard Thurman was never a fire-
brand, and to some, who did not pay close attention to his message, he
seemed to be an otherworldly mystic with little time to spare for any
down-to-earth realities, including the practical politics of American
minorities fighting for their civil rights. But for those who listened
carefully, including many in the rising generation of African American leaders in the 1930s and 1940s, among them James Farmer, Pauli
Murray, and Martin Luther King Jr., they heard a call for a new
Christianity—one without dogmas, dedicated to the principles of
pacifism and nonviolence, and utterly committed to the task of eradi-
cating Jim Crow in all its varieties and manifestations. It is true that
Thurman was never primarily a writer or speaker on political topics.
But in his public appearances, articles, and teaching in the 1930s and
1940s, and both in his own right and through his broader contagion,
he was one of the creators of a distinctly African American path to
radical Christian nonviolence.

On October 21, 1935, Howard Thurman reached Ceylon's major
port and capital city, Colombo. When Thurman arrived in Colombo

he had been traveling by rail and boat for a month, since he and his party had left New York Harbor.[1] He was in Ceylon as chair of the four-person Negro Delegation, undertaking a "Pilgrimage of Friendship" to South Asia on the behest of the Student Christian Movement in the United States (basically an alliance between the YMCA and the YWCA), and its Asian counterpart, the Student Christian Movement of India, Ceylon, and Burma. He was accompanied by the other members of the delegation: his wife, Sue Bailey Thurman, and another couple, Edward and Phenola Carroll. The delegation would remain in South Asia for a hectic four months, crisscrossing India (including stops in what is now Pakistan) and visiting Ceylon (now Sri Lanka) and Burma (now Myanmar).[2] Their path would take them from the subtropical waters of the Indian Ocean to the wintry foothills of the Himalayas, from the Khyber Pass on the Indian border with Afghanistan to the Irrawaddy Delta in Southeast Asia. They would visit fifty cities, and Thurman, who took the lion's share of the speaking engagements, would make at least 135 appearances, on occasions ranging from small, intimate gatherings to mass meetings.[3] They would meet with thousands of people, among them the two most famous Indians of the time. In his ashram (which doubled as one of India's most distinguished institutes of higher learning) the delegation would meet with the poet and educator Rabindranath Tagore. And early one morning in a little town in outside Bombay, they would become the first African Americans to meet with Mahatma Gandhi, who, at the end of their meeting, imparted the famous message that "it may be through the Negroes that the unadulterated message of nonviolence will be delivered to the world."[4] The time Thurman spent in India would be a turning point in his life and a watershed in the gathering struggle of African Americans for racial equality.

At the time of his arrival in Ceylon, Thurman was thirty-five years old. He was an ordained Baptist minister and a professor of religion at Howard University, where he led the weekly services at Howard's Rankin Chapel. If Thurman was, as one of the organizers of the Pilgrimage of Friendship remarked, somewhat long in the tooth to be a "student" Christian, there was no doubt that he was already acclaimed as one of the leading young ministers of his generation and a man who had already amassed a considerable reputation as a preacher and religious thinker, before audiences both white and black.[5] He was, the organizers of the Negro Delegation thought, the perfect person to bring the message of American Christianity to India.

The delegation was in India at the request of the head of the Student Christian Movement in India, Ceylon, and Burma: Augustine Ralla Ram. Ralla Ram had wanted a delegation of Negroes to visit because he felt they could relate better and would be more fully accepted than the white missionaries who comprised the vast majority of the overseas Christians coming to India. Unlike most of their predecessors, the Negro Delegation was not coming to India as evangelists, as would-be savers of souls, or as bringers of Christ to India. (Thurman found it typical of Western pretensions that most missionaries ignored the fact that Christianity had been in India since about the third century CE, long before any Angles or Saxons had adopted the new faith.[6]) Rather than proselytize or in any conventional way preach the gospel, the Negro Delegation was in Asia to represent one version, their version, of African American Christianity to an Asian audience and to present the complexities of being black and Christian in 1930s America. How this would be received, how the members of the Negro Delegation would meet or disappoint expectations, they were about to find out.

The first moments in Ceylon were not promising, as the delegation had their initial tangle with British officialdom. The customs officials wanted to hold on to their passports until they provided the address at which they would be staying in Colombo (which they didn't know) and until they were met by their local hosts (which Thurman, not very impressed with the competence of the committee in New York City that had made the arrangements, did not think would happen in a timely fashion). But they were eventually met by a local committee, and, passports in hand, were allowed to disembark. "With this," Thurman noted with some relief in his journal, "I turned away ending my first contact with B.G. [British Government]." It would be the first of many. Thurman was warned the next day, before their initial press conference—and they had been coached on this point long before they left the United States—"Do not say anything to offend the white man lest our journey be cut off before it started."[7] The delegation had developed careful rules about what to say and where to say it, with the certainty (at times confirmed) that they were under a constant, if generally discreet, surveillance.

But what was most striking about Colombo was how un-British it was. Once in Colombo, Thurman would write in his autobiography, he entered "a totally new world." He was entranced by the "strangeness of the dress, the unfamiliar language," the new smells and the new food, which he found uncomfortably spicy.[8] Although the tour was planned to coincide with the end of the summer monsoons and the coolest months of the year, the climate remained humid and the weather subtropical. Thurman was a scion of the pre-air-conditioned South, but he nonetheless found Ceylon's weather so "enervating" that it "took an act of will" for him to "prepare for the day." He learned to start every day by carefully unwrapping his mosquito netting and gingerly watching his footfalls lest he step on an unsuspecting scorpion or cobra.[9] (He also, like many new visitors to Asia from the United States, had to experiment with the squat privies, which he deemed "a much more rational and natural arrangement" than the American toilet.[10])

But above all he was fascinated by the Ceylonese. Everyone around him had dark skin, some as dark as his own deep-brown complexion. "The dominant complexions all around were shades of brown, from light to very dark." All around "were the many unmistakable signs that this was *their* country, their land. The Britishers, despite their authority, were outsiders." And yet they ruled the country. This was the paradox of imperialism. For all their power, the British would always remain outsiders and unwanted intruders. And for all their powerlessness, the native inhabitants of Ceylon knew it was their country.[11]

Thurman's perception of the complexities of racial difference, always acute, was heightened during his time in Asia, because he knew he was dealing with a racial world both like and unlike that with which he was familiar. It was unfamiliar in that Thurman suddenly had vaulted to the top of the racial hierarchy, with all the privileges accorded Europeans and other Westerners in British Asia: first-class train compartments, entrance to European-only waiting rooms, and a servile class to attend to his comforts.[12] And of course it was familiar because there were the usual vast differences between the powerful and the powerless, with the gulf, if anything, wider than what he was used to at home. He found this very strange and uncomfortable. He found the Europeans on the whole to have a profound disregard for the personality of native people. "Servants were everywhere" and everywhere degraded, he wrote in his Colombo journal.[13] He remembered having dinner with an eminent academic in Colombo, who "was making a crucial point to me and was frustrated because he had to pay attention to boning the fish on his plate. In disgust he put down his fork and fish knife and yelled, 'Boy—come bone this fish!' Shades of the United States."[14]

What was also familiar to Thurman was the experience of some whites not quite hearing what he had to say. He started his first full day in Colombo being interviewed by local reporters, and, following the warnings against opining on local politics, he spoke instead on conditions in the United States. He was rather upset with the result, feeling the main topic of concern to the local press was the boxer Joe Louis and his supposedly comical gormandizing and sartorial style. Thurman tried to convey a sense of the ferment rippling through contemporary black America, and he was dismayed that the reporters were primarily interested in blacks who seemed to embody fading ideals of racial subservience and deference. "They wanted to know about Negroes who had achieved things in life—I mentioned several but true to the mentality of the white world they did mention only Booker T. [Washington] & [George Washington] Carver."[15]

Although being for the first time in his life in a place where people of color were the overwhelming majority was remarkable, perhaps the most novel aspect of Colombo for Thurman was that he was in a country where Christianity was not the dominant religion. Thurman would spend much of the next four months comparing Christianity with the three great religions that dominated South Asia: Buddhism,

Hinduism, and Islam. The comparisons were often not flattering to Christianity. That first morning he was taken to see Buddhist and Hindu temples and an old Dutch church. He was impressed by the Buddhist temple, and the Hindu building "was not very clean but there was present a strange kind of serenity." The Dutch church, on the other hand, "was severe, stolid, cold" and did not "stir a single emotion related to worship or religion in my own mind or heart." At the local branch of the Student Christian Movement he heard a lecture by a local minister on Christianity in Ceylon—"of course he meant Protestant Christianity"—which struck Thurman as narrowly European in its condescension to the native population, and Thurman was "not impressed with him or with what he said."[16]

If anything Thurman was even more upset by a worship service led by a native Ceylonese student at the YMCA. "He was Pentecostal in his emphasis and said that the second coming of Christ was universal because he had come in fulfillment of the word, thus before the end of time the gospel would be preached to all people. It was a wretched disappointment and I saw trouble ahead if there were many like him ahead. I appreciated his seriousness but it was all so sad because he had been completely duped."[17] Thurman's first days in Colombo were spent observing the limitations of official Christianity in Asia, an exotic implant that seemed jarringly out of place, and an institution used by European and natives alike not as a means to greater spiritual insight but as a crutch for unexamined dogmatism. "On the whole," Thurman wrote, with experience of official Christianity in mind, "the days in Colombo were not very satisfying."[18]

Perhaps not, but they were certainly very interesting, and the most memorable moment occurred almost at the beginning of his stay, probably on his first full night in Asia, when Thurman was asked to speak before a meeting of the law students at the University of Colombo.[19] His encounter that evening would be the most vivid of his meetings in Colombo, and in some ways it would provide the framework for the remainder of his time in Asia, and indeed, in many ways, for the rest of his career. There probably was no single incident in his life that Thurman would write or speak about more frequently than his conversation that evening with an anonymous Ceylonese lawyer. He first did so less than a week after it happened while the delegation was still in Colombo.[20]

Although in his many tellings of this tale he would elaborate it differently each time, the basic story always remained the same. Thurman had been asked to speak on "aspects of the Racial Parity in America."[21] As a rule, Thurman did not speak about race relations, at least in such bald sociological terms. It was not, he felt, what he did best, and Thurman found it faintly patronizing that race seemed to be the only topic that whites wanted to hear blacks speak about, as if they were fit to speak on nothing else but some aspect of the "Negro Question." For Thurman, to speak about race before predominantly white audiences perhaps smacked too much of the hypocrisies of a revival meeting, the preacher ritually invoking the hellfire and brimstone of racial oppression, the cowed listeners making skin-deep and insincere confessions of sins before quickly returning to their old ways.

But in October 1935, Thurman was of course not addressing white audiences in the United States but Asians in Ceylon who were genuinely interested in getting accurate information about race in the United States and were not complicit in the system of racial discrimination they were asking Thurman to discuss. Despite his professions of being incapable of giving talks on current affairs, the sort filled with statistics and acute political observations, Thurman was a very close student of all aspects of American race relations and had prepared extensively for just such meetings before going to India, intensely studying race and politics in both America and Asia and speaking to many experts in the field. He probably gave more explicitly political talks while in Asia than at any other time in his career.

The interest in Thurman's talk at the Law Club at the University of Colombo was, he noted, "most keen," and the attentive listening of the audience was followed by many pertinent and sharp questions.[22] They asked Thurman if it made "any difference in race feeling on the part of white Americans when Negroes become Christians," and they queried why the federal government was powerless to enforce the Fifteenth Amendment, guaranteeing all citizens the right to vote.[23] Thurman was fascinated to discover that his audience "knew all about Scotts-boro," the international cause célèbre arising from nine teenage blacks arrested on spurious rape charges in Scottsboro, Alabama, in 1931. He was asked very specific questions about it, such as the implications of the recent U.S. Supreme Court case *Norris v. Alabama*, decided in the spring of 1935, which held that the systematic exclusion of African Americans from juries constituted a violation of the Fourteenth Amendment.[24]

When the hour was up Thurman was invited downstairs for some coffee and further discussion in a more informal setting. He was somewhat inconsistent about who had invited him, sometimes describing him as a law student, sometimes as a lawyer, and sometimes as principal of the law college.[25] He is at times described as a Hindu, which might mean that he was a member of Ceylon's Tamil minority in the predominantly Sinhalese and Buddhist city of Colombo.[26] Whomever he was, he was certainly not a Christian, though he knew a lot about Christianity, in part, presumably, from it being force-fed him in the Christian schools that were just about the only way in British Asia for a native to receive a Western education.

He got right to the point. "What are you doing here?" he asked. Thurman, startled, asked him what he meant. He repeated the question. "What are you doing here?" He told Thurman that he knew about the publicity surrounding the Negro Delegation, and how it was a pilgrimage of friendship from the students of the United States to the students in India, Ceylon, and Burma. "But what, really," he wanted to know, "are you doing here?"[27]

He told Thurman that he hadn't planned on speaking to him, assuming that it would be a waste of his time. He had thought that Thurman would be a mere mouthpiece, a flunkey and messenger boy for Western Christianity, and that his answers would be bland and evasive. But instead, Thurman seemed to be bright and politically aware, fully alert to the depth of the problem of racial oppression in the United States, and not to be offering any easy solutions. This only made it worse. "I think that an intelligent young man such as yourself, here in our country on a Christian enterprise, is a traitor to all of the darker peoples of the earth. How can you account for yourself being in this unfortunate and humiliating position?"

The lawyer proceeded to offer his indictment. He had read deeply in the history of the Atlantic slave trade. "More than three hundred years ago your African forebears were taken from the west coast of Africa by slave traders who were Christians. You were sold in America to other Christians. You were held in slavery three hundred years by Christians." One of the first British slavers, he told Thurman, had sailed to Africa on the good ship Jesus, referring to Sir John Hawkins, the privateer and hero of the victory over the Spanish Armada and one of the founding fathers of the British slave trade. Hawkins had indeed used the *Jesus of Lübeck* as his flagship on his foray to the Guinea Coast in 1567–68. Two centuries later, the lawyer continued, another captain of a British slaver wrote hymns like "How Sweet the Name of Jesus" in his spare time, referring to John Newton, the eighteenth-century hymnodist best known as the author of "Amazing Grace."[28]

And Albion's perfidies soon became America's. American Christians ought not to take any pride in the ending of slavery, he said. Its chief architect, Abraham Lincoln, "was not a Christian, but was the spearhead of certain political and economic, and social forces, the full significance of which he himself did not understand." Slavery ended in the United States not because Northern whites hated slavery but because it had become inconvenient as they sought to expand their economic system to the South. That is, the lawyer seemed to be saying to Thurman, the freeing of the slaves was almost an accident, an inadvertent byproduct of other economic trends, and had nothing to do with abolitionism or goodwill by Christians in the North toward those mired in captivity. (This was a standard interpretation of the American Civil War at the time offered by progressive historians such as Charles Beard. By the 1930s it had percolated into all sorts of accounts of American history favored by those with a Marxist slant, who saw history as largely created by the economic self-interest of the powerful parading as the higher benevolence.)

And, the lawyer told Thurman, in the end the Civil War changed very little. Ever since, he said, "you have lived in a Christian nation in which you are segregated, lynched, and burned," and in which the church itself was perhaps the most segregated institution in the country. He told Thurman that he had read that in the South white worship services were sometimes dismissed so that the congregants could go and lynch a poor black soul, after which they return to the church "to finish their worship of their Christian God," the descendents of slaveholders undeterred in their confidence of their continuing possession, like John Newton, of God's amazing grace.

Now, he concluded, you are in Ceylon as a representative of American Christianity. "You will pardon me sir, I do not wish to seem rude or disrespectful to you, a visitor in our midst," he said, but continued, "I think that any black Christian is either a fool or a dupe." If Thurman wanted to try to convince him that he was neither, he would be interested in hearing his arguments.

Thurman's reaction to this diatribe was not one of anger or taking offense. He told the lawyer he was moved by his frankness, and that he had entertained similar doubts and questions for years. The two men spoke for a long time. Despite coming at the end of a busy day, and before another full day of personal appearances, they had a very lengthy conversation, which Thurman estimated as lasting as long as five hours.[29]

Thurman said that he had not come to Ceylon "to bolster up a declining or disgraced Christian faith in your midst." He had not come to seek or make converts or to be an "exhibit A as to what Christianity has done for me and my people." He told the lawyer that he not only agreed with his critique of American Christianity but also thought that in many ways it didn't go far enough. Thurman said that while his host's view of American racism and slavery was from the vantage of an outsider, his own was experiential, and his entire life had unfolded under its yoke and burden—his grandmother, probably the biggest single influence in his young life, spent the first two decades of her life in bondage—and that as a result "my judgment about slavery and racial prejudice is far more devastating than yours could ever be."

But Thurman went on to say that he made a "careful distinction between Christianity and the religion of Jesus." He was a Christian "because I think the religion of Jesus in its true genius offers me very many ways out of the world's disorders." It was not a message limited to Christianity or to Christians. Later in the same week as his en-counter in the law school, Thurman spoke to the Buddhist warden of the hostel at which he was staying in Colombo about Christian education, and argued that, if properly conducted, it was inclusive of all religious traditions. "It seems to me Christian education has suc-ceeded if it makes a man a true Christian or makes of him a better and more completely intelligent Buddhist. For I believe that Jesus reveals to a man the meaning of what he has already. When the prodigal son came to himself, he came to his father."[30]

Thurman had long made a contrast between Christianity and the religion of Jesus. (This contrast had become something of a common-place among Protestant modernists in the first half of the twentieth century.)[31] Thurman's conception of the division was starkly dichoto-mous. He told the Ceylonese lawyer that "in my opinion the churches and all so called Christian institutions are built and prevail upon the assumption that the Strong man is superior to the weak man and as such has the sound right to exploit the weak and be served by him." He was "dead set against most of the institutional religion with which I am acquainted." Thurman's conception of religion was intensely per-sonal. He was at his core a mystic and would become a distinguished interpreter of mysticism. Religion for Thurman was always a personal relation between an individual and the divine. Anything interposing itself in this relationship was a distraction, a detour, an impediment. And for Thurman, progress in race relations was also premised on personal relationships, of people honestly and forthrightly discussing their differences in the way he was discussing race with the Ceylonese lawyer. It was only through intense dialogue that people could really come to know each other, and only by coming to know one another could real change—transformation—become possible.

But Thurman never believed that intense discussion or dialogue was in the end a substitute for social change. Thurman told the lawyer that he belonged to "a small minority of Christians who believe that society has to be completely reorganized in a very definite egalitarian

sense if life is to be made livable for most of mankind." By this Thurman certainly included racial discrimination, but his egalitarianism
was not limited to this and included other inequalities as well: between the rich and the poor, between the hoarders and accumulators
of property and the unpropertied, between the laboring masses and
the elites who set the conditions of their labor, between the coloniz-
ers and the colonized, between men and women, and even between
humanity and the world of nature. (Thurman, rather unusual for a
1930s thinker, questioned whether humanity's self-appointed dominion over nature was good for either humankind or the planet.)[32] But
at the center of his social thought, radiating outward into all these
other spheres, was the basic inequality he confronted his entire adult
life: between whites and blacks in America.

For blacks in America, during slavery and its aftermath, Thurman said, "Christianity was a way out." But Christianity was never
accepted on the terms in which it was offered by white slave masters
and preachers. He would write in 1938 that "I have never quite understood why the Negro freedman became a Christian unless it was due
to the fact that he saw in the message of Jesus Christ something which
was deeper and more profound than what he was taught about the
meaning of that message."[33] In speaking to the Ceylonese lawyer he
drew on an article he had recently published, "Good News for the Underprivileged," in which he made an essential distinction between the
religion of Jesus and that of Paul.[34] Jesus and his disciples were poor
Jews in first century CE Palestine, colonized subjects under a Roman
overlord, "an underprivileged minority in the Greco-Roman Empire."
Thurman told the lawyer that their religion reflected this reality, less
in overt political rhetoric and more in the need for religion to address
a profound sense of powerlessness and lack of control over one's destiny. Meanwhile, Paul, a Jew of the Diaspora, was a Roman citizen,
and this made him less sensitive to disparities in power and more
willing to dismiss all questions of political and social status (such as
the difference between slaves and their masters) as simply irrelevant
to the true message of Christianity. It was Paul who transformed the
religion of Jesus into Christianity. "When Christianity became a world

religion, it marched under banners other than that of the teacher and prophet of Galilee."[35]

The tragedy of American Christianity, Thurman said, is that the true message of Jesus has rarely been heard and even less frequently been heeded. But in the end, American Christianity is not a monolith. "The work of the minority interested in changing society is just as much a fact as the iniquity of the majority." We will be reckoned with, he told the lawyer, we will not be moved, we will not be ignored. This minority "is concerned about and dedicated to experiencing that spirit that was in Jesus. Christ is on the side of freedom and justice for all people." With this, the lengthy conversation drew to an end. The two men had spoken far into the night.

What was this "minority interested in changing society" that Thurman mentioned to the Ceylonese lawyer? In 1935 it had no single name, and it would never march under a single institutional or ideological banner. It certainly included many Negro organizations, like the NAACP and the Brotherhood of Sleeping Car Porters, dedicated Christians like Thurman and Christian organizations such as those that sponsored the trip of the Negro Delegation, and Christian pacifist groups, notably the Fellowship of Reconciliation. But it also included labor unions associated with the newly formed Congress of Industrial Organizations (CIO), Communists, and militant atheists, as well as a host of other left-wing organizations in their teeming sectarian profusion, along with liberal Democrats and progressive Republicans.

By the 1950s this loose affiliation of peoples, groups, and organizations was further modified (and to some extent limited in its scope) by acquiring the label "civil rights movement." Of books on the civil rights movement and its origins there has been no end. Many start their narratives in the 1950s. Others go back farther, to the 1940s or to the period we are considering here, the ferment of the mid-1930s. Some authors emphasize the role of labor, others the influence of the church. Some look to its roots in the South and its profoundly Christian character; others point to the North and the crucial role of the Communist and the non-Communist left. They are all, in part, correct. The civil rights movement was the most important social transformation in American life in the second half of the twentieth century. Success has many parents, and many rightly clamor for and deserve credit.

Howard Thurman was one of the many who were present at its creation, and his contributions have been relatively overlooked. He would be a mentor to many better-known names, and he was an important influence on Martin Luther King Jr. But this was not his greatest significance to the nascent civil rights movement. In his thought and by his life example, he showed a way forward through the contradictions and dichotomies of his time. Thurman was Christian, but at the same time profoundly sympathetic to non-Christian and even anti-Christian turns of thought. Thurman tried to craft a new Christianity, one that could speak to the many learned despisers of religion among the black intelligentsia of the interwar years and yet could retain a spiritual depth and resonance and language to communicate with the learned and unlearned alike. He sought to fashion a religion that accepted the gritty particularities of worship in America, with its forced racial, ethnic, and denominational divisions, and yet aspired to universality, an enemy of any parochialism, white or black. Thurman's Christianity embraced and transcended contradiction. He was a child of the South, but had his most crucial education in the North. He was close in the 1930s to the radical currents surging through progressive politics, but always based his politics on the need for the United States to live up to its democratic potential and make true citizenship a reality for all Americans. Thurman's vision was capacious, seeing in the unity of God the necessity for the unity of all people. Only a Christianity that had been purged of racism and of the historical divisions that had kept whites and blacks apart could be an instrument for social change. And the way to accomplish this was not by exhortation but by example. In 1944 he left his comfortable position at Howard University to cofound the Church for the Fellowship of All Peoples in San Francisco, one of the first churches organized on an explicitly interracial basis.

Throughout the late 1930s and early 1940s, Howard Thurman was

ubiquitous, speaking constantly, gathering admirers and planting adherents wherever he went. What he preached was a vision of a better
world: one without war, without violence, without barriers between
religions, peoples, or classes; one in which the powerful and the powerless could meet as equals; one in which fractured humanity would
try to re-create, through their deeds, thoughts, and prayers, their one-
ness. In the birth years of the civil rights movement he helped to give
it its shape, its impetus, and its religious meaning. He had promised
the lawyer in Ceylon no less.

CHAPTER ONE

Southern Boy, Morehouse Man, Rochester Scholar

HOWARD THURMAN'S ARRIVAL IN Colombo was timed to coincide with the end of the monsoon season, though Thurman noticed its "last dying gasps" in "the high sprays that rose in the morning sunlight as the waves dashed madly against the breakwater."[1] He had been a careful student of the many moods of the ocean since his lonely, somewhat introverted boyhood in Daytona, Florida, where he had been "befriended" by Daytona's beaches with their seemingly endless expanses of sky and sea.[2] Thurman loved the beaches when they were calm, but what he really waited for were the storms, the mighty autumn hurricanes that would swirl up the Florida coast commanding attention; showing no respect to people, institutions, or human authority; reducing the giant evils of his time and place to their true Lilliputian dimensions. He would watch the storm assault the beach and would become one with its fury. "The boundaries of self would not hold me. Unafraid, I was held in the storm's embrace." The storm gave him a connection to a power that was otherwise unavailable to him, a strength that gave him "a certain overriding immunity against much of the pain I would have to deal with in the years ahead."[3]

Thurman's ability to find power and comfort in the fury of a storm was only one of the unique spiritual gifts he honed over a lifetime. In some ways they had been predicted at birth. On November 19, 1899, Alice Ambrose Thurman's baby boy was born with a caul. The membrane of the amniotic sac was still covering his face. A caul is a very rare phenomenon. It is an eerie, powerful, and mysterious sight; the newborn baby's face masked, in the world but not yet entirely out of the womb. Every culture has its own folklore about the caul, and the meaning and the powers it confers to the rare baby born with one.

In the African American culture in which Howard Thurman was raised, being born "behind the veil," as it was called, was both a blessing and a curse. It conferred "second sight," the powers of clairvoyance, the ability to predict the future. But this was also a dangerous talent; those given the gift of prophecy were also given sad and grief-stricken lives. In order to lose the gift and the curse attached to it, one had to pierce the ears of the newborn, thereby deflating, but not entirely eliminating, the power of the veil.

When he was a young boy, Thurman discovered a bit of scar tissue in the middle of both ear lobes. He asked his mother and his grandmother, Nancy Ambrose, an experienced midwife, what it meant. They told him about the veil, the abilities it conferred, the perils it posed, and why they had pierced his ears. Perhaps, he thought, they had not entirely removed his powers. From his boyhood he would have, often at critical moments of his life, what he called "visitations" when "there emerges at the center of my consciousness a face, a sense of urgency, a vibrant sensation involving some particular person." Writing about this toward the end of his life, Thurman was unsure how much the stories of the veil influenced him, but they probably made him believe that in some way, he possessed an awareness, a special sensitivity to extranatural occurrences and seeming coincidences, an ability to look deep into the heart of things.[4] While never writing much about it, Thurman, in most ways the model of a modern religious liberal, always quietly believed that hidden possibilities and realms lay beyond rational explanation.[5]

Howard Thurman was also born within another kind of veil, the one that W. E. B. Du Bois wrote about so memorably in *The Souls of Black Folk*: the veil of the color line casting its deep shadows on every black child born in the South, behind and beneath which they seemed destined to live out their lives wrapped in a shroud; dishonored, disfigured, and disinherited in the land of their birth.[6] Thurman's caul was, perhaps, a foretelling of his extraordinary gifts, and he would exercise every opportunity to realize them. But he knew early on that only by immensely difficult and painful exertion would he be able to pierce this second veil and triumph over the inextricably linked handicaps of being born poor, being born black, and being born both in the Jim Crow South. "The fact that the first twenty three years of my life were spent in Florida and in Georgia," he would write in the 1960s, "has left its scars deep in my spirit."[7]

II

Thurman was born on November 19, 1899, most likely in West Palm Beach, Florida.[8] He spent all of his boyhood in Daytona and environs. His autobiography tells us very little about the background of his father, Saul Thurman, probably because he did not know much about him. Saul was a large man, sturdy and strong, as you might expect of a railroad laborer, and yet Thurman describes him as quiet, soft-spoken, gentle, and thoughtful; a man of great dignity and pride. Every two weeks young Howard would wait outside the barbershop as his father got a fresh shave before returning home. Saul Thurman was born in Florida in 1850, presumably into slavery, and was more than twenty years older than his wife. He didn't like going to church, and when the rest of his family went off on Sunday mornings, he stayed at home and sat on the porch reading his favorite authors, among whom was the famous nineteenth-century American agnostic Robert Ingersoll.[9]

Thurman also tells us that, probably in 1907, Saul Thurman came down with a terrible case of pneumonia. He staggered home, struggled for five days, and his young son saw him die. Near the end of the vigil, his wife heard the guttural chokes of the death rattle. She asked him, "Saul, can you hear me?" He nodded yes. "Are you ready to die?" Summoning all of his strength, he said, "All of my life I have been a man, I am not afraid of death. Alice, I can stand it." Shortly thereafter his body shuddered with a final spasm, and Saul Solomon Thurman was gone. He was, his son would write, the first person he ever saw die.

The death of a parent is always a life-shattering event for a young child, particularly when the death is sudden, and it was for the acutely sensitive young Thurman. But if anything, the immediate aftermath was even more traumatic. Not being a church member in a black community in which the church was by far the strongest and most visible institution made one an outsider, one to whom respectable people felt no obligation. There was no local black funeral home, and the deacons of Mount Bethel Baptist Church, the congregation to which Thurman's mother and maternal grandmother belonged, refused to bury Saul Thurman because he died "out of Christ." The Thurman family was very short on options. Nancy Ambrose, Thurman's grandmother, always a very determined and forceful person (Thurman's mother was quite a bit shier and quieter), went back to the deacons and demanded that the church hold the funeral. They agreed, but the church's pastor refused to participate. Alice and Nancy then felt fortunate when a traveling evangelist, Sam Cromarte, volunteered to conduct the service. But he had offered to lead the service only to make an example of the deceased, and in his eulogy proceeded to preach Saul Solomon Thurman into hell, telling the assembled that he was an evil reprobate who deserved the tortures of the damned, which he was beginning to endure and would continue to do for all eternity. Thurman asked his mother again and again, "He didn't know Poppa? Did he? Did he, Momma?" But he was unconsoled, and during the long ride back from the cemetery, he told his mother and grandmother that when he grew up and became a man, he would have nothing to do with the church.[10]

In a sense he kept that promise. This was Thurman's first real introduction to institutional Christianity, and it was a searing indictment of its theological narrowness, its heartlessness, and the cruelty that passed for teaching unfortunates lessons. He came to view evangelizing and saving souls to be a profoundly amoral undertaking. He felt that dividing humanity into those inside and outside the boundaries of particular creeds and denominations was the source and inspiration of all later attempts to divide humanity into included and excluded classes.[11] He had no interest in the church of rituals and symbols. "Even to this day," he wrote in 1959, "I find that whenever I see the cross, my mind and my spirit must do a double take, because the thing that flashes instinctively in my mind is that of the burning cross of the Klan."[12] And if historically the church was a haven for black people, it also left its own victims, like Thurman's father. For Thurman the church was the home of the best and the worst in American society, and he did not spare black churches from his indictment. In many ways he always remained his father's son. He became a deeply and profoundly religious man, but he always felt that true religion had at best an ambiguous and compromised relation with "the church."

But Howard Thurman was also his mother's, and grandmother's, child. Nancy Ambrose had been born in 1842 in Madison County in northern Florida. This was classic plantation country with a cotton economy dominated by large and middle-sized estates. She grew up a house slave on the plantation of John C. McGhee, the county's second largest plantation owner. Thurman grew up in a world where almost every adult he knew was either a former slave or the child of slaves. But if slavery's presence was still palpable, hovering over everyone and everything in black Daytona, it seems to have been rarely discussed, no doubt because of the painful and unsettling memories it evoked. This was certainly the case for Nancy Ambrose, who spoke little of the twenty-two years of her life spent in bondage. Yet every summer she would return to Madison County, often with young Howard in tow, to visit family. This was, Thurman wrote, "Grandma's pilgrimage. The slave plantation where she grew up was in this area. She never spoke of it; she did not point out landmarks. Her thoughts were locked behind a wall of fierce privacy and she granted to no one the right of passage across her own remembered footsteps."[13]

There was one exception, however, to Grandma Nancy's refusal to talk about slavery. It was one of Thurman's favorite stories, and one that he told often in his writings. When she was growing up, the master's white minister sometimes held services for the slaves, and he invariably used as a text Paul's notorious injunction "slaves, be obedient to them that art your masters."[14] This was why Nancy Ambrose, who never learned to read or write, and would have Thurman read to her from the Bible, never let him read from Paul. The master, "old man McGhee," would occasionally allow the slaves to listen to a black preacher from a neighboring plantation. He would invariably preach the crucifixion of Jesus—his arrest, his trial, his torments, his seven last words, his mother at the foot of the cross, the darkness at noon—and his resurrection, acting out the whole story, building up to a tremendous emotional crescendo. At the end, he would pause, look at the congregation, and tell them, "You are not niggers! You are not slaves! You are God's children!"[15] For Thurman this was the essence of Christianity. Through the primacy of the connection to God, all temporal bonds and limitations were transcended and loosed; the despairing, the marginal, and the disinherited found the courage to go on; and those who sought a more just and better world would do so knowing they were seeking God's kingdom. If all this was not apparent at first to the young Thurman, he became increasingly aware as he got involved in his mother's and grandmother's Baptist church "that whatever I did with my life *mattered*."[16]

Both his mother and his grandmother were extremely devout members of the Mount Bethel Baptist Church in Daytona, a one-room, cross-shaped church in which young Thurman logged much time. He remembered burying his head in his grandmother's taffeta-covered lap "during the endless hours of the Sunday worship service." Those were serious, sober services, and Thurman wrote that contrary to stereotypes of black Baptists, "the preachers in my church were not 'whoopers'; they were more thoughtful than emotional," and they read their sermons. Many of the ministers supplying his congregation had college educations. Yet in other ways Mount Bethel was still a traditional Baptist congregation.[17]

When he was twelve, after a children's revival, Thurman decided he wanted to join the church. As was the custom, he presented himself to the deacons for examination, telling them he wanted to become a Christian. The deacons rejected this as inadequate, explaining to him that he could join only after he had already become one. Perhaps his decision to join the church was too rational, lacking the normal theatrics of evangelical conversion experiences. When he told Grandma Nancy about the church's rejection of him, she marched him right back to the church before the meeting had ended, demanding that her grandson be accepted for membership, and he was. But even as a young boy he was of two minds about his relationship with the church. He possessed an innate suspicion of over-dramatizing inner experience, along with a deeper ambivalence over whether participation in the church was a betrayal of the memory of his father. "Very early," he would write, "I distinguished between the demand to surrender my life to God and thus become a follower of Jesus, on the one hand, and the more prescribed demands of our local church, on the other."[18] But slowly he found himself drawn ever more deeply into his local religious community with its endless rounds of prayer meetings, services, and other obligations. By the time he was a junior in high school, he knew he would pursue a religious vocation, and his conviction in this never wavered.

III

If one had to grow up black and poor in the Deep South at the nadir of the Jim Crow era, there were worse places to do this than Daytona. Like much of Florida, Daytona had no antebellum history and had been founded as recently as 1876. Many of the town's founders were Northerners who hoped to develop the citrus industry and were attracted by the salubrious climate. It became a winter resort for wealthy "snowbirds," like John D. Rockefeller Sr. (certainly the wealthiest), who seasonally migrated to the region. Eventually, some chose to stay year round. They became active in the life of Daytona and took a serious interest in the plight of the less fortunate. Northern women founded a civic organization that provided the funds for the kindergarten Thurman attended. In addition, snowbird James Gamble (of Procter and Gamble fame) provided financial support to Thurman throughout his high school and college years. As Thurman would write, "The tempering influence of these northern families made contact between the races less abrasive than it might have been otherwise." By 1910 Daytona had grown to a town of three thousand five hundred, with more than half of the population consisting of African Americans attracted by the growing citrus industry, and perhaps by its reputation for a somewhat temperate racial climate.[19]

To be sure, Thurman's Daytona was a Southern town, where the whites were in charge and the races were separate and unequal. As Daytona grew and more white Southerners moved to the town, it became more punctilious in observing Southern mores. One observer remembers "White" and "Colored" signs going up in the first decade of the twentieth century. In March 1910, when Thurman watched the famous auto racer Barney Oldfield set a new land speed record of 131 miles per hour on the hard, flat surface of Daytona Beach, he was impressed by white and black spectators mingling together behind ropes on the sand dunes. Within a few years, he remembered, that sort of interracial contact became impossible.[20]

Still, for all the profound separateness of white and black Daytona, black Daytonans were not insular and inward-looking. They were able to vote in local elections and exercised the franchise wisely, helping to defeat the Ku Klux Klan in the 1920s and getting local officials to be attentive to their demands. By 1905 the town's black communities of Midway and Waycross had black police officers and other amenities unusual for black communities in the Deep South, such as new school buildings, cement sidewalks, and storm sewers. The city of Daytona Beach was established in 1926, uniting Daytona, Daytona Beach, and Seabreeze, with the not inadvertent consequence of diluting black voting strength. But as late as 1940, Daytona Beach was the only city in Florida where blacks voted in substantial numbers.[21]

The civic pride of Daytona's blacks was palpable and inspired the young Thurman. Perhaps no one was more important in this regard than Mary McLeod Bethune who founded the Daytona Educational and Industrial School for Girls in Waycross in 1904, which would eventually become Bethune-Cookman College. Bethune, in a long and distinguished career as an educator and administrator, would become probably the most prominent black woman in America in the first half of the twentieth century. Her school and her personality gave, as Thurman would write, "boys like me a view of possibilities to be realized in some distant future."[22]

But before that distant future could be realized, Thurman had to pass through the usual trials and tribulations of boyhood and adolescence. It was a difficult passage. The death of his father left him the only male in a household of women—his mother, his grandmother, and his two sisters, Henrietta, born in 1897, and Madaline, born in

1908, probably after his father's death. After Saul's death, Alice had to take jobs with white families as a maid and a cook, and Nancy would be the stable force in the household. Alice remarried twice, first to Alex Evans in 1909, and for a few years they lived with him in Lake Helen, a community about twenty-five miles from Daytona. Alice was able to stay home with her children, and this was a happy marriage. But her second husband died after a few years, and Alice and her brood returned to Daytona. She later married James Sams, whom Thurman never liked and never trusted, and who played little role in his life, other than making him worry that his stepfather was stealing his mother's money. Without a father or an elder brother, he felt the lack of an older male protector. He sought what he would call his "masculine idols in those early years." From the women in his early life Thurman learned to love and need religion, and from the men in his life he learned to be skeptical of its excesses. In his maturity, he tried to honor both sides of his family and both sides of his personality.[23]

Thurman was an awkward adolescent: shy, acutely self-conscious, and easily embarrassed. By his own testimony, girls avoided his company, and boys did not seek him out to play in their games. He was uncomfortable with his appearance—unathletic, somewhat overweight, and pigeon-toed. But it was his mental unease that was really crippling. He would later speak of being "haunted by a feeling of awkwardness in all of my relationships. I felt clumsy. As I walked, it was as if my feet felt fearful of being together." This is the psychological profile of a loner. "When I was young," he would write, "I found more companionship in nature than I did among people." He was, he said, befriended by the woods near the Halifax River and by the vast ocean on the unbroken beach at Daytona. It was the sublimity and not the prettiness of nature that attracted him. Thurman would go to the beach at night, especially those cloudless, moonless nights when the stars were like lanterns, and he "could hear the night think, and feel the night feel."[24]

But he was especially attracted to the beach and ocean during those mighty autumn Florida hurricanes. And if it was too dangerous to go all the way to the beach, he would go into his backyard and watch the way the great live oak tree swayed in the storm, bending without breaking. He would pour out his soul to the tree, knowing "that I was understood."[25] If Thurman was a mystic, he was essentially a nature mystic who felt that God could be most directly perceived and experienced through nature rather than in any human-made representation. Thurman found his way to God in his early years in Daytona, and it was a God that could never be claimed by any one person, one theology, or one denomination. It required nothing more than a sense of awe and exhilaration in the beauty of a gale.

Of course, conversations with live oak trees, even at their most numinous, tend to be a little one sided, and Thurman did also seek human companions. Surely one of the reasons why he was attracted to the church, like generations of shy, awkward adolescents before and after him, was because it was one place he felt comfortable, where he did not feel he was being judged on things that were not in his control, and where he could participate in "a feeling of sharing in primary community" with others.[26] It was a place where, increasingly, his gifts could be nurtured and appreciated. The other place where this was so was in school, and it was in the sanctuary and the classroom that Thurman began to discover himself.

Education had a special meaning in the Thurman household, as it had for many black households in the first generations after slavery. Grandma Nancy bitterly remembered the daughter of her slave mistress being punished for trying to teach her to read. Alice Ambrose Thurman could read—Thurman would regularly write her and send her copies of his books and other reading material he thought would interest her—but her writing was halting and unpolished. The ethos of "uplift," which saw education as one of the few readily available forms of self-advancement, pervaded black communities at the time, and Thurman was a typical if an unusually distinguished product of the system. Its values—propriety, dignity, refined elocution, the avoidance of vulgarity, and the necessity of living one's life as an example to those less fortunate—were instilled in him early. These are typically seen as the values of the black middle class, and it is worth stressing that however one defines that vexed notion, young Howard and his family were not in it. Certainly after the death of Alice's second husband, the family had to scrounge, and Alice worked as a maid and a cook, Nancy took in laundry and worked as a midwife, and Howard picked up any job he could. During his adolescence he helped his grandmother with the laundry, raked leaves (at one house a young girl stabbed him with a pin because she had been told that black people can't feel pain), worked in an ice cream parlor, sold fish, shined shoes, worked as a chef, and was a dog sitter. When Thurman was eighteen he wrote that his mother—"God bless her holy name"—had "toiled morning noon and night that we may be permitted to go to public school," and when he told her that he wanted to go to high school, she said that she had no money to spare and needed to take care of his sisters. Thurman told his mother all he wanted from her was her prayers. The need to earn extra money, the occasional skipped meal, the need to get the best possible grades to earn partial scholarships for his tuition, which continued through his college years, gave Thurman a sense of urgency, a drive to succeed that was perhaps absent from those from higher economic status. He knew how lucky he was to be pursuing his education, how many obstacles he had already cleared away, and how many were still in his path.[27]

He was always an excellent student, and in seventh grade he received maximum marks in seven of his nine subjects. By all odds this should have been the end of his formal education, as it was for many bright black students in the South in the first decades of the twentieth century who lacked the encouragement and opportunity to go further. Public education for blacks in Daytona ended with seventh grade, and without an eighth grade, as Thurman would write, "there could be no demand for a black high school; and if by chance a demand were made, it could be denied on the ground that no black children could qualify." Then the principal of Thurman's elementary school, R. H. Howard, tutored Thurman in the eighth-grade curriculum and told the local school superintendent that he had a student ready for the eighth-grade examination. During the year Thurman established a fish market (which came to the notice of the *Chicago Defender*, the earliest known reference to Thurman in print), and every day he would get up early, catch fish in the Halifax River, study his lessons in the fish stall, and go to school to recite them, after which he went to an evening job. Despite this, he proudly wrote when he was eighteen that he had "completed my grammar school education with an average of 99% receiving the first Certificate of Promotion given to the colored people of my County."[28]

But with his certificate of promotion in hand, Thurman's difficulties in pursuit of a high school education had only begun. There obviously was no public high school for blacks in Daytona—there were only three in all the state of Florida, along with a few private high schools. The nearest school was in Jacksonville, the Florida Baptist Academy, founded by the American Baptist Home Mission Society in 1892.[29] Thurman was admitted to the school, but before he was able to get to Jacksonville to start high school, an incident occurred that would remain with him his entire life. He came to the Daytona train station with an old, borrowed trunk with no lock and no handles, secured only with a rope. He purchased his ticket but the stationmaster refused to let him to check his trunk because regulations stipulated that all checked trunks required handles, and thus Thurman would have to ship it by railroad express, which would cost far more than the few dollars and cents he had on hand. So close to his goal, and yet so distant, and completely frustrated, Thurman sat down on the steps on the railroad station and started to cry, the tears pouring down his face. Let us tell the story in his own words:

> Presently I opened my eyes and saw before me a large pair of work shoes. My eyes crawled upward until I saw the man's face. He was a black man, dressed in overalls and a denim cap. As he looked down at me he rolled a cigarette, and lit it. Then he said, "Boy what in hell are you crying about?"
> And I told him.
> "If you're trying to get out of this damn town to get an education, the least I can do is to help you. Come with me," he said.[30]

The man went to the stationmaster, paid for the trunk, gave Thurman the receipt, and without saying another word, left, and started walking down the railroad track. Thurman never saw him again.

This event had a deep significance to Thurman, for reasons he never quite made clear. But we can imagine what they might have been. It took place at the precise moment of what is always the most crucial transition in any young life—leaving home for the first time. He couldn't even get on the train taking him away from Daytona. It was a story of racial solidarity and of the hopes and expectations that were placed on his shoulders. It was a story of human solidarity, of people coming to the aid of others without being asked and without asking for anything in return. It was a reminder of just how precarious his pursuit of further education was. To get the money for the fare, he had obtained some sort of advance on his or his mother's insurance policy, clearly pushing his meager financial resources to the limit.[31] The story on some level reflected his belief in a divine presence in the world that subtly shapes our destinies. To call it providence would probably be too strong, but it informed his sense that nothing of importance in life can be purely serendipitous or accidental.[32] Whatever it meant for Thurman, he dedicated his autobiography not to his wife, his daughters, his mentors, or his friends but to "the stranger in the railroad station in Daytona Beach who restored my broken dream sixty-five years ago."[33]

Once he arrived in Jacksonville, things didn't get much simpler. "The four years in high school," he wrote, "were not easy years." For his first year he roomed with a cousin, walking two and a half miles to school every day, and worked all day Saturday and most evenings pressing clothes. There was never enough food or money. The remaining years he boarded at the school, but the boarding fee of five dollars a month was beyond his reach without a series of odd jobs, in addition to which he took on responsibilities at the school, such as a dormitory supervisor. After his long day he would study half the night. His health suffered, and just before graduation, he suffered a nervous collapse (the first of several the sensitive Thurman would experience in his life). He wanted to stay at school to deliver the class oration, his right as valedictorian. But his mother insisted on his coming right home afterward. Completely exhausted, he spent several weeks in bed catching up on rest, writing a teacher that his physician was making him pay his "big bill to Dr. Sleep." He soon recovered enough to spend the summer working in a Jacksonville bakery six days a week for ten hours a day.[34]

As a sophomore, in the summer of 1917, Thurman attended his first YMCA conference at the Lincoln Academy at Kings Mountain, North Carolina, the site of an annual conference for black colleges and normal schools (teacher colleges) in the South. It was a new world for Thurman, one filled with dynamic, young college-educated ministers speaking of their ambitions for black America and for making Christianity a true ally in the fight for racial equality. The next year he returned to Kings Mountain, and by the time the conference was over, he was convinced that he had received a calling to the ministry. He wrote to the person who had impressed him the most, Mordecai Wyatt Johnson, one of Thurman's "masculine idols," initiating what would be one of the longest, most fruitful, and most complex relationships in his life. Johnson was only ten years older than Thurman, a native of Tennessee, a 1911 graduate of Atlanta Baptist College (which was renamed Morehouse College the following year), and a 1916 graduate of Rochester Theological Seminary. He worked briefly as a student secretary for the YMCA before resigning in 1917 over the organization's failure to challenge discriminatory practices at a national conference in Atlantic City, New Jersey. At the time Thurman wrote him he was pastor of First Baptist Church in Charleston, West Virginia, where he remained until 1926 when he was named president of Howard University, the first black to hold that office. If there was one model for Thurman's career, it was Johnson, and like him, Thurman would attend Morehouse and RTS and work briefly as a Baptist minister before commencing an academic career, with his single-longest stint spent with Johnson at Howard from 1932 to 1944.[35]

Thurman wrote Johnson in June 1918, the first extant sample of his writing, and it is everything a teenager's letter to an idol should be: proud, ardent, a bit naïve, and deeply felt; a young man pouring out his heart to a stranger simply because he was convinced someone would care. He opened by saying that he had let Johnson "slip into my heart and occupy the place of a precious friend," that he longed to tell Johnson of his "hopes, ambitions, and discouragements." Thurman went on to tell the story of his life, his impoverished, widowed mother's efforts to raise her family, and his own hardships and academic accomplishments. He wrote Johnson that "I want to be a minister of the Gospel, I feel the needs of my people, I see their distressing condition," and, expressing himself in a traditional Christian vocabulary that he would soon eschew, went on to say that God's "precious love urges me to take up the cross and follow him." As a result he had "offered himself upon the altar as a living sacrifice in order that I may help the 'skinned and flung down.'"[36]

Johnson's response was all Thurman could have hoped for. He told him that "your perseverance under difficulty, your reverence for your mother, and your yearning to serve mark you as a God-chosen man." Johnson recommended that Thurman be patient and take the time to attend a first-class college and a first-class seminary. He also encouraged Thurman to start thinking about the Bible critically and historically and acquaint himself with the latest scholarship on Christianity. The days of the less than fully educated black preacher were over.[37]

A year later, in the fall of 1919, Thurman entered Johnson's alma mater, Morehouse College, though this was probably less the consequence of Johnson's example or prodding than the fact that Thurman, by virtue of being the valedictorian of a Baptist secondary school, was awarded a partial scholarship. Without it, he would not have been able to attend college, and he never forgot—Morehouse men (it was, and remains, an all-male school) were not allowed to forget—how rare a privilege this was. In 1919 less than one hundredth of one percent of African American men in the South attended a four-year college. "We were always inspired to keep alive our responsibility to the many, many others who had not been fortunate enough to go to college."[38] (Before he graduated Morehouse, he wrote college president

John Hope proposing an elaborate scholarship scheme, never acted on, to aid indigent black college students.)[39]

Morehouse College, founded in 1867, was one of the many educational institutions for blacks founded by white Northern Protestants in the years after the Civil War. By the time Thurman entered Morehouse in 1919 it had emerged, under the direction of John Hope, its first black president, as one of the most academically distinguished black colleges in the Deep South. In the epic division between Booker T. Washington and W.E.B. Du Bois, Hope retained the friendship of both men, but he was firmly on the side of Du Bois's commitment to academic education, and under Hope's leadership Morehouse had steadily improved the quality of its teaching staff and curriculum. It was a small and intimate place during Thurman's years—there were only forty young men in Thurman's 1923 graduating class—and the students and faculty were on close terms.

Like many black (and white) college presidents of the time, Hope governed autocratically and instituted strict regulations against smoking, drinking, dancing, card playing, or fraternizing with female students at nearby Spelman College without chaperones. Students who failed to uphold the honor code were expelled, and to prevent temptation from rearing its ugly head, their routines, from rising in the morning to going to bed at night, were closely supervised. Thurman once got into trouble himself when his complaints over the quality of the grits in the dining hall sparked a short-lived student rebellion. Faculty members were expected to report students for infractions, and Hope freely offered the faculty advice about their private lives. Hope, Thurman wrote, inspired more respect and fear among his classmates than genuine affection, though Thurman and Hope had a fairly close relationship. In this closely regulated, somewhat paternalistic environment, Thurman flourished.[40]

Thurman pushed himself at Morehouse with his accustomed relentlessness, in part because there was additional scholarship money available to men finishing at the top of their class, which Thurman did every year, once again graduating as valedictorian. Thurman took only one course in religion during his four years at Morehouse and concentrated instead in courses on economics and sociology. His main professor in economics, Lorimer Milton, who went on to become a successful bank president in Atlanta, urged Thurman to pursue a career in business. Thurman was very fond of Garrie Moore, a Columbia-trained sociologist who died during Thurman's senior year, and saw him as a real friend. His relationship with another sociologist, E. Franklin Frazier, then at the beginning of his distinguished career, was more antagonistic. Although Thurman found his course in social theory with Frazier to be "spellbinding," these two strong-willed men frequently clashed, until at one point Frazier ordered Thurman not to say another word in class for the remainder of the semester.[41]

But a summer course he took at Columbia University in New York City became "the most significant course I ever took, certainly during this critical period of my life." Thurman was persuaded by Garrie Moore that he needed to take a serious course in philosophy to develop his ability to think critically. Thurman used his scholarship money to take "Introduction to Reflective Thinking." The dominant figure in the Columbia University philosophy department was John Dewey, and the course had a decidedly Deweyian cast. The class instructed its students that all problems, from simple factual inquiries to complex social and religious matters, could be analyzed from a common framework of inquiry, one that subjected all a priori assumptions to rigorous and skeptical inquiry. This sort of rigorous philosophical pragmatism would become a basis for Thurman's emerging religious thought. He came to feel that serious philosophy had been deliberately excluded from the curriculum of black colleges by their white founders so that their students wouldn't be obliged to examine the fundamental contradictions of their education and lives too closely. He would do something about it. When Thurman taught at Morehouse and Spelman in 1928, the first course he offered was "An Introduction to Reflective Thinking."[42]

The Columbia course was just one example of the lengths to which Thurman went to obtain the education he believed was rightfully his. During his Morehouse years, like many bright young people coming into their own, Thurman soaked up experiences, people, and knowledge. He tried, and by his own account succeeded, in reading every book in the (rather small) Morehouse College library, as if he could assimilate the world's store of knowledge through the power of his will. And it seems as if he also tried to participate in every extracurricular activity he could cram into his waking hours. To summarize the rather breathless account of his accomplishments in his yearbook, he was class president, editor of the yearbook, writer of the class poem, winner of the Edgar Allan Poe Short Story and Athenaeum literary prizes; acted in productions of Hamlet and Othello; was a member of the varsity debating team; sang with the Glee Club; delivered the Paxon Prize and Emancipation Day orations; and still had time to be class valedictorian and a speaker on commencement day. He was, his yearbook claimed, "the personification of the Morehouse Ideal." He was voted the busiest, the most dignified, and the most brilliant member of his class, and the amply proportioned Thurman was in the running for the title of "biggest eater" as well.[43]

One of Thurman's proudest accomplishments during his student years were his various literary efforts for the Morehouse literary magazine, the *Athenaeum*. Sixty years later he still remembered the "thrill in seeing my name in print" for the first time for a short prose poem that, appropriately enough for a man for whom the ocean was one of his earliest sources of religious inspiration, described his emotions on watching a sunrise on a beach. The *Athenaeum* also published his other earliest poems, short and derivative, lauding his willingness to die for the flag, the godliness of his mother, and the spiritual intensity of the night, along with several sentimental fictional vignettes.[44]

But the most telling of his student writings, and the only piece that enables us to get a real glimpse of his thinking, was "Our Challenge," his 1922 Emancipation Day oration (delivered on January 1, the anniversary of the Emancipation Proclamation). The Emancipation Day oration was, like all Thurman's Morehouse writings, tailored to a specific rhetorical framework, in this case the ideology of uplift that dominated black colleges in the early twentieth century, which on public occasions typically combined praise for the progress blacks had made since emancipation with a castigation and critique of the failure of blacks to advance farther and faster. Thurman was comfortable with its tropes, and it would remain a part of his thinking, though in increasingly muted ways, for the rest of his life. Its cadences can be observed in some of the speeches he gave in India, and even in his autobiography, which has in places an "up from slavery's aftermath" feel. But he was also from the outset sensitive to its limitations, and this can be observed in "Our Challenge," which was far more a relating of black failure than a smug paean to black progress, and if it offered the expected self-critique, it saved its ripest rhetoric for a lacerating attack on white supremacy.[45]

Thurman opened by declaring that "physical slavery is no more," but "psychic slavery" was stronger than ever. Blacks had grown "complacent" and "intoxicated" with their progress since emancipation and had forgotten that "our thoughts, our attitudes, our ideas and in many respects our destinies" are "being shaped and planned by those who love us not." Blacks remained too dependent on the white man, who demanded to be worshiped like a god. Unable to control their own lives, blacks were too much the product and reflection of their desires and needs, and as a result the "masses of our people" lived in "a state of darkness," held "mercilessly in the thralldom of shiftless and desultory habit." "Our Challenge" is the earliest version of an argument Thurman would make his own in *Jesus and the Disinherited* and elsewhere: blacks, denied true citizenship and a real ability to direct and order their own lives, fell prey all too easily to the triple ills of fear, deception, and hate.[46]

His proposed solution was a purple patch of operatic violence: blacks must pull down the pillars of racial prejudice as "smoke and flames [fly] upward, fire the entire civilized dome, and then, and only then, will the car of Negro freedom, physical and psychic, rumble on forever, over the bleak and dismal loneliness of an exterminated slavery." His Wagnerian vision was not one calling for revolutionary violence but rather a metaphorical cleansing of the obstacles that remained in the way of black advancement. He would soon learn to express similar thoughts in rhetoric less obscure and overripe and in language less threatening and inflammatory. But he never abandoned the outrage and anger on exhibition in this early oration, and beneath the calmer language of his later work lurked the race man of "Our Challenge."

The general feeling of "Our Challenge" is one of entrapment and claustrophobia. Blacks are penned in, dominated by whites in ways that often they do not even understand. And there is no easy way out. Thurman's overheated rhetoric at the end only disguised the paucity of his proposed solutions. Of course Thurman's dilemma was the dilemma that confronted all African American intellectuals in the opening decades of the twentieth century: the need to declare independence from white domination, and then the need to continue to live within a white-dominated society on their own terms. Even in the relatively immature rhetoric of "Our Challenge," Thurman does not underestimate the difficulty of the task. His evolving understandings of Christianity began to point to a solution, to a way out.

We do not really have a good sense of Thurman's religious views while at Morehouse. His yearbook describes him as "brainy and sympathetic he is our ideal of a minister, one who will furnish us with a rational and practical Christianity." This sounds as if, following advice from Mordecai Wyatt Johnson and others, he was already on the road to a modern progressive Christianity. On the other hand, there is an anecdote from a classmate, Gamewell Valentine, on how E. Franklin Frazier, a professed atheist, would regularly taunt Thurman in class: "Dr. Frazier would ridicule certain Scriptural stories with bitter sarcasm, and Howard Thurman would be moved to such a point that he would fold his arms, look up to the top of the ceiling, and audibly groan." He went on to say that Thurman started "by responding to Frazier's taunts, but eventually let them pass in silence." Perhaps Thurman was responding less to the specifics of what Frazier was saying than his general mocking tone or Frazier's thinking that pointing out logical inconsistencies in the more far-fetched Bible stories was a serious critique of religion. In any event, it seems reasonable to suppose that Thurman at Morehouse was not quite the full-fledged Protestant modernist he would be a few years hence.[47]

But Christian organizations offered Thurman a path to another

world, outside Morehouse and Atlanta. Thurman's involvement with
the YMCA, as we have seen, began while he was still in high school
when he attended (and was profoundly influenced by) YMCA conferences at Kings Mountain. His involvement with the YMCA expanded
during his undergraduate years. At Morehouse he was president of
the campus YMCA, which made him the unofficial "religious leader
on campus." Thurman attended local and national YMCA conferences and had a chance to observe what was praiseworthy about the
YMCA, the YWCA, and the Student Christian Movement they
animated. They were massive organizations with many branches and
with large contradictions when it came to race. Most of their local
branches were segregated and would largely remain so until 1946. On
the other hand, white philanthropists had helped make black branches
of the Y some of the most important civic institutions in many cities.
Their Colored Men's and Colored Women's Divisions, which would
establish chapters at almost every black college, would become an in-
valuable training ground for black leaders, including many that would
play significant roles in Thurman's life, among them Mordecai Wyatt
Johnson, Channing Tobias, Jesse Moorland, Max Yergan, Juliette
Derricotte, and Thurman's second wife, Sue Bailey Thurman. If the
black leaders of the YMCA and YWCA deeply resented the policy
of local segregation, they also appreciated working in an organization that gave them great visibility and responsibility. For those like
Thurman, who soon found himself as a regular on the YMCA and
the YWCA speaking circuits, involvement in the Student Christian
Movement afforded an opportunity to travel, to meet interesting
people, to address both black and interracial audiences, and to work
with whites as equals to a degree with few parallels among prominent national organizations at the time. From his undergraduate years
through World War II, the Student Christian Movement in America
was a second home for Thurman.[48]

The YMCA and kindred organizations such as the Christian pacifist Fellowship of Reconciliation, which he also joined as an undergraduate and which will be discussed more fully in the next chapter,
were so important to Thurman in part because he found Atlanta so

oppressive. Perhaps the relatively mild race relations in Daytona did not fully prepare him for living in a city where the memory of the ferocious 1906 race riot remained fresh in the minds of its black residents, and the black community seemed for the most part to be cowed and intimidated. He would later write about living in Atlanta "during a period when the state of Georgia was infamous for its racial brutality. Lynchings, burnings, unspeakable cruelties were the fundamentals of existence for black people. Our physical lives were of little value." He would write on more than one occasion of hearing a man sing in Beaver Slide, an impoverished black neighborhood near Morehouse, "Been down so long / Down don' worry me." For Thurman this was "a Negro man whose soul had given up the ghost."[49]

But if progressive blacks could find a home in the YMCA, they often found themselves fighting uphill battles against the racial conservatism and paternalism that often dominated the organization. Thurman remembered going to a YMCA meeting with John Hope as a Morehouse senior to discuss a forthcoming Atlanta recital by the Negro tenor Roland Hayes, where the concession to blacks (made solely because there was a black performer involved) was to segregate the concert hall vertically rather than horizontally, with whites to one side and blacks to the other, rather than relegating blacks to the balcony. Thurman felt this was little better than nothing, and to the extent the whites thought they were doing blacks a favor, perhaps less than nothing. He walked out of the meeting. Hope followed him out, placed a hand on his shoulder, and said, "Thurman, I know how you feel about what is going on in there, but you must remember that these are the best and most liberal men in the entire South. We must work with them. There *is* no one else. Remember." Thurman appreciated what Hope was saying, and Thurman understood why people like Hope felt that it was important to engage in dialogue with Southern moderates. But it would not be Thurman's way. Still, within the many mansions of the Student Christian Movement, Thurman began to find an alternative to the terrible divisive certainties of Jim Crow, a place where whites and blacks could, however haltingly and imperfectly, begin to treat one another as equals.[50]

By the time he graduated from Morehouse in the spring of 1923, Thurman was identified as one of three class pacifists, and was almost certainly among his fourteen classmates who identified themselves as socialists (along with twenty-two Republicans and one Bolshevik). His way out of the dilemmas of "psychic slavery" that he outlined in "Our Challenge" was to try to overcome his fear and his hatred of whites by engaging with them, treating them as real people, and refusing to concede them moral or intellectual superiority. It was a lesson Thurman began to learn in Atlanta, and one he would have to apply in a different way and much more comprehensively during his three years in Rochester.

IV

As valedictorian of his graduating class, Thurman had a number of options. Morehouse offered Thurman an instructorship in economics and to assist him financially in attending the University of Chicago for a fifth undergraduate year, a process known as validation. (Because black colleges were not formally accredited, many good students opted to spend a fifth undergraduate year at a prestigious white college, thereby obtaining a recognized bachelor's degree.) Thurman turned down these offers. He was determined to go to seminary. His first choice, Newton Theological Seminary in Massachusetts, rejected him because the school did not admit Negroes, and suggested Thurman attend a black seminary, such as one at Virginia Union College. Thurman chose instead to apply to Rochester Theological Seminary, in part because of the example of a teacher at Morehouse, Charles Hubert, as well as that of Mordecai Wyatt Johnson. But one suspects that one of his reasons for wanting to go to Rochester was to demonstrate to himself that he was any student's equal. He knew that RTS only had two black students in residence at a single time (so that they would be able to room together). He applied and was admitted. The letter of admittance, in Thurman's remembrance, underlined how privileged and fortunate he was, in ways he found somewhat objectionable, to be able to study at RTS.

When Thurman came to Rochester it was "the most radical period of adjustment of my life." He was living in the North for the first time and living in a "totally white world." Nearly all his classmates were white, and his teachers entirely so. This was also more or less true for the city of Rochester itself, which out of a population of 295,000 had fewer than two thousand residents of color in 1920. Although there were local black churches, which Thurman attended whenever he could, the black community, compared to the cities in Florida and Georgia where he had lived previously, was minuscule. In any event, his life revolved around his studies at RTS. There was a formality at the seminary he found at first intimidating. He had been used to instructors at Morehouse, like E. Franklin Frazier and Benjamin Mays, who were only a few years older than himself. At RTS, his professors seemed hoary and white bearded, and all students were addressed as "mister." The daily chapel services were also formal beyond anything in his experience.[51]

Thurman did not know if he could fit in at RTS and measure up to his classmates, most of whom had gone to undergraduate schools that were considerably higher up on the academic pecking order than Morehouse. He tried to compensate by his willingness to push himself to his limits, requesting extra reading from his professors. He was bedazzled by the size of the RTS library, several times the size of that of Morehouse, and once again he tried to read as many books as he could, filling his bag to the breaking point with borrowed books. By planning strategically (leaving one book in the bathroom, one in his bedroom, and so on), he ensured that he was never far from choice reading material. But as much as he tried to fit in, he felt his classmates had one "unyielding advantage. They were at home in the world, and I felt a stranger. Whether they were gifted intellectually, or mediocre, the fact remained that this world belonged to them." Thurman's frustration was heightened by the ignorance people displayed to his world, such as instructors who asked the rather urban Thurman to talk about things outside his ken, such as rural camp meetings, as if this was the only way Southern blacks worshiped. But for all the occasional insensitivities, he had very good relations with most of his classmates and instructors, and he soon found that intellectually he could more than hold his own. As with every other academic institution he ever attended, Thurman graduated RTS as valedictorian.[52]

Helping with his adjustment was the fact that the city of Rochester seemed "fabulous" to him. RTS was located in the heart of downtown Rochester. (In 1928, two years after his graduation, the school moved to a new campus on the outskirts of the city and adopted a new name, the Colgate-Rochester Divinity School.) Thurman enjoyed window shopping in Rochester's trendy stores and eating in the city's restaurants, especially those with the cuisines of recent Italian, Jewish, and German immigrants, which he found quite exotic. He especially liked that "generally, I was not troubled by questions of race. I was never refused service or otherwise insulted in any of the stores." He attended weekly films at the opulent and newly opened Eastman Theater, just a few blocks from his school. On Fridays he attended weekly orchestral concerts. If his love of classical music does not date from this period of his life, it was surely strengthened and intensified, and plumbing the depths of Beethoven, especially the late quartets—whose music "consumes all foibles and mediocrities, leaving only a literal and irreducible reality"—would be a lifelong quest.[53]

The only drawback to Rochester for Thurman was that it "seemed to me to have the most consistently cold weather in the world." For a Floridian who had only seen snow once before in his life this was hardly surprising, especially since he had to do battle with Rochester's formidable snowstorms without the benefit of a proper winter coat. But by uncomfortable-sounding expedients of bundling himself tightly in heavy wrapping paper and taking cold showers and alcohol rubs, he survived. By his second winter he acquired appropriate outerwear. Beyond the charms of Rochester itself, the city's location was reasonably convenient for weekend trips to New York City where Thurman would continue his hungry acquisition of high culture, going to the theater to see Shakespeare and Ibsen, to the ballet to see Tchaikovsky. After Atlanta, a city defined by its racial antagonisms, Rochester, if not a racial utopia, was a breath of cold, fresh air. And at times Thurman found something else in the city. He would write of coming home very late one night to the seminary, crossing Main Street, the city's central traffic artery, when there was almost no traffic. "As I walked along, I became aware of what seemed to be the sound of rushing water. I realized that I had been hearing this rumbling for quite some time, but had only suddenly become aware of it." The next day he asked one of his professors about this, who told him that part of Main Street crossed over a submerged and invisible section of the Genesee River. He would later write, "The sound itself was continuous, but when there was the normal traffic in the daytime, the sound could not be heard. It was only when the surface noises had stopped that the sound came through. This is analogous to the mystic's witness of God within, whose Presence may not become manifest until the traffic of the surface life is somehow stilled." Thurman discovered himself in Rochester.[54]

Rochester Theological Seminary had been founded in 1850 by German Baptists. In the late nineteenth century, under the leadership of respected theologian Augustus Hopkins Strong, the seminary hewed to a fairly conservative course, politically and theologically. This would change in the early twentieth century when its best-known faculty member, Walter Rauschenbusch, would become the leading figure in the Social Gospel, the liberal Protestant movement that insisted that the social ills created by industrialization and urbanization were a central problem for religious belief and practice. The seminary also became a center of Protestant modernist thinking, subjecting the truths of Christianity to a searching historical and anthropological examination. Rauschenbusch died in 1918, but when Thurman arrived in the fall of 1923, his presence was still hovering over the seminary. If Thurman was not a full-fledged modernist and Social Gospeler before he arrived in Rochester, he soon became one.

Despite the gaps of age and race between himself and his professors, Thurman rapidly developed close bonds with many of his instructors, along with considerable intellectual debts. Conrad Moehlman, who taught the history of Christianity and wrote pioneering works on the history of Christian anti-Semitism, surely helped fix in Thurman's mind the inseparability of the life of Jesus from the persecution of the

Jews. With Henry Burke Robins and Justin Wroe Nixon he would form lasting friendships, and many of these would be renewed when he spent a sabbatical year at Colgate-Rochester Divinity School in 1937–38.[55]

If Thurman learned much from his professors, he soon discovered that few had any specific interest in the Christian dimensions of the race questions. This was a habitual blind spot not only among the RTS faculty but also among proponents of the Social Gospel in general, for whom the problems of blacks and racial minorities did not figure high in the hierarchy of social problems requiring redress. To the extent it was considered at all, it was seen as a Southern problem (the small size of the black population in Northern cities such as Rochester in these days before the Great Migration accentuated this bias), and one that did not require any special attention to blacks per se, beyond the help extended to all classes and peoples on the lower rungs of society. This had been the position (or the lack of one) of Walter Rauschenbusch, and it continued, with some differences between the individual RTS faculty members, into Thurman's day. As his biographer Christopher Evans has noted, Rauschenbusch's inattention to racial matters, his paternalism, and his casual racism were, as compared to his Social Gospel peers, "neither exceptional, nor intentionally malevolent—they were tragically typical."[56] Thurman had an unusual ability when dealing with people to focus on their gifts and not to be overly burdened by their limitations, which is evidently how he dealt with the lack of interest or the misconceptions about race on the part of RTS faculty. And presumably he entered RTS with low expectations in this regard to begin with. If there was one thing he did not need to learn from the middle-aged white men on the RTS faculty, it was the reality of American race relations.

Thurman's main professor at RTS was George Cross, professor of systematic theology. Cross, who earned his PhD in 1900 at that bastion of modernist theology, the University of Chicago, brought liberalism with him to Rochester when he arrived in 1912, much to the consternation of his illustrious predecessor, Augustus Hopkins Strong, who wrote that he regarded Cross's selection as "the greatest calamity that has come to the seminary since the foundation. It was the entrance of an agnostic, skeptical, and anti-Christian element into its teaching, the results of which will be only evil."[57] Strong knew what he was talking about. Thurman described his initial impression of Cross by writing, "He dismantled the structures of orthodoxy with scrupulous scholarship. At first he seemed to me both pious and iconoclastic, ruthlessly dethroning our inherited orthodoxies. I was by turns fascinated and outraged by what seemed to me to be his supreme self-confidence." The two would frequently meet on Saturday mornings to discuss the week's lecture: "With the utmost patience and understanding, he would reduce my arguments to an ash." If anything was left of Thurman's traditional Baptist faith when he came to Rochester, it was soon merely embers.[58]

Our glimpses of Thurman's work at RTS certainly reveal him in high modernist mode. His earliest surviving student paper, "Virgin Birth," probably written in the spring of 1924, denies this central Christian tenet, dismissing it as a remnant of primitive mythological thinking, an idea "born in error." Following contemporary anthropological theories that now sound as quaintly archaic as the theories they were criticizing, Thurman argues that the virgin birth was a lingering residue of a time when humans were generally ignorant of the connection between coition and conception and attributed human births to miraculous intervention, and it had survived into historical times as an explanation for the birth of heroes. Thurman's intolerance of traditional Christian dogma was further demonstrated the following summer when he was ordained into the Baptist ministry in the First Baptist Church in Roanoke, Virginia, where he was working as an assistant for the summer. He was reluctant to affirm the traditional dogmas of the Baptist faith, including the doctrine of the virgin birth, and after hours of tense quizzing by a panel of Baptist ministers, he was somewhat reluctantly approved for ordination, but only after he dropped his objection to the traditional laying on of hands during the service (which in the end he found very moving). Thurman then, and ever after, would see the dogmas of Christianity, or any religion, as barriers to the true understanding of religion.[59]

In its stead, drawing on his own strong religious instincts and the tutelage of George Cross, Thurman began to advocate a religion of direct experience, of actual contact with the divine, rather than a religion intermediated through a set of dogmas or fixed principles. The closest he came in his seminary years to providing a theological exposition of his religious principles was in a paper he wrote in the fall of 1925, "Can It Be Truly Said That the Existence of a Supreme Spirit Is a Scientific Hypothesis?" Thurman's debts to pragmatism, and especially to the Deweyian course he took on reflective thinking at Columbia in 1922, are clear, including extensive unacknowledged borrowings from the texts he used in that course. After answering the question posed in the paper's title in the negative, he concluded "the validity of the faith that there is a supreme spirit is determined by whether or not it will stand the test of experience." This is the faith of pragmatism, though Thurman pushed his experiential faith to the borders of mysticism, writing that for him religion was "when I am supremely conscious that I make contact with *somebody* and I know that I am not alone," and in these moments "I do not only say 'I believe' but when I am most myself I say 'I know.'" This would always be Thurman's religion, in which there was no substitute for direct contact with the divine.[60]

The main challenge that confronted Thurman in seminary was neither intellectual nor theological but the basic dilemma that confronts individuals trying to live moral lives. (And it was the particular genius of Thurman to treat all such questions as theological, and vice versa.) Thurman was confronted with (as he would jocularly entitle an article some twenty years later) "the White Problem." Before coming to Rochester, whites for him were at best distant or benign and at worst abusive and oppressive, but they were always somewhere else, not among the real people, not people he would ever try to seriously befriend, whose hopes and fears he would listen to, or to whom he would talk to about his own. While he knew that most white people were Christians, and most of his seminary mates were, like him, Baptists, it had never really occurred to him that they really shared the same religion or that they could really pray together. It had never, he wrote memorably in his autobiography, "occurred to me that my magnetic field of ethical awareness applied to other than my own people."[61]

Thurman was a popular student at RTS, and his single room became a meeting place for his classmates. At the beginning of his second year, two classmates across the hall, occupying a suite intended for three students, asked Thurman to join them. To do this, he knew "if I were to make the move I could never be as I was before; a lifetime of conditioning would have to be overcome." Thurman told them that RTS had many informal rules that he was frequently bumping into, including one that prohibited black seminarians from having white roommates. The two men, Seldon "Red" Matthews and Dave Voss, said they would ignore the rule, and Thurman moved in. Nothing was said to Thurman, but Matthews and Voss were spoken to by the administration. The three would become lifelong friends.[62]

Thurman further expanded his "magnetic field" to include whites outside the RTS community. From almost the beginning of his time in Rochester, he was in demand to speak in local churches. During his three years in Rochester, we know of at least seventeen appearances in central and western New York, almost all before white audiences, and this is probably just a small fraction of his total number of speaking engagements. In many of his appearances he was shadowed by local members of the Ku Klux Klan, then making a short-lived revival in New York and other Northern states. Although the northern Klan did not engage in the night ridings and lynchings that made their southern brethren so notorious, they were certainly capable of acts of wanton cruelty, such as burning down the churches of ministers who were too vociferous in their criticisms. Thurman was monitored by the Klan in all of his appearances at local churches, and on one occasion had to walk past a silent, menacing, and unhooded gauntlet of Klan members on his way to a local church. The presence of the Klan, if nothing else, was a constant reminder to Thurman of the stakes involved in his speaking to white audiences.[63]

By the late 1920s Thurman was already being lauded as "one of the best young black ministers of his generation," and his rise to celebrity started during his seminary years. At the end of 1923 he was a delegate to the International Student Volunteer Convention in Indianapolis, and the next year he was a delegate to the quadrennial YMCA convention in Washington. Before he graduated he also spoke at Union Theological Seminary in New York City, at Newark, New Jersey, and in Evanston, Illinois.[64]

None of Thurman's sermons survives from these years, but his extant writings give a good sense of his main messages. He was, first and foremost, a thoroughgoing exponent of the Social Gospel. In a short article published in the *Roanoke Church News* in 1924 (Thurman was working in Roanoke as a summertime assistant pastor), "The Sphere of the Church's Responsibilities in Social Reconstruction," he argues that one of the lessons of World War I was that "religion was powerless to stay the carnage" and was not doing a much better job in the postwar period when many of the major combatants, having learned nothing, were simply rearming for the next war, and religion seemed powerless to prevent it. The "great task of social reconstruction" required that the "social order," shot through with "a thousand ills," be transformed. But too many ministers focused on saving individual souls and leaving Jesus in the sacraments and on the altars. The only way forward, he wrote, was for the church to boldly and directly address "economic ills, political corruption and social injustice."[65]

Thurman also felt the church in the 1920s had to learn to speak to young people, who had such a vertiginous sense of difference from the prewar generation. Rather than treat God as something apart from life, gray and churchly, modern Christians had to seek God elsewhere and in different guises, to try "to find Him as a part and parcel of all experience." This is what Thurman argued in a 1925 article published in the *Student Volunteer Movement Bulletin*, "The Perils of Immature Piety." He criticized a preening evangelical style he found distasteful for assuming an unearned and unmerited spiritual superiority, for its sedulous aping of real piety, and for naïvely assuming there was a simple "religious formula" that one could follow to achieve "spiritual power." Too many Christians invoked what Thurman called a "Twentieth Century Monastic Concept," as if Christianity required a narrowing of one's focus and restriction of one's sympathies; for

him, "any conception of 'full time Christian service' that does not
synthesize *all* of life around that ideal is barren." Thurman called for
a spiritual creativity that was a response to and a genuine product
of its time, and one that was comfortable with not having all the
answers.[66]

Above all, Thurman thought the Student Christian Movement
needed to be more frank and open in addressing race issues. Thurman's early essays on race are among the most interesting he ever
wrote, in part because they are implicitly autobiographical, exploring
his newfound involvement—as speaker, colleague, and friend—with
whites. In "College and Color" and "Let Ministers Be Christians!,"
published in 1924 and 1925, he offers a taxonomy of the ways white
college students interact with blacks. There are the tolerators, those
who "condescend to smile 'Hello' or wave 'Good-bye.'" And then there
are the indifferent and the thoughtless, the sort who laugh unembar-
rassed at racist jokes or speak casually with friends about purchasing
tickets for a performance in "Nigger Heaven" (then a common term
for the top level of a theater's balcony). These groups outnumber the
overtly hostile, the person who "intentionally and maliciously brushes
against the Negro student in the corridor" and says nasty things to
his face.[67]

One thing that could be said for the open haters, Thurman acknowledged, is "their utter lack of hypocrisy." This was more than
could be said of most other interracial interactions, where the hypocrisy was patent, as when a black student found himself surrounded by
a cordon sanitaire ("all the chairs in his immediate vicinity are marked
by an invisible 'Unclean'"), or experienced a sudden change of dinner
plans when someone discovered he would be eating with a Negro. No
institution was more guilty of racial hypocrisy than the church itself.
In "Let Ministers Be Christians!," Thurman related the story told him
by a (presumably white) friend of a young woman who confided that
"I can't understand why I am going to Africa as a missionary. I hate
'Niggers.'" When it came to confronting the truth about racial inequalities, far too many ministers were afraid to raise controversies,
confront members of their congregation, challenge discriminatory

practices, and were content to "pussy-foot and wabble by the truth in the name of Jesus of Nazareth."[68]

The way away from hatred and hypocrisy started with personal honesty. Thurman often told the story of meeting a little girl of four who had never seen a black person before. She wondered if his color would rub off and whether he was black all over, and then, after a few questions, she forgot about it and they chatted as friends. In the end, her attitude "was one of sympathetic understanding—which leads to respect for personality." Sympathetic understanding was "not a patronizing attitude or anything that is cheap and sentimental. Nor do I mean an attitude that is so swollen with condescending pride that its stench is intolerable. But I do mean an attitude which says a man of another race is essentially myself, and I feel towards him as fundamentally as if he were myself." For Thurman, this was the "Christian way in race relations," which leads to "respect for personality."[69]

This was Thurman's attitude in April 1924 when "College and Color" appeared in the *Student Challenge*, and it would be, with very little variation, the position he would hold for the remainder of his life. His student essays on race are deceptively original and deceptively radical. He argued that respect for personality meant realizing an individual's potential, and only when individuals are treated as persons, and not as faceless and soulless extensions of their group or race, can society as a whole begin to realize its potential. Anyone who "strangles personality and inhibits its highest growth" is committing "a crime against God." And those Christians who "take unprotesting comfort" in the "unbrotherly, castelike inequalities of opportunity that prevail in the world" are teachers of "an anti-Christian ethic." If Thurman was not absolutely the first to argue that liberal Christianity would succeed or fail in how it dealt with the question of race, he would be among the most persuasive and influential. As Gary Dorrien has suggested, Thurman was the spiritual leader of a generation of black religious intellectuals, progressive in their politics, liberal in their theology, for whom "the social gospel movement had barely begun; what was needed was an American Christianity that took

seriously its own best preaching and ethics on behalf of equal opportunity, racial integration, and peace."[70]

And if Thurman taught others, he also learned from those he spoke
to and with. He would often look to a Student Christian Movement
retreat he participated in during the fall of 1925, at the Hudson River
town of Pawling, as a spiritual turning point in his life. About twenty-
five men and women from some of the finest colleges in the East were
in attendance, probably with few if any blacks besides himself. One
night, because of a shortage in accommodations, he was obliged to
share a bed with Allan Hunter, a Congregational minister who would
become a leading pacifist. As Thurman told the story:

> With frank simplicity he told me that although he had been
> unaware of harboring any racial prejudice until that moment,
> he also had never faced the prospect of sharing a bed with a
> Negro. Social relationships with Negroes were beyond the
> scope of his experience. We explored our souls together that
> night and helped each other exhume ghosts of racism each of
> us had considered buried forever. We talked until early light,
> and then we went to sleep. When we awoke, our lives were
> bound together in friendship.[71]

Thurman would record a few similar experiences in his life that
shared this sort of naked soul-bearing and mingling and the great
significance they had for him. It was this sort of very hard work that
was a precondition for the "sympathetic understanding," the deep empathy that he had discussed the previous year in "College and Color."

There was another reason why the Pawling retreat was so memorable for Thurman. One night, George "Shorty" Collins (all of six feet
five) read to the group an allegory, "The Hunter," the story of the quest
for a vast, beautiful white bird and the suffering the hunter endured
on his way. Thurman was overwhelmed. He had never heard anything that moved him as did "The Hunter," and "it seemed that all my
life I was being readied for such an encounter." It was written by the
South African novelist Olive Schreiner. Thurman became an instant,
fervent, and lifelong devotee, and she was perhaps his single most
important intellectual influence. He would read all of her writings in

short order, name his eldest daughter Olive in her honor, and in 1973 fulfill an ambition of thirty years by publishing an anthology of her writings.[72]

Schreiner was born in 1855 in what is now South Africa, the daughter of white missionary parents, though she would in time come to rebel against her evangelical upbringing and considered herself a freethinker from an early age. After working as a governess, she moved to England in 1883, where in 1885 she published her first and best-known book, *The Story of an African Farm*, which is generally seen as the first significant feminist novel. Another novel, *Trooper Peter Halket of Mashonaland* (1897), attacked Cecil Rhodes and British imperial designs on southern Africa. In England she became involved in a number of leftist causes, among them socialism, pacifism, and feminism. (Her 1911 treatise *Women and Labor* was one of the major theoretical statements produced by the British feminist movement in the early 1900s.) In 1891 she published *Dreams*, the first of several volumes of allegories, which would always be the most important part of her work for Thurman. World War I strengthened her pacifism, and in part because of her familiarity with South Africa, she was one of the earliest prominent British supporters of Mahatma Gandhi's satyagraha campaigns. Never in robust health, she died in South Africa in 1920. Schreiner and Thurman make for an odd intellectual couple. When Thurman discovered who she was and where she was from, "I became immediately suspicious and felt guilty that I was so affected by her." How could "a white woman born and reared in South Africa" feel like such a soul mate? And Thurman found her racial views to be challenging. She was not unsympathetic to the plight and rights of native Africans (though this wasn't a major component of her work), but she was not above using *nigger* as a passing description, something that evoked "shock and anger" in Thurman.[73]

What then did Thurman see in Schreiner? Probably most important, they shared a religious sensibility; both were products of an evangelical upbringing they rejected, embracing a far looser spiritual sensibility, though Schreiner had moved beyond Thurman in her rejection of Christianity. (Thurman says his understanding of the world was religious; Schreiner's was metaphysical.) But both Thurman and

Schreiner were, at their cores, nature mystics. Thurman quotes her approvingly in the introduction to his anthology as saying, "All nature is alive, even so-called inanimate matter; a stone has no apparent energy and so *seems* dead; but life runs through everything." For both, the unity of all life was the single most fundamental, overriding spiritual reality. Schreiner would write that "when I was a little girl of five and sat alone among the tall weeds at the back of the house, this perception of the unity of all things, and that they were alive, and that I was part of them, was as clear and overpowering to me as it is today. It is the one thing I was never able to doubt." A lonely, sensitive black boy turned to the ocean for spiritual solace; a lonely, sensitive white girl turned to the veldt. It was only when he read Schreiner that Thurman was able to understand that his own childhood experiences of nature were not unique and was able to view them with sufficient distance. In the end, what Thurman most admired about Schreiner was her unbounded imagination, her ability to fashion herself to transcend the limitations of a harsh childhood, and the subordinate role assigned to her by an unfeeling society. He would write of her: "It is difficult to identify the influences that shape and fashion the life of an individual. . . . It has been aptly said that the time and place of a man's life is the time and place of his body, but the meaning and significance of a man's life is as creative, as vast, and as far-reaching as his gifts, his dreams, and his response to his times can make them."[74] He was of course also writing of his own journey.[75]

For both Thurman and Schreiner, nature was not only to be admired in reverie; it was also a primary source of personal and collective strength. As Schreiner wrote, quoted by Thurman, "You cannot by willing it alter the vast world outside of you; you cannot, perhaps, cut the lash from one whip; you cannot, perhaps, strike the handcuffs from one chained hand." But when you start to help the weak and those in pain, you get a feeling "not easy to put into words . . . you also are a part of the great universe; what you strive for something strives for; and nothing in the universe is quite alone; you are moving on toward something." The romantic vitalism in Schreiner's writings and its teleological force; her sense of controlled, purposive (and non-

Darwinian) evolution; its slow, providential twisting toward a better future were ideals Thurman greatly admired, and it suffuses his writings. Schreiner's allegories can be read as a pilgrim's progress of the soul, or the people's progress toward some distant, difficult goal, and Thurman read them both ways.[76]

Olive Schreiner's most important cause was feminism and the oppression of women. She cataloged the means and varieties of their oppression: by their inability to participate as equal citizens in the political process; by their lack of vocational choice; all too often by their marriage and relations with men; and by a society that at every turn thwarted their ability for artistic, religious, and sexual self-expression. There were of course profound differences between the situation of the (predominantly white and middle- and upper-class) women Schreiner wrote about and the condition of blacks in America, but Thurman knew oppression when he saw it, and Thurman became a feminist. If this was not entirely unique among his male, liberal Protestant peers, white or black, it certainly was unusual. He had always been a man with dominant female figures in his life, starting with his indomitable grandmother. But from Schreiner he learned how to understand the plight of women historically and politically and the scope of its broader implications. Thurman's feminism decisively shaped who he was and who he would become.

This would be most apparent in the work that served as the culmination of his seminary years, his bachelor of divinity thesis, "The Basis of Sex Morality: An Inquiry into the Attitude toward Premarital Sexual Morality among Various Peoples and an Analysis of Its True Basis." The thesis was a summation of the person Thurman had become at Rochester. It was the product of many things: of the changing sexual mores of the roaring twenties; of many frank conversations with men and women, whites and blacks about their desires, their frustrations, and their worries as to whether Christianity had any message for them besides abstinence until marriage; and of his new appreciation of the special problems faced by women. But above all, the choice of the topic and the way he wrote it was a tribute to his newfound intellectual passion for the works of Olive Schreiner.[77]

After an impressive display of feminist erudition, he argues that the purpose of premarital chastity had been primarily to confine women to the home and to render them dependent and inferior to men. "At no point," he wrote, "has the domination of men been more disastrous than in the conventional attitude toward pre-marital unchastity," which was the basis of the double standard that expected "respectable" women to be prudish and ignorant of sex, while allowing lower-class women to be available to fulfill the extramarital sexual desires of men. Like Schreiner in *Women and Labor,* Thurman argued that the dominant sexual choice for women was between being a wife in a male-dominated marriage or a prostitute. (In his only comments on race in the thesis, he argued that antimiscegenation laws had the effect of making all sex between whites and blacks extramarital, thereby exposing "the girls of the minority group to the lustful ravages of men in the majority group.")

But, Thurman argued, attitudes were beginning to change. Women "have revolted against the selfishness, injustice, and domination of the 'Man's State.'" They have demanded an end to an educational system that was "segregated" and left them "in ignorance." (Separate is always unequal.) Women had achieved the vote, but that was merely the beginning of what feminists sought. Feminists would realize a "true equality of men and women," which Thurman called "a form of Socialism." Feminists also wanted "free love," which would make marriage "the result of a common decision to live together" and "destroy all vestiges of the male monopoly." They were also demanding the "complete economic freedom of women." All this would lead to a new legal and societal recognition of "a woman's right over her own body," wrote Thurman. This would end what Thurman, again referencing Schreiner, would call the Parasitic Woman, the woman denied a useful function in society. Women were fighting for their own advancement, but all oppression and all fights for equality are linked: "It is impossible to separate the struggle for freedom on the part of women from the general wave of democracy that has swept the world."

The roots of the thesis lay in the myriad conversations he had enjoyed with students at various Christian conferences over the previous few years. And though he doesn't really call attention to it, many of these conversations had been with white women, like the story he relates of the Swarthmore co-ed who had initiated sexual relations with her boyfriend. One can't imagine that there were many precedents for this, and it was a combination of the growing sexual frankness of the 1920s—what Thurman and others were calling "the revolt of youth"—and Thurman's remarkable gifts as a confidant that made this possible. Most of his confidants shared "a flagrant disregard for anything which savored of external authority," and their interest and use of sex to challenge what they saw as a stifling convention. For Thurman the frankness of the talk no doubt reflected changing racial mores as much as changing sexual mores. If black men and white women could talk about sex, then people could talk about anything.

In the final section of the thesis, he argues that if an unmarried man and woman come together on "the basis of spiritual unity," premarital sex was acceptable. Quoting Schreiner and her referencing her close friend, the pioneering sex researcher Richard Havelock Ellis, he calls "sex intercourse the great sacrament of life," and that woman, "by reason of the very sexual conditions which in the past have crushed and trammeled her," will be "bound to lead the way and man to follow" toward a new "history of sex with its great power and its beauty of holiness," one still "in its infancy."

In the thesis, if Thurman was writing about its ostensible topic, women and sexuality, he was hinting at something else as well. He saw women (and, following Olive Schreiner and most of the feminist authors he cited, he was primarily writing about white women) as an example of a marginalized group in American society challenging the basis of their oppression, demanding full citizenship, and being accepted as equals. If white women were somewhat farther along on this path than blacks (male and female), then their achievements could only hearten and give lessons for those still waiting their turn. When Thurman was writing about sex, he was writing about the overwhelming power of true human intimacy as well. Intimacy and religion, like sex, were not primarily something to be written about or logically explained; they needed to be viscerally experienced.

Thurman's thesis was a unique work in his output. Never again would he write at length on sexuality. Never again would he write with such passion on women or feminism. And never again would he write on what was such an important part of his ministry, his private and frank conversations with young people and college students. But the main tenets of the thesis would be assumed and incorporated into later work: the spiritual importance of physicality, the importance of interpersonal dialogue, and an abiding commitment to the absolute equality of the sexes. In its combination of worldliness and spirituality, of the personal and the political, and its plea for the deep unity of all aspects of the human experience, it was a crucial step forward in his intellectual and religious maturation.

Thurman's thesis was a fitting culmination to his career at RTS, where he graduated as valedictorian from his class of twenty-nine. A thesis was not mandatory for RTS graduates, and many never completed one or completed one years later. The RTS faculty was proud of their brilliant student but knew he could never follow in their footsteps and aim for a teaching career at a place such as RTS. Either as a pastor or a professor, he was destined to spend his life within black institutions where the realities of social inferiority would be a constant companion.

It was perhaps similar considerations that led George Cross to have one final conversation with Thurman shortly before his graduation. He told Thurman that he had superior gifts and that he could and probably would make an original contribution to the spiritual life of the times. But there was a caution. "You are a very sensitive Negro man, and you doubtless feel under a great obligation to put all the weight of your mind and spirit at the disposal of your people for full citizenship. But let me remind you that all social questions are transitory in nature and it would be a terrible waste for you to limit your creative energies to the solution of the race problem, however insistent its nature." Instead, Cross advised, "Give yourself to the timeless issues of the human spirit." Thurman was astounded and more than a little offended by Cross's comments, and an awkward silence followed before Cross added, "Perhaps I have no right to say this to you because as a white man I can never know what it is to be in your situation." Thurman remained silent, and Cross changed the subject.[78]

It was a critical conversation for Thurman, one that he would repeat word for word half a century later when writing his autobiography. Cross was speaking to (without really challenging) an asymmetry, a double standard, that was at the heart of the education of blacks in places like RTS. White seminarians could study and write on any topic of their choosing from the entire intellectual edifice of Christianity without raising any questions; black seminarians were presumed to be most interested in and most capable of writing on some aspect of the race question, and this was seen, as Cross implied, to be an ephemeral question of secondary interest. This had been a crucial question for all blacks in Thurman's situation: proving they were the equal of white students and proving that their intellectual interests were as catholic as any of their peers'. It was one reason Thurman, as far as we know, wrote nothing about African American religion while at RTS, and why many other blacks in similar circumstances, such as John Hope Franklin and Martin Luther King Jr., were reluctant to write on African American topics in their graduate education.

But this was of course a trap. To be concerned with the universals of the human condition while ignoring the particulars of one's own circumstances, especially when those conditions in the America of the early twentieth century were so problematic, was to risk intellectual and emotional sterility. As Cross was speaking to him, Thurman couldn't say what he was thinking: "I pondered the meaning of his words, and wondered what kind of response I could make to this man who did not know that a man and his black skin must face the 'timeless issues of the human spirit' together." But if Cross's comments were somewhat patronizing, he was also responding to a very real issue that Thurman was confronting: balancing his need and gift to speak on the "timeless issues of the human spirit" with the basic facts of his racial identity without submerging one beneath the other, learning how to speak to white audiences without either ignoring race or focusing on it to the exclusion of everything else. They were questions he began to address while at RTS, and he would continue to wrestle with them for the remainder of his life.

CHAPTER TWO

Starting a Career

ON MAY 18, 1926, Thurman graduated from Rochester Theological Seminary, his formal education completed. Two milestones followed in quick succession. On June 11, in LaGrange, Georgia, in an early morning ceremony, he married Katie Kelley. She was twenty-six months older than Thurman, born in September 1897, the daughter of Charles H. Kelley, a prominent LaGrange educator, and Frances Kelley. Her parents were Morehouse and Spelman alumni. She followed her mother's path, and graduated from Spelman in 1918. She continued her studies briefly at the University of Chicago before returning to Atlanta to pursue studies at the Morehouse-affiliated Atlanta School of Social Work in the fall of 1921. It was presumably at this point that her path crossed Thurman's, and the two were probably introduced by her brother and his classmate, Charles Kelley Jr. She worked as a visiting health educator in the black branch of the Anti-Tuberculosis Association of Atlanta for several years before becoming director of an antituberculosis clinic in Morristown, New Jersey, where she remained until a month before her marriage. How Kelley and Thurman conducted their romance is not known, but perhaps the many trips to New York City Thurman took during his seminary years that he mentions in his autobiography had some connection to her living in the greater metropolitan area in northern New Jersey.[1]

We know relatively little about Katie Kelley. She was not granted a long life, and her health was already fragile by the time of her marriage. She was a bright, socially committed woman, determined to give herself the best education possible. Her radiant beauty looks out from surviving photographs, and she had a happy marriage with Howard Thurman. Their only child, Olive Katherine Thurman, was born in

October 1928. Shortly thereafter Katie Kelley Thurman would develop a full-blown case of tuberculosis, presumably contracted during
her years of social work with consumptive patients, and she would be
dead by the end of 1930. Her death would plunge Thurman into the
deepest and most prolonged depression he would ever experience.

Their wedding was a perfect day—Thurman remembered "the soft-
ness of the rising sun reflected in the mysterious beauty of Katie's
eyes"—but there was no time for a honeymoon.[2] Right after the ceremony the Thurmans boarded a train for the Midwest, and on June 13
Howard Thurman preached his first sermon as pastor of the Mount
Zion Baptist Church in Oberlin, Ohio, his first pastorate and his first
full-time job. Thurman would only spend two years in Oberlin, but it
proved a fruitful starting point for his career. He took advantage of the
town and gown possibilities that life in the college town of Oberlin
offered, continuing his theological studies at the Oberlin School of
Theology. (He registered for a master of sacred theology, but never
completed the work.)[3] He engaged in his lifelong interest in theater
by directing two productions staged by a local black drama troupe.[4]
He found his work at Mount Zion Baptist Church exciting and re-
warding. Like many newly minted seminary graduates, he had much
to impart to his "flock" about new ways of thinking about old questions. He would offer sermon series on the meaning of love and on the
dangers of medical quackery, among other topics. He modernized
the communion service, making it more inclusive, and also campaigned
for Oberlin College to do a better job in admitting local blacks.[5]

In time Thurman outgrew what he thought was an initial cal-
lowness and didacticism in the pulpit. He felt that when he arrived,
his public prayers at Oberlin were highly self-conscious, as if those
hearing him were rudely intruding on his inner spiritual life, or his
efforts to address his congregation's spiritual needs were forced and
artificial. He soon transcended this false dichotomy. He discovered
that there was no reason "to differentiate human needs, theirs and my
own" and learned to "pray in public as if I was alone in the quiet of
my own room." His sermons became less "motivated by the desire to
'teach'" and more by "the meaning of the experience of our common

quest and journey." He would help an old ex-slave come to terms with the bitter hatred he had always felt for the master who had savagely beat him, enabling him to die with the act of Christian forgiveness he had long sought. A Buddhist visitor from China would become a sometime attendee at the church, telling Thurman shortly before he returned home that "when I close my eyes and listen with my spirit I am in my Buddhist temple experiencing the renewing of my own spirit." Thurman would write in his autobiography that he knew, on hearing this, that "the barriers were crumbling," though it would take many years for him to fully understand the implications of this breakthrough. Nonetheless, the pattern of his entire career was set in Oberlin. His passionate commitment to challenging the social and political injustices outside the walls of his church always started with the exploration of his own spiritual life and that of his congregation.[6]

Thurman remained much in demand as a speaker, writing Mordecai Wyatt Johnson in September 1926 of his engagements that "things are opening up in a way which is positively embarrassing." In his two years at Oberlin, his engagements would be as far flung as Prairie View State Normal and Industrial College in Texas, Iowa State Teacher's College in Cedar Falls, and Vassar College in Poughkeepsie, New York, where he would be the first black to preach in the chapel. Once Mordecai Wyatt Johnson became president of Howard University in September 1926, Thurman preached there regularly. He was a featured speaker at the annual black YMCA conferences at Kings Mountain, North Carolina, with the leading black progressive Christians of his era. During these years he was developing his craft, trying out themes and topics that he would spend years polishing and honing. Before a Congregational church in Oberlin in November 1927, he preached on "Barren or Fruitful," five years before its published version appeared, and that same year a YMCA audience in Indianapolis heard "Christian, Who Calls Me Christian?" a decade before the sermon would be published. By the time Thurman left Oberlin in the summer of 1928, he was already being described in the *Pittsburgh Courier* as "an outstanding pulpit orator and one of the greatest thinkers of the age."[7]

Perhaps his most notable appearance during his Oberlin years was at a National Student Conference in Milwaukee at the turn of 1927, with 2,500 people in attendance.[8] After a stirring address by Mordecai Wyatt Johnson, the conference passed a resolution affirming the equality of the races. Thurman would be the only other black to address the conference in a sermon called "Finding God." As would become typical for him, he said little about race (and that obliquely) before the predominantly white audience. He opened by observing that the 1920s were a time of protest against the "bondage of formulae" in all areas of life, including religion. When the rubrics and formal rituals of religion are discarded, the believer is left with the God who is the source of all life, the "underlying unity" for all creation. One could by striving at special moments "make contact with that unity." It could be reached through personal achievement—Thurman gave the example of great musicians and actors at peak moments in the creative process. But one need not be an artist to realize this sense of creative unity. Everyone can and must reach out, and when we do so, include the excluded in our circles of comfort and friendship, the marginal people Thurman here called "the lost," another term for what he would later call "the disinherited." "God needs them [the lost], and God will never be what He hungers to be in His world until these people are what they ought to be." One can find God, Thurman concluded, only by demanding for oneself "the kind of energy that God releases" and not resting until it is found. Over the next half century, Thurman would find many different ways to say this, but this would always be his essential message to audiences white or black, big or small. Discrimination or any other artificial distinction between classes of people is, above all, a rupture in the unity of God, which can only be repaired by becoming a vessel of God's purpose.[9]

Thurman's message in "Finding God," his distrust of cant, of routine, of any expressions of self-satisfaction, speak to an inner intellectual and spiritual turbulence for Thurman during his Oberlin years. In April 1927, he would write Mordecai Wyatt Johnson (at the time Thurman's favored confidant) that "I am going thru a veritable upheaval in my thinking—I do not know where I shall come out—

and it hardly matters."[10] We have few other clues to the nature of this spiritual crisis, but it seems likely that it pushed Thurman to further separate himself from what he saw as the pernicious values of mainstream American society, writing Johnson a few months later that "we are fed and clothed by a vast system built upon deceit and adulteration."[11] Like many sensitive souls in the 1920s influenced by Sinclair Lewis, Upton Sinclair, and others, Thurman was struck by the emptiness and hollowness of American civilization in which getting ahead of one's fellows and the accumulation of material possessions seemed to be the only ideals, where, as he would write in 1927, there was "no sacredness of life, nothing but the survival of the fittest and every man for himself."[12]

This situation placed blacks in a familiar double bind. In the same essay, "Higher Education and Religion," published in a black Baptist journal, he wrote of a conversation with the "head of the department of sociology in a very influential college in the Middle West," possibly Robert Park at the University of Chicago, who told Thurman, "The thing you must tell young Negroes is to get money. They must learn to speak the language of economic power and control, that is, the language of the American white man generally." This was sound, familiar Washingtonian advice, the language of uplift that had been drilled into Thurman from an early age. But Thurman felt that there was no point in making blacks as superficial and power-obsessed as whites. Forfeiting one's soul was too steep a price for racial equality. "The only people who are going to save our civilization, if it can be saved or ought to be," he told the sociologist, "are those who have learned to *live*, so as to reveal the superiority of the human spirit to the domination of things." For blacks to embrace the "religion of materialism" as ardently as whites "means death, and that quickly."[13]

The religion of materialism had far too many black adherents already. The black church had moved from an otherworldly apocalyptic faith to a this-worldly faith in things and institutions, following the lead of their white brethren in building ever bigger, gaudier churches and seeing this as a sign of progress. Thurman wrote in another essay in a black religious journal, paraphrasing Nietzsche, "People

always build temples to their dead Gods." He recognized that formal structures are necessary evils. It was "a very interesting paradox"
that "a dynamic idea cannot continue to persist unless it is housed
in some form of organization."[14] But those within institutions must
continually fight against their deadening embrace. He wrote Johnson
in September 1927 that "there *seems* to be something about joining
a church which deprives an individual of the keen obligation to be
exercised increasingly about being Christian." The best church members were those, he continued, "who apparently have transcended the
church."[15]

So what was needed, he continued to Johnson, was a way "to release
to the full our spiritual powers, [so] that there may be such a ground
swell of spiritual energy that existing systems will be upset from
sheer dynamic" as a prelude to a "genuine uprooting." The only way
for blacks to truly join American society as equals was to transform
it. In his two articles in 1927 and 1928 addressed to a black audience,
Thurman outlined what this spiritual and social revolution might en-
tail. Blacks, their ministers, and their churches must embrace the best
of modern American society, but only on their own terms. They must
avoid "the current demand for things" and seek "the spiritual tasks to
which He has set our hands," and realize this task involved directly
experiencing "the contagion of the spirit of Jesus" rather than placing
their faith in institutions that at second- and thirdhand sought to
perpetuate a weak and watered-down Christian message. Following
from this, he argued, "we must seek to demolish the artificial barrier
between religion and life" that left religion neutered and life without
a guiding principle, perhaps the most tragic and most fundamental
form of segregation.[16] And yet, there still seems something unformed
about Thurman's religious writings during his Oberlin period. If he
was clear about what he opposed in organized Christianity, his alternatives remained abstract and unspecific. From his boyhood he possessed an almost innate sense of mysticism, but this remained little
developed or explored, either intellectually or spiritually. This would
soon begin to change, in part because of an encounter with a book
Thurman purchased for a dime at a used book sale.

II

Thurman would often write about the power of serendipity, those accidental occurrences that belie the seeming randomness of the world. One of those moments occurred in late 1927 or early 1928 when he was attending a religious conference at a church in a town near Oberlin. Thurman was bored and left before the conference was completed. As he was leaving the church, he chanced upon a table of books with a sign saying, "Your choice for 10 cents." He purchased *Finding the Trail of Life* by Rufus Jones. Thurman wrote in his autobiography that he "was intrigued by the title and sat on the steps of the church and began reading. I did not move until I had read the entire book."[17]

What attracted Thurman to Jones's book, a short autobiography of his childhood years? Perhaps it was a sentence on the book's second page. "I am convinced, too, by my own life and by wide observation of children that mystical experience is much more common than is usually supposed."[18] Thurman had found a kindred spirit. Jones first became aware of his own openness to mystical experience as a young boy, experiencing God through nature. Jones writes in the book of his finding God in water, in the lakes and rivers of Maine, and in extreme natural events, in storms, in thunder, and in lightning. He was a lonely boy, surrounded by strong female figures, and he grew up in and outgrew his strict religious upbringing, a rigorous brand of Quakerism. (Jones would write elsewhere, "There are few crises to compare with that which appears when the simple childhood religion, imbibed at mother's knee, and absorbed from early home and church environment, comes with collision with a scientific, solidly reasoned system.")[19] The little book, less than one hundred and fifty pages in length, concluded by saying that "if a man can succeed in telling about the building of his soul, it is more worthwhile than the telling of any other tale." There is no doctrine, no theology in *Finding the Trail of Life*, just autobiography mingled with stray religious reflection. Thurman's own autobiography, written half a century later, owes much to the example of Jones, for both men had the same purpose in writing their life stories—to convey the message that, as Gary Dorrien has written of Jones, "Religion and theology either begin with personal experience, or they have no real starting point at all."[20]

In 1927, when Rufus Jones published *Finding the Trail of Life*, he was not only an accomplished popular author but also one of the most prominent and influential theologians of his generation. Born in Maine in 1863, a student of philosophy at Harvard during its golden era at the turn of the twentieth century, he was much influenced by William James and his emphasis on religious experience rather than abstract theorizing about religion. We will reach the kingdom of God, Jones wrote, through "a new experience of God as Father—not as a new theory of the Fatherhood of God."[21] In his most influential book, *Social Law in the Spiritual World* (1904), and in many subsequent works, he made a distinction between ascetic world-denying mysticism and a positive mysticism that embraced the world and its concerns, which he saw as characteristic of George Fox and the Quakers. If Jones was concerned with a variety of social issues—for example, he was a pacifist, a principal founder in 1917 of the American Friends Service Committee, and he traveled overseas frequently on its behalf—he wrote little about social issues directly, but in his voluminous writings he returned again and again to questions of personal religion. In all these things, his understanding of religion as experience, of the distinction between the mysticism of affirmation and negation, and of the need to approach social questions from the vantage of personal religious experience, Jones would be a profound influence on Thurman.

If, when Thurman read *Finding the Trail of Life*, he did not know that Jones was an expert on the history and theology of mysticism and a distinguished professor at Haverford College, he soon found out. Jones was, as Leigh Eric Schmidt has written, as close as early twentieth-century American Protestantism "came to having a mystic and a saint," and Thurman was determined to study at his feet.[22] For Thurman, real learning always required the intimacy and intensity of personal mentoring. He had always sought out teachers who could provide this, and he would try to be that sort of teacher himself, giving several generations of students the same sort of close spiritual encounters that had been so important to him. Writing to John Hope in 1926, he would quote with approval a prayer of Walter Rauschenbusch's, "We remember with gratitude to thee the godly teachers of our own youth who won our hearts to higher purposes by the sacred contagion of their life." With Hope, and more particularly with George Cross and Mordecai Wyatt Johnson, he had found that sort of mentor, and he hoped that with Jones he would have a further exposure to the "sacred contagion" of extraordinary teaching.[23]

Thurman also hoped that Jones would in some way be his final mentor, a way to finish his education. He had already largely decided by 1928 not to obtain a doctorate in theology. This would have been the natural and expected next step for him, especially after his sterling record as a student and his ambitions for his own academic career. But he had deep reservations about this, deciding, as he wrote in his autobiography, "that if I were to devote full-time to the requirements of a doctoral program, academic strictures would gradually usurp the energy I wanted to nourish the inner regions of my spirit."[24] He was afraid of the dangers of routinization and formalism, as much in writing about religion as in the experience of religion itself, and at no stage in his career had he much interest in formal theology. But at the same time, he felt his education was incomplete; there was much more to study, especially in the presence of a master. Studying with Rufus Jones would be the way to finish his education.

But there were a number of obstacles in the way of Thurman studying with Jones. First, he had a full-time job at Mount Zion Baptist Church in Oberlin. Second, he had a wife who was seriously ill with tuberculosis and a baby daughter who needed to be cared for. Third, he needed to find a way to fund his period of study with Jones. And fourth, as he rightly suspected, Haverford College, a Quaker college outside Philadelphia, like most Quaker Colleges at the time (shamefully, given their heritage), did not accept black students.

All of these things would be worked out. He resigned his position in Oberlin. Although he was offered a position at Howard, he chose instead a joint appointment at Morehouse and Spelman, in large part so that his wife could be near her family. He would start teaching in

Atlanta in the fall of 1928, but would spend the spring 1929 term at Haverford as a special student of Jones, who had arranged for Thurman's admittance. He would stay in graduate housing and there would be no cost of tuition. Thurman obtained a fellowship from the National Council for Research in Higher Education, usually reserved for doctoral work, to defray his expenses.[25]

Thurman found his months with Jones to be "seminal times." He attended all Jones's lectures at Haverford as well as a special seminar on the fourteenth-century German mystic Meister Eckhart. Jones and Thurman had weekly meetings, and Thurman also attended Wednesday worship at the Haverford Meeting House. He found Jones to be "utterly informal" but penetrating, quickly getting to the core of the matter, with the "gift of intimacy, which allowed him to go to the heart of his personal experience without causing embarrassment to himself or his listener." And if Jones was vitally interested in social matters, like most Social Gospel exponents of the time, race was not a matter of great concern to him, and it did not come up in his talks with Thurman. He found this surprising, and would write, "I felt that he transcended race; I did so, too, temporarily," though whether Thurman thought this was a good thing is unclear.[26]

Their discussions ranged over the history of Western mysticism. Thurman wrote papers for Jones on the great Spanish mystics St. Teresa and St. John of the Cross, on the seventeenth-century French Quietist Madame Guyon, and what Thurman called a "definitive study of the mysticism of St. Francis of Assisi." (Alas, none of these papers are extant.) At the conclusion of his study with Jones, he would write him to offer "my most sincerely personal thanks for the huge share you have had in the enrichment of my life during the past five months. I cannot now estimate the significance of the days with you at Haverford."[27]

What was the significance of his study with Jones? First, he learned about mysticism and its history from perhaps that era's leading exponent. If Thurman was in many ways a mystic from his earliest years, this had never been systematically cultivated. Mysticism played little role in Rochester Theological Seminary curriculum during his years there, and Cross was not particularly sympathetic to mysticism.[28]

In his exposure to the Quaker way, Thurman found the perfect expression for his mystical tendencies, how to communicate religious feeling without any preacherly affectation, the necessary alliance between religious speech and religious silence, and the difference between speaking with or for a congregation rather than from a place of privilege, simply speaking to it. In time he would learn to preach in the Quaker way, without formal texts, with few notes, his words essentially dictated by the voice within. In 1951 he remembered his first attendance at a Quaker meeting during his time at Haverford. "Nobody said a word . . . just silence. Silence. Silence. And in that silence I felt as though all of them were on one side and I was on the other side, by myself, with my noise. And every time I would try to get across that barrier, nothing happened. I was just Howard Thurman. And then . . . I don't know when it happened, how it happened, but somewhere in that hour I passed over the invisible line, and I became one with all the seekers. I wasn't Howard Thurman anymore; I was a human spirit involved in a creative moment with human spirits, in the presence of God." The Quaker meeting, with its quiet, its spontaneity, its emphasis on "centering down" and meditation, was for him perhaps the ideal venue for authentic religion, one that in his various ministries he would try to re-create for the rest of his career.[29]

What Jones and Thurman called mysticism or experiential religion, we today might call spirituality, and as Leigh Eric Schmidt has argued, both Jones and Thurman were key individuals in the development of a distinctive American spirituality holding itself outside of and as an alternative to formal, creedal religion.[30] If Jones had discovered at the heart of the Quaker way a formless, creedless religion prior to any attempt to qualify or describe it, his spiritual quest remained essentially Protestant and Christian in its nature, whereas Thurman would slowly and steadily move beyond his own Christian moorings to a freer, utterly interreligious experience of God. While he would soon teach courses on mysticism at Morehouse and Howard, he would write or speak little about mysticism for a decade, but eventually his deepening understanding of it and its broader implications and ramifications would become the basis of both his religious and his social thought.[31]

III

Thurman did not really want to return to Atlanta when he resigned his position in Oberlin. Although he had fond memories of his undergraduate days, he never really liked the city, which had always struck him as a menacing place for blacks to live, especially for blacks who were willing to hold their heads up high. Howard had the advantages of prestige and a president who was actively seeking Thurman's presence. But his wife's illness made relocation to Georgia necessary. He wrote Johnson in May 1928, "After going thru the whole matter of coming to Howard *next year* I have decided against it. Until we are surer of Mrs. Thurman's health I must work either in Atlanta or nearer there than Washington." So for the interim, Thurman would devote himself to "develop the spiritual tone of the students at Morehouse and Spelman" in his joint appointment. They were not particularly happy years for Thurman, personally or professionally.[32]

Atlanta remained as inhospitable as he remembered it. And far from improving, the racial climate was, if anything, deteriorating. In 1930 the Morehouse-Spelman-Atlanta University area was roiled by the murder of a Morehouse undergraduate for the supposed crime of insulting a white woman. The possibility of a race riot was ever looming.[33]

Also complicating Thurman's return to Atlanta was his difficult relationship with one of his bosses, Florence Read, the formidable president of Spelman College. When appointed in 1927, she was an official of the Rockefeller Foundation, which through its General Education Board was the primary financial spigot for both colleges, though she had little experience in college administration. She took the lead in trying to implement the board's effort to engineer a formal "affiliation" between Spelman, Morehouse, and Atlanta University, which was finalized in the spring of 1929. John Hope was named president of the new Atlanta University and remained president of Morehouse as well, but he was in declining health (and would pass in 1936), and increasingly Read was the real authority.[34] Thurman felt that the era of white presidents of black colleges had passed, and Spelman, unlike most black colleges in the late 1920s, still had a predominantly white faculty. Although Read was an effective administrator (and would remain president of Spelman until 1953) and more enlightened in her racial attitudes and progressive in her pedagogy than her immediate predecessors, the two did not get along. Thurman found her attitudes toward Spelman and its students colored by more than a whiff of condescension, and she tried to control his off-campus speaking engagements (something that happened in every college in which Thurman was employed, and something that always left him enraged). Typical of the paternalism that persisted at Spelman, Thurman felt, were the Sunday services in the chapel led by the president, with a sermon usually preached by a visiting white minister. In all, Thurman recalls, "Almost imperceptibly at first, the breach between Miss Read and me widened," and their enmity was never resolved.[35]

But Thurman's deepest source of sadness and melancholy during his Atlanta years was the steady decline of his wife's health. For much of the time she stayed in the MacVicar Infirmary on the Spelman campus, a teaching facility for nurses.[36] By the fall of 1930, it was clear that she was losing her battle with tuberculosis. On the shortest, darkest day of the year, December 21, Katie Kelley Thurman died in Atlanta. She was buried in her hometown of LaGrange. We know little of Thurman's immediate responses, and indeed we know little of his life over the next two years, as he kept his deepest feelings to himself and corresponded little with others. Whether as a relief or not, Thurman soon plunged into his usual busy schedule of speaking engagements, and on January 1 he was back home in Daytona Beach, speaking at the Emancipation Day ceremonies at Bethune-Cookman College. He would preach at Howard University later in the month, before engagements that semester at Fisk University, at Rochester, and in Detroit where he would preach the first of many Holy Week engagements at the St. Antoine Street YMCA.[37]

Nonetheless, when the summer break came, he was "physically and emotionally exhausted. I needed to get my bearings on my future, personally and professionally." He traveled to Europe to do some sight-seeing in Britain and on the continent, where he visited Paris and

Geneva (and was joined for part of the trip by his closest friend, Herbert King), but the greatest advantage that Europe had over America was that he knew almost no one there and could be left alone with his thoughts. After finding a hotel that would rent to blacks, he walked the streets of London from morning to night, and then spent time on a sheep farm near Edinburgh where his days were spent walking in the moors and napping in the fields. (One wonders if Thurman caught a glimpse of another visitor to London that summer, Mahatma Gandhi, in town for the Round Table Conference with British authorities.) In all, his time in Europe was restorative. "My life seemed whole again," he would later write, "and the strains of an unknown melody healed my inmost center."[38]

IV

If the four years Thurman spent in Atlanta, from 1928 to 1932, had plenty of low points, they were not without their achievements and personal accomplishments. Certainly by the time he left Atlanta, his reputation was nicely burnished. In the space of one year, 1932, the *Atlanta Daily World* described him as "brilliant and illuminating," and one appearance as rising a "to a vast pinnacle" of "mysticism and philosophy."[39] His profundity was no bar to his popularity. Any place he would speak "will be embarrassed for seating space," claimed another article, which went on to describe seeing Thurman emerge from a drugstore as if it were a sighting of Plato in Woolworth's: "The noted philosopher was seen in animated handshakes with good friends and admirers on the Avenue."[40] By the time he was thirty-two years old, he was already being acclaimed as "Howard Thurman the Great."[41]

He may have been embarrassed by some of the hyperbole, but his intellectual achievements during his Atlanta years were considerable. In some ways he used the inhospitable racial climate to his advantage.[42] In the fall of 1928, in a series of five chapel talks at Spelman, Thurman introduced what would be one of his most enduring themes, his reflections on the Negro spirituals. He had always loved the spirituals, but he first began to think about the complexities of their meaning five years earlier as a senior at Morehouse during a mandatory chapel service. A few directors of the all-white General Education Board, a major source of funding for Morehouse, were present. They were introduced and then awaited their traditional serenade, the singing of spirituals by the entire student body. The signal was given. All was silence. The signal was given again, with the same result. John Hope was deeply embarrassed, and he called for a special assembly that evening at which Morehouse students were severely reprimanded. The response of the students was simple, according to Thurman. "We refuse to sing our songs to delight and amuse white people. The songs are ours and a part of the source of our own inspiration transmitted to us by our forefathers."[43]

This was a common response to the spirituals in the 1920s. At Howard University in 1925 a similar situation—the refusal of the student body to sing spirituals for white visitors—precipitated a student strike that led to the resignation of J. Stanley Durkee, the university's last white president.[44] By the 1920s Negro spirituals had become, among broad classes of black intellectuals, a sign of servility, because, as Thurman's friend James Weldon Johnson wrote in 1926, the "chief effect of this slave music upon its white hearers was that they were touched and moved with deepest sympathy for the 'poor Negro.'"[45] The new Negro of the 1920s didn't sing spirituals. Thurman, like Johnson, was in the forefront of a current in black intellectual life that was urging the rehabilitation of the spiritual. Thurman wanted to talk about the spirituals, as he told his audience at Spelman, because their "religious message" had been forgotten or submerged (and then safely aestheticized) beneath "the beauty of the melodies."[46] Thurman wanted his listeners to hear the spirituals anew without the patina of docility and supplication.

If Thurman's explanations of the spirituals rooted them in their necessary contexts, as slave songs of the antebellum South, his real interest in the spirituals was in their universality and their applicability to other times and other peoples. He was far more interested in looking forward and establishing their continuing relevance to the plight of blacks in the America of the 1920s than in looking backward and tying the spirituals to their African roots. Although by the 1920s there was already quite a literature on the possible African roots of the spirituals, this held little interest for Thurman.[47] Following from E. Franklin Frazier and others who emphasized the discontinuity of antebellum slaves from their African origins, the spirituals were less reflections of Africa than the cry of the deracinated offered in a religion stolen from their masters. As he would write in a 1939 article on the spirituals: "The slave was a man without a home. . . . His primary social grouping had been destroyed, so it was not possible for him to perpetuate his own tongue. . . . Slavery stripped the African to the literal substance of himself, depriving him of the props on which men commonly depend—language, custom, and social solidarity."[48] The spirituals were an attempt to find meaning in circumstances of radical discontinuity when old truths lost their power to explain, comfort, or succor.

The spirituals were not panaceas. There was no "get out of jail free" card from the prison of slavery save emancipation. The spiritual "Jacob's Ladder" spoke to the necessity of hope for even the most hopeless, though Thurman cautioned that looking to escape the realities of the world into another realm can all too easily be "a defense mechanism, the symbol of cowardice and fear." According to Thurman, the message of "De Blin' Man" was that "God is the answer to human suffering," though he cautioned that when God comes "sometimes the pain is relieved but very often it is not!" Thurman's 1928 exploration of the spirituals was also his first extended exploration of the lives of those on the bottom rungs of society. As always with Thurman, it was not a heroic portrait. For Thurman the meaning of the spiritual "Heab'n, Heab'n" was that "people who live under social pressure as in a master-slave society and its posterity find it almost impossible to be honest with each other." And little was changed. Whites and blacks in contemporary Atlanta remained "monumental hypocrites" in their furtive, cautious interactions, never saying what they were really thinking. The contemporary challenge of the spirituals, Thurman suggested, was to respect the creative, synthetic, religious genius of their creators and to go beyond them, forging new, contemporary answers to the old dilemma of white dominance and black powerlessness.[49]

One of Thurman's most creative efforts to forge a new understanding of social consequences of religious belief appeared the same year. It is relatively unheralded but was in its historical significance one of the most important articles he ever wrote, the first significant essay by an African American author to suggest that the techniques of Christian nonviolence could be part of a Christian solution to the race problem. Thurman was by the mid-1920s a prominent member of the Fellowship of Reconciliation (FOR), the preeminent Christian pacifist organization. FOR was founded in 1915 to protest the cataclysm of World War I. Thurman joined FOR after meeting George "Shorty" Collins, FOR's southern field representative, while still a sophomore at Morehouse when the horrors of the late war were still very fresh. He would write in 1924 of the not-too-distant past when "Horsemen of the Apocalypse swam across Europe in a sea of blood" fomenting "the most terrific and bloody carnage the world has ever seen."[50]

Thurman's article on pacifism appeared in two forms, as "Peace Tactics and a Racial Minority" in the *World Tomorrow*, a leading socialist and pacifist journal in late 1928, and, with somewhat different contents and a new title, "'Relaxation' and Race Conflict," in a collection published the following year, *Pacifism in the Modern World*. Though Thurman would be a firm opponent of militarism throughout his career, this was never the prime motivation of his pacifism. Instead it was the search for a way, a Christian way, a nonviolent way, of addressing the violence—real, threatened, or implied—that he and people like him faced every day. It was in FOR that he found "a place to stand in my own spirit—a place so profoundly affirming that *I* was strengthened by a sense of immunity to the assaults of the white world of Atlanta, Georgia." That pacifism was perhaps the crucial tool in achieving what would become perhaps his most important and fundamental social belief. As he would say in 1952:

> I became interested in peace long before I had any concern about war. This is a contradiction because to me peace meant working out reconciliation in areas where you were fighting. And I wasn't fighting in Europe and some other part of the world but I was having a very rugged time living on a little col-

lege campus in the fabulous city of Atlanta, Georgia. And peace meant, for me, not whether I would join the army, whether I would ever bear arms against some other lands, or whether I would take up arms to defend my flag. It meant nothing like that. But peace meant for me, could I live in Atlanta, Georgia and walk the streets of Atlanta, Georgia without fear and without hatred and without bitterness.[51]

If pacifism was hardly uncommon in the progressive Christian circles in which Thurman traveled, he was in the forefront of those who believed that pacifism might be of at least equal utility in fighting violence at home rather than only concentrating on military actions overseas. By the end of the 1920s this view, in part through the example of Gandhi, was becoming increasingly widespread, and the volume *Pacifism in the Modern World* was, in the words of its editor, Devere Allen, dedicated to the "new pacifism," which "directly challenges imperialism, industrial autocracy, punishment as a basis for penology, race prejudice, indeed every phase of the existing social order which thwarts fellowship and love." The volume included a chapter by George Collins on "Pacifism and Social Injustice," largely about the use of pacifism in labor disputes, and A.J. Muste wrote a similar chapter on "Pacifism and Class War." Devere Allen wrote on "The New White Man," asking whether whites could abandon their "imperialism and arrogant race consciousness," their ignorance, fear, and superstition, and meet "the new Negro, the new Chinese, the new oppressed and submerged colored people everywhere" as equals. But in FOR in the late 1920s, it still was primarily white men and women who were reaching out with these laudable sentiments. Thurman's was the only essay in the volume by an African American.[52]

Thurman opened his essay by scolding some of his fellow pacifists for ignoring the plight of America's minorities. "It is a very simple matter for those who form the dominant group in a society to develop what they call a philosophy of pacifism that makes few, if any, demands upon their ethical obligations to minority groups with which they may be having contact." He went on to argue that the majority group dominates the minority through violence and its metaphorical extensions, using all means at its disposal, including media, the church, and education. All these techniques were subtle forms of violence based on the conviction on the part of whites that without controlling blacks their own lives would be profoundly menaced, or in Thurman's words, "the will to dominate and the will to live are one and the same." This pattern traces back to slavery, and Thurman, as he often did when writing about slavery, talked about the experiences of his grandmother and the extent of control exerted over her by her slave master. "The slave was not an underling, for that implies belonging to the same order, but lower in the scale," a thing, a "body," as Thurman wrote. This attitude, he argued, had persisted.[53]

For blacks, fighting the majority's will to dominate was immensely difficult, in part because many of the seeming ways to fight domination only reinforced it. The minority group had its own complacencies, more understandable perhaps, but just as regrettable. There is imitation of the majority group, and as Thurman pointed out, it is possible "to hate people so bitterly that one becomes like them." That was his diagnosis of the black middle class, and, sounding much like E. Franklin Frazier, he pointed to rampant imitation of whites "from the cut of clothes and small-town economic 'imperialism' to religious ceremonials." The worst thing about this form of self-hatred is that it often took "the form of compensation" and looked for someone else to hate, as people abused at work take it out on their families and the black middle class takes it out on those deemed "beneath" them. "Those who ride on top in a minority group may treat those below them, so to speak, as they themselves are treated by the dominant majority," Thurman wrote.

The solution he offered, or at least the path that led away from this unequal contest of wills, was religious pacifism. "A philosophy of pacifism implies the will to share joyfully the common life and the will to love all." This means different things for the dominant and dominated group. The majority group must "relax their will to dominate and control the Negro minority." But the main work would have to be done by the minority itself and would require "a will to relaxation" that would be "sufficiently operative in group life to make vast creativity, with no corresponding loss in self-respect." Relaxation is a difficult concept to understand precisely, and perhaps it owes something to the mystics Thurman was then studying with Rufus Jones, for whom relaxation was often a preliminary state before mystic elevation, a way of not responding to external stimuli, and it had a similar role in works of religious psychology of the time with which Thurman was probably familiar.[54] Social relaxation was much the same thing, a way an individual could find freedom by "transcending his environment" and not responding to hostility, domination, and control by refusing to recognize its power. In some ways this was a familiar technique used by Southern blacks, particularly those in the lower classes, who "in the midst of a hostile, dominating, controlling white majority relaxes and oftentimes becomes remarkably creative. When he swears or laughs or sings the gods tremble." In Thurman's opinion, it might be more difficult for educated blacks, their lives fringed by "discouragement, despair, pessimism, and bitterness" to achieve this natural relaxation because, for the most part, "individual and group experience is against it." But it was absolutely necessary for the minority to detach themselves from their habitual routines, patterns, and grievances to interpret the relation between themselves and the majority group "in the light of a will to share and will to love." When this is done, he wrote, the dominant majority will have lost their power to dominate.

What were the social consequences of relaxation? As usual for Thurman, he was not interested in spelling out the detailed political and social consequences. But it is clear that ceasing to be in the majority's thrall would have political consequences. It would start with personal belief and religious conviction. "I am profoundly convinced, however, that the change must be an individual as well as a social one." The process "must be formal and informal, direct and indirect, studied and spontaneous"; it must involve the school, the church, and the home. In the end, it would require "a new philosophy of education, a more adequate philosophy of religion, and a higher quality of religious experience." But all this would lead to a "harnessing" of "all social forces operating separately and jointly" among both blacks and whites. Thurman argued that the ultimate consequences of the relaxation of "the Will to Hate the Man who Tries to Dominate and Crush Me" would be a religiously based social movement, secure enough to love and strong enough to overcome hate and oppression. Thurman's essay "'Relaxation' and Race Conflict" is the beginning of a distinctively African American understanding of the potential for Christian nonviolence to address the African American condition, and its message would reverberate in the decades ahead.

If Thurman's four years in Atlanta were darkened by tragedy, they came to an end with one of the happiest days of his life. On June 12, 1932, Thurman married Sue Bailey, a YMCA national secretary, at the annual Kings Mountain conference for black student Christians. Sue Bailey, a native of Arkansas, a graduate of Spelman and Oberlin colleges, and a national secretary of the YWCA, was a forceful, intelligent, gracious woman who would accompany Thurman on the remainder of his life's journey and would contribute immensely to his life and work. They had known each other for many years and had many mutual friends. She came into his life seriously sometime in 1931 and their engagement soon followed, as would their daughter, Anne Spencer, born in 1933.[55]

By the time he was married, Thurman knew he was leaving Spelman and Morehouse and was moving to Howard University to be reunited with his mentor, Mordecai Wyatt Johnson, and to be university chaplain, presiding at Howard's Rankin Chapel, and a professor in the school of religion. From his first letter to Thurman on being appointed president of Howard in 1926, Johnson had tried to recruit him, and now he finally got his man.[56] Thurman would be joining what was, in no small part due to Johnson's unstinting efforts and eye for talent, the most prosperous and prestigious of all the black colleges, with as glittering an array of African American intellectual star power as has ever been assembled in a single academic institution before or since.[57] Thurman was excited to be there. As he would write in his autobiography about coming to Howard, "I was caught up in Mordecai Johnson's vision to create the first real community of black scholars, to build an authentic university dedicated primarily to the education of black youth."[58] But the School of Religion Thurman was joining was generally viewed, as historian Rayford Logan put it, as Howard's "poor cousin," not eligible for the federal funding that was a key to the university's success, and perceived by the rest of the university as second rate.[59] The hiring of Thurman was in part an effort to remedy this, as would be the hiring a few years later of Benjamin E. Mays as its dean.

Thurman arrived at Howard during that university's golden age when leading scholars such as sociologist E. Franklin Frazier and political scientist Ralph Bunche challenged many of the standing pieties of black life, such as what they perceived as the ossified and inward-looking class structure of the black middle class and the NAACP's painfully slow efforts to achieve legal equality for blacks through the courts and conventional politics. In its stead, Bunche and others recommended creating new interracial structures based on common economic interests of blacks and whites, to seek both political and economic equality.[60] Thurman would be influenced by their critique. (This is most apparent in his 1940 lecture, "A 'Native Son' Speaks.")[61] But for many black intellectuals of the 1930s, perhaps the most reactionary, hidebound, and ultimately irrelevant institution of all was the Negro Church, which for generations had been a bulwark for blacks but at the price of turning their attention from politics and this-worldly matters. This only sharpened Thurman's dedication to fashioning a new type of Christianity, one that at once could speak to the spiritual needs of worshipers and yet address the doubts of religion's many skeptics. His trip to Asia in 1935 and 1936 would prove crucial in this quest.

CHAPTER THREE

Planning the Pilgrimage of Friendship

THURMAN HAD BEEN AT Howard for almost two years when, in April 1934, he received a letter from a committee of the Student Christian Movement (the combined YWCA and YMCA) inviting him to be the chairman of the Negro Delegation that would undertake a "Pilgrimage of Friendship" to India, Ceylon, and Burma. His first reaction was not at all enthusiastic. He did what he often did when he was unsure of his course of action; he prayed, held long discussions with his wife, and meditated, hoping, as he said on a different occasion, "for the light of God [to] make it clear to me what is the path to take."[1] After a weekend of discussions, the Thurmans came to a "place of calm and decision." Howard Thurman concluded that "under no circumstances would it be possible for me to accept" and wrote a letter (unfortunately no longer extant) explaining his reasoning.[2]

Reviewing the events in retrospect in 1938, he gave two main reasons for his initial hesitance. He was, he told the committee, "an American Negro, a member of a relatively underprivileged minority in American life," and to the extent that organized religion, as it was wont to do, "made its peace with the powerful of the earth," it was a peace made against people like him. Therefore, he could not go to Asia as a representative of organized American Christianity and could not apologize for its flaws or be exhibited as an example of its advances in dealing with the race problem. Furthermore, while he told the committee that he was "committed to the Christian way of life," he was in no way an evangelist and could not participate in any delegation that had evangelical trappings. He was not a saver of souls.[3]

The committee that had selected Thurman as the unanimous first choice to head the delegation was understandably upset by his rejection of the offer, and rather than try to negotiate with him through correspondence, they sent an emissary to Washington, Winnifred Wygal, a national official of the YWCA, with full power to negotiate on their behalf. Wygal, who was to speak at Howard's Rankin Chapel on May 6, was one of Thurman's closest friends in the Student Christian Movement and had special qualifications in speaking about India. In 1928 she had been a delegate to a World Student Federation Conference in Mysore, and during her time in India, much as Thurman would do, she met with both Gandhi and Rabindranath Tagore. Wygal and the Thurmans had an "exhaustive discussion," speaking "far into the night," in a "climate of honesty and trust."[4] She tried to convince them that Thurman was wanted for the delegation because of, and not in spite of, his reservations. Wygal assured him that he would be free to present his own interpretation of the religion of Jesus as he saw it. If he was seen as an official mouthpiece for American Christianity, there was no point in going to India. After this explanation, Thurman later wrote, his "course was clear."[5]

Possibly, though Thurman doesn't mention it, Wygal dangled a sweetener before the Thurmans, the inclusion of Sue Bailey Thurman in the delegation. She had not originally been asked to participate, perhaps out of concerns over nepotism, but by the middle of May 1934, both Howard and Sue Bailey Thurman had given their assent to be members of the Negro Delegation to India.[6]

Contributing to Thurman's initial reluctance was an ambivalence about the Student Christian Movement itself. Although it had been his spiritual home for many years, he did not want to become its official spokesman. Part of this was his feeling, one shared by many blacks in the movement, that despite the relative equality in the higher echelons, many of the local facilities remained segregated, and there was a general reticence about confronting racial discrimination head-on. As Thurman's friend Juliette Derricotte, who had spent years working as an official of the YWCA, had said around 1930, it was asking a lot of blacks to be representatives of the YMCA and YWCA when they could not go into some of the branches "to eat or sleep or, sometimes, to ask a civil question."[7] Beyond racial considerations, Thurman's general feeling, dating back to the mid-1920s, was that the Student Christian Movement was often too willing to be self-satisfied with grand statements and professions of piety, too evangelical and traditionally Protestant in its emphasis. Shortly before the India Committee had contacted him about the India trip, he had written to his good friend Wygal about plans to reorganize the Student Christian Movement. For Thurman it was a meaningless gesture. "In all of the movements there is a lot of deadness. And if you make the tragic error of attempting a vital connection between something that is dead and something that is less dead, we simply increase the sureness of death. Zero multiplied by infinity is still zero."[8]

There were many who shared Thurman's ambivalence about the Student Christian Movement. His close friend Herb King, who could always be counted upon for frankness, wrote that he was delighted about the delegation if for no other reason than that Thurman could "get out of this miserable country for a while," though he wondered, "Lord only knows what price you are paying for it." Although King found something "inestimably hopeful" about the work of the delegation, this was "despite the *auspices* of the thing."[9] Thurman was more than a little peeved when he heard that the wife of a prominent Harlem minister was suggesting the members of the Negro Delegation, all Southern blacks, had no doubt been chosen because, unlike Northern blacks, they exhibited a well-known tendency to docilely acquiesce in white racism.[10] Another friend in Harlem asked for some political advice in 1935, writing "I suppose you are a poor one to seek advice from, suppressed as you will be by the conservative YW, but you might tell me anyway."[11]

Thurman dealt with this sort of criticism about his participation in the Negro Delegation by reaching out to his critics and asking them to tell him what they would want him to say and do in India, and promising all that he would be no one's proxy or mouthpiece. But if there were political reasons for not going to India, there were also political arguments on the other side, promises to keep, debts to be paid. Among those who were skeptical of the Negro Delegation was Paul

Hutchinson, an editor at the *Christian Century* who wrote Winnifred Wygal in March 1935, wondering how the delegation "will be saved on the one hand from sentimentalism, and on the other from a false sense of representativeness." Above all, he wrote, the delegates needed to remember Juliette Derricotte. "Suppose," he wrote, "the Indians begin to ask what became of her?"[12] He needn't have worried. She was very much on the minds of both Howard and Sue Bailey Thurman.

In 1928 Derricotte, a national secretary of the YWCA, had been one of two African Americans who were included in an American Student Christian Movement delegation to a conference in Mysore, India. (One of her closest friends was her replacement as national secretary, Sue Bailey, not yet married to Howard Thurman.) Although she did some traveling while in India, she was unable to arrange a meeting with Gandhi, much to their mutual regret.[13] Derricotte would write in the *Crisis*, in 1929, "How can I tell you that I am no longer free; that the wealth as well as the poverty of India haunts me, that I ache with actual physical pain when I remember the struggles of all India today—religious, economic, social, and political?"[14]

In 1929 Derricotte left the YMCA for a position as dean of women at Fisk University in Nashville. In 1931 she was critically injured in a traffic accident near Dalton, Georgia, and the nearest (all-white) hospital refused to admit her. After spending the night in the home of a black family, she was transferred to a black hospital in Chattanooga, where she died the following day. The incident became a cause célèbre, and Howard Thurman delivered the eulogy at her funeral. "There is work to be done," he said, "and ghosts will drive us on. . . . This is an unfinished world, she has left an unfinished task. Who will take it up?"[15]

The Thurmans would not forget Juliette Derricotte while they were in India or after they returned to the United States. Sue Bailey Thurman would establish a Juliette Derricotte Scholarship Fund to send black women to study in India, a project disrupted by the coming of the war.[16] For all that was wrong with the United States, the YMCA, the YWCA, and the Student Christian Movement, and for all the questions raised by being overseas representatives of these institutions, Thurman knew that he also had to honor the ghosts of

people like Juliette Derricotte, and that one of her unfinished lega-
cies was establishing a deeper, more vital connection between African
Americans and the native people of South Asia.

II

The main impetus for the Negro Delegation came from Rev. Augustine Ralla Ram, the executive secretary of the Student Christian
Movement of India, Burma, and Ceylon. He had been born in the
Punjab region of India in 1888, the son of Brahmins who had converted to Christianity. After graduating in 1915 from the Saharanpur
Theological Seminary (run by the United Church of Northern India,
a combined Presbyterian and Congregationalist denomination), he
became a chaplain to Indian troops overseas (serving in 1919 in Iran
and Iraq), a pastor in Allahabad, and in 1928 he was named general
secretary of the Student Christian Association of India, Burma, and
Ceylon, staying in the position until Indian independence in 1947.
As a second-generation Christian and a committed Indian nationalist, he was a leader in the effort to remake the Indian church as an
authentically Indian institution, freeing it as much as possible from
its Western trappings. He would attract much attention (both favor-
able and unfavorable) by decorating his church in the bright colors
of Hindu temples rather than drab Protestant browns, replacing the
organ with Indian music accompanied by tabla drumming, and leading services in which the congregation sat cross-legged on the floor,
eschewing the pews.[17]

Ralla Ram was also a frequent overseas traveler on the World Student Christian Federation circuit. He visited the United States in
1931, speaking of the Indian Church and Indian problems in general.
Ralla Ram was a friend and associate of Gandhi, and when he visited
Spelman College, presumably with Thurman in attendance, he told
his audience that "Gandhi's outlook and plans for action are identical
in tone and purpose with those set forth by Christ—so certainly alike
that many think of him as a second corporate Christ, the living spirit
of Christianity."[18]

While in the United States, Ralla Ram discovered a deep affinity with American blacks. The *Spelman Messenger* reported that he had a particular interest in "the social and class distinctions to which Negroes in America are subjected" because "they seemed to parallel, to some degree, caste distinctions in India." Ralla Ram made a plea that "the colored people of America pray for India and identify themselves sympathetically with problems so nearly akin to their own difficulties in this country."[19] When Ralla Ram returned to India the initial planning for the Negro Delegation commenced. By 1933 there were already murmurs in American Student Christian Movement publications of plans afoot to sponsor a Negro delegation to India.[20]

The main reason Ralla Ram wanted the delegation was because "Christianity in India is the 'oppressor's' religion." He thought that "there would be a unique value in having representatives of another oppressed group speak on the validity of the contribution of Christianity."[21] Much in the spirit of his namesake, St. Augustine, who had tried to demonstrate that Christianity was not fatally implicated in the declining fortunes of the Roman Empire, Ralla Ram attempted a similar theological and political divorce of Indian Christianity from the British Empire, writing in 1934 that the purpose of a Negro delegation was that "in the minds of our young people belonging to other faiths, Christianity is identified with western imperialism, and they all think that Christianity is a part and parcel of western cult[ure]." Ralla Ram conceived the mission of the Negro Delegation not as evangelizing but as obtaining for Christianity a respectful hearing from people who tended to view it less as a religion than as a form of organized treason to the Indian people.[22]

Ralla Ram's notion of a Negro delegation to India found a receptive audience among the American Student Christian Movement, which from the other side of the colonizer-colonized divide had been having similar thoughts. World War I saw the end of the golden age of the Protestant missionary enterprise. A new critique was developing by the 1920s that saw traditional missionary efforts as far too single-mindedly focused on soul saving, as providing political cover to whatever colonial regime happened to be in power, and as culturally insensitive, a bull in the china shop of native sensibilities. What the non-Western world needed, this critique maintained, was not more Christians but a new hearing for Christianity based on the demonstration that it could respect other religions and be a positive force for social change.[23]

Thurman, in his time in India, would have the opportunity to observe missionaries closely and would come to similar conclusions. Thurman was not without sympathies for the missionary effort. "I found many instances of highly devoted, conscientious missionaries who were sacrificing their health, their strength, themselves, for the masses of the people, many of whom were healing the sick, feeding the hungry, administering in a wide variety of ways to the social needs of the people." But he found their religious thought and practice to be rigid and orthodox, their basic predilections in this regard reinforced by their difficult political position. "Almost everywhere," he would write, "I encountered what amounted to a fear, practically, of the social emphasis of Christianity," and this made for a dour, conservative, and straightened faith in which personal salvation was all.[24]

Thurman thought the inherent hypocrisies in the Western missionary enterprise created an insuperable handicap. He wrote that the Western missionary was "devoted to Jesus of Nazareth whose teachings cannot be compatible with much to which the missionary must give his approval to in order to function. He has all the prestige of power as he tries to live humbly, he represents economic security to people the masses of whom are insecure and many of whom are hungry, he must live without arrogance, even as he is called upon to uphold the dignity of the white man in that part of the world." Missionaries ministered to their flocks with benevolence, but "very few times was I convinced of their love for the Indian stripped bare of condescension." In the end, Thurman concluded, it was possible for the Western missionary to overcome the contradictions of their roles, but only by those possessing towering spiritual powers granted to few.[25]

The World Student Christian Federation (WSCF) was in the forefront of the effort to reconceptualize international Christianity away from missionary work. The Pilgrimage of Friendship was a frequent tool of the WSCF to connect its various national movements. Sue

Bailey participated in a tour of this sort to Europe in the late 1920s,[26] and Augustine Ralla Ram in 1932 had been a part of Mission of Fellowship to the British Isles that seems to have been a model for the Negro Delegation, a four-person, three-month tour of Great Britain and Ireland.[27] The WSCF and its president, Willem (Adolf) Visser't Hooft, saw the Negro Delegation as part of a more general effort to have persons of African or Asian descent head delegations to non-Western lands, and Ralla Ram was one of the most energetic advocates of such an approach. At the same time he was planning for the reception of the Negro Delegation, Ralla Ram was planning to send a delegation to Java and China.[28] By the end of 1933, the talk about a Negro delegation to India had become more concrete, and the American Student Christian Movement had created an India Committee to select the personnel, set the agenda, and handle the arrangements.

The India Committee consisted of six persons, equally divided between men and women and including two African Americans. All the members were associated with the YMCA or the YWCA. (Although it is easy to criticize the American Student Christian Movement for its limitations—and Thurman's catalogue of grievances was extensive—there were few, if any, major organizations in the United States in the mid-1930s that had gone farther down the road to gender equality and racial integration.) The two black members were Frank Wilson and Marion Cuthbert. Wilson was one of Thurman's oldest friends, and he had been the other African American, along with Juliette Derricotte, to visit India under WSCF auspices in 1928.[29] Marion Cuthbert was a national secretary of the YWCA, a close friend of Sue Bailey Thurman, and a prominent writer on educational topics. Elizabeth Harrington and A. Roland Elliott, both prominent officials of the Student Christian Movement, functioned as cochairs of the committee and would frequently dominate its deliberations.

Among the first of the committee's tasks was to establish objectives for the Negro Delegation. Frank Wilson developed a series of "General Principles" in April 1934, drawing in part from suggestions made by their Indian counterparts. The delegation would consist of four persons, and it would be a team, with complementary talents and abilities. It would have an equal number of men and women, and at least one person under age twenty-nine. While there was some sentiment in the broader American Student Christian Movement for an interracial delegation, with two or three blacks and one white, this was rejected as being contrary to the invitation of the Indian movement. The Indian movement had wanted people with a history of "vital contact" with the Student Christian Movement in the United States, comfortable in meeting with leaders from other religions, and who were equally adept in speaking before large public gatherings and intimate meetings. They also wanted the members of the Negro Delegation to combine a "philosophical, mystical approach of personal religion" with a "practical and ethically compelling demand for social justice."[30]

There were decisions made on other issues, such as how to split expenses between the United States and India and whether to extend the tour of the Negro Delegation to China and Japan—Thurman was very much interested in such a possibility but the India Committee finally decided that there weren't enough funds to make this extension possible.[31] A more significant matter, and one that would plague the tour of the Negro Delegation throughout its duration, was the question of whether it would have an evangelical component—Thurman would later write that the nonevangelical character of the tour would have "to be explained over and over again in our journey." In response to a somewhat ambiguous comment in a letter, Ralla Ram quickly clarified to the India Committee that he did not conceive of the tour to be an adjunct to evangelicalism, and he wanted only for Indian students to "see for themselves that Christianity is universal in its sweep," believing this would be accomplished by inviting "Negro friends from America, . . . those who have suffered acutely at the hands of the white people," to testify about their religious faith.[32]

The committee accepted Ralla Ram's understanding, but purging the tour of evangelical expectations was more easily said than done. If Ralla Ram was a religious liberal, the Indian Student Christian Movement as a whole was far more evangelical and oriented to conversion than its American counterpart, with missionaries often the leaders of local chapters. In the end, Thurman concluded, "If the pilgrimage of friendship was a disappointment at any point it was in connection with the whole question of evangelicalism." For many, the brand of Christianity Thurman brought to India was simply beyond their ken.

At the same time, Thurman would develop considerable sympathy for the typical Asian convert, such as the Ceylonese man in Kandy who spoke to him after a sermon, complaining that "you did not call my Master's name!"[33] Thurman would have to repeatedly explain his position and that of the delegation, and some accepted his explanation that he was offering an alternative path to Christian truths; some did not. Part of the emphasis on evangelization in Asia, Thurman felt, was that the stakes were simply higher. In America, the convert adopted a new religion; in Asia the convert had to adopt a new civilization as well, and often faced ostracism from the old one. Those who adopted Christianity in India, both Hindu and Muslim, generally did so knowing that they would endure a form of social death. This gave them little choice but to embrace their new religion with a sense of desperation, like a drowning person clinging to a life preserver. The resulting dependence "of the Indian Christian upon the West *tends* to rob him of independence of thought, and actions based upon the dictations of his own heart and mind."[34]

On the whole, Thurman concluded, the Indian Christian "strikes me as being singularly a man who is halfway between two worlds." This in-betweenness was a place he knew well. The pull of evangelicalism among the poor and disenfranchised was all too familiar to him, and he saw it as a grasping for narrow and unambiguous truths in a harsh and unforgiving world, making for "over simplicity, conservatism, and 'cock-suredness.'"[35] (On the other hand, Thurman noted that evangelical and especially Pentecostal sects in India often lacked the pomposity and social hierarchies of the more established Protestant denominations, and among the European Christians in India he most admired were members of a Pentecostal sect who truly shared their lives with their native followers.)[36]

Thurman had spent much of his adult life in navigating the distances between white and black America, alert to the myriad pitfalls of such a journey. He would observe something similar in Asia. A woman he befriended in Ceylon, a Sinhalese official of the Student Christian Movement, whom he described as one who "understands much but does not become effective," reminded him of many people he knew at home. Thurman wrote that she "admires the advantages of being European, wishes she were at times and yet underneath carries a burning bitterness against all the things that hold her and women back, which bitterness is gradually killing her soul."[37] Often, he would write, while talking to Indian Christians, he thought of Carl Sandburg's description of a flying fish: "Child of water, child of air, wing thing, fin thing, I have lived in many half worlds myself, so I know you."[38]

Besides evangelicalism, another issue of contention between the Indian and American sponsors of the Negro Delegation was the question of their singing voices. Augustine Ralla Ram had initially wanted the members of the delegation to be "expert singers," performing popular Negro spirituals. The India Committee was alarmed and had visions of the delegation taking regular minstrel turns. Frank Wilson wrote Ralla Ram that the Negro Delegation would be taken seriously as thoughtful African American representatives of American Christianity and not put "on exhibition either as singers or anthropological specimens." Ralla Ram was somewhat taken aback by this criticism and made clear to the India Committee that he wanted preachers, not recitalists, to come to India. But, he added, if the ability to sing was not a necessity or requirement, it wouldn't be a bad thing if the members of the Negro Delegation knew how to carry a tune. It would enable the delegates to "enter into our hearts," noting that he only mentioned this because "Negro Spirituals have begun to be loved in India a great deal and our students sing them all over the country."[39]

To Thurman's considerable distress, some news of the intention of having the delegation come as singers percolated to the broader Western community in India, and E. Stanley Jones, an American Methodist who was perhaps the most prominent American missionary in India, famous as the author of *The Christ of the Indian Road*,[40] announced early on that he was looking forward to seeing the Negro

Delegation come to India as "singing, soul-saving evangelists." This was just the image Thurman had wanted to avoid, and he would write in his autobiography that Jones no doubt had wanted the delegation to appear in India with wide grins plastered on their faces, ready to testify that they were "full of the grace of God as that grace had manifested itself in what it had done for us as black people in American society."[41]

But Ralla Ram was certainly correct that Indians (not limited to Indian Christians) were just mad about Negro spirituals, the first genre of African music in the Americas to achieve worldwide fame. Spirituals had been popular in India since the 1880s when the Fisk Jubilee Singers had spent much time there during an Asian tour.[42] Indeed, Thurman received a letter from an elderly woman in Calcutta who had seen the Fisk Jubilee Singers at that time and emphasized the continuities between the two tours; she praised the delegation as bringing proof to "our non-Christian brothers and sisters" that "*Jesus is alive and well.*"[43] For many in South Asia, Negro spirituals were a distinctive, non-European form of Christian expression, forged in bondage, and one they rarely heard from authentic Negroes. Adolf (later Willem) Visser't Hooft wrote to Frank Wilson in 1934 that Asian Christians "love to sing these spirituals because they express to them a Christianity more congenial than Western music does."[44] Indeed, after hearing of the delegation's reluctance to sing spirituals, representatives of Judson College in Rangoon, Burma, wrote to Thurman begging the delegation to relent and sing some spirituals in their performances because "we cannot do justice to the deep religious experience which they express for we cannot enter into the soul of your people."[45] Even Gandhi expressed interest in hearing the delegation sing spirituals. In the end, a compromise of sorts was reached. The delegation was not treated as entertainers, though they certainly did sing spirituals. While the delegation had no vocal auditions, Sue Bailey Thurman had both an excellent voice and a degree from the Oberlin Conservatory of Music. (One suspects this worked in her favor in her selection.) In India, she would both sing spirituals and train native choruses to do the same. And Thurman, a close student of the spirituals, would frequently speak on this theme in India, delivering his talks on "Deep River" and the "Meaning of the Spirituals" on numerous occasions.

One other significant question the India Committee had to address was the freedom of speech of the delegates, particularly on political matters. This was an issue of great concern to Thurman and was one of the major reasons for his initial reluctance to participate. Ralla Ram clarified his understanding to the India Committee in the summer of 1934 during a U.S. speaking tour: there would be no censorship, no list of acceptable topics. Winnifred Wygal wrote Elizabeth Harrington, after a meeting with Ralla Ram on the permissible limits of political speech, that even "Howard Thurman would have been completely reassured could he have been talking to him."[46]

However, Ralla Ram also made clear that prudence dictated in public meetings, with journalists present, the delegates refrain from offering opinions too freely on Indian politics. If not, it "may defeat the primary purpose of the mission to India."[47] He suggested that the delegation reserve any pointed comments to private, smaller gatherings where more frankness was possible. Thurman accepted this restriction, which was after all how determined supporters of Indian independence generally had to live their lives anyway, amid the constant specter of surveillance and threats of incarceration. As Thurman would write in 1938, "I was determined also not to discuss or deal with situations of a political nature, our understanding on this was clear before leaving this country."[48] He soon found, even before the trip started, that he could make reference to the social situation of Indians without directly commenting upon it. All he needed to do was discuss the situation of blacks in the United States and let his audience draw the inevitable comparisons. As he wrote an admirer in the summer of 1935, "Due to my daily experiences as an American Negro in American life, I think I can enter directly into informal understanding of the psychological climate in which these people live. While the details of our experiences differ, they do not differ in principle and in inner pain."[49]

In any event, British officials, aware of their tenuous grasp on

their Asian colonies, looked askance at all possible sources of distur-
bance, particularly if the potential agitators were from outside Asia.
The plans of the Negro Delegation were no doubt aided in that they
made their trip during a period of relative calm and quiet in British
Asia. The Government of India Act of 1935 had just been passed.
The last comprehensive effort at governmental reform under the Raj,
it enhanced powers of local self-government without significantly
modifying British control over the political process, and as such it
was broadly disliked (for opposing reasons) by both India's Congress
Party and conservatives back home such as Winston Churchill. (In
1978 Thurman would describe the act as "England's last great gasp to
try to revive the lungs of the Empire by squeezing some more energy
out of its Indian people.")[50] Gandhi, out of prison since August 1933,
had not forgotten the struggle against the British, but was spending
much of his time touring India campaigning to end discrimination
against the untouchables, or in his coinage, the *harijan*, or "children of
God," the object of a fast he had undertaken in the summer of 1934.[51]

But on all sides, everyone knew that the calm was a deceptive lull
before the next storm, whether its source was from the increasingly
troubled international situation or from the fissiparous tensions between Hindus and Muslims at home. Above all, throughout British
Asia, there was a growing restlessness; independence seemed at once
inevitable and unobtainable. Nowhere were these sentiments stronger
than among British Asia's educated elites, clustered in the very colleges
the Negro Delegation was planning to visit. There is no doubt that
Ralla Ram had been correct; the British would monitor the Negro
Delegation closely, alert to any political transgressions, and Thurman
and the others needed to mind their words. There was a reluctance
to allow the delegation into India in the first place; the initial impulse
of the British authorities was to turn down the request. Thurman
reported British officials in New York City telling the members of the
India Committee that the mere presence of educated American blacks
in India would "create many difficulties for our rule," to say nothing of
having them travel the breadth and width of India giving speeches.[52]
The Negro Delegation was not singled out for this sort of scrutiny;

W. E. B. Du Bois, writing in 1936, commented how difficult it was for African Americans to obtain the necessary papers to travel to India and the restrictions placed on their speech once they got there.[53]

In the end, permission was granted for the Negro Delegation to come to British Asia. Nonetheless, they would be kept on a short leash and under constant scrutiny. (Thurman suspected that every letter he sent or received was opened by the authorities.)[54] On his first day in Ceylon, as we noted earlier, Thurman would be warned before his first meeting with the press "not to say anything to offend the white man lest our journey be cut off before it started."[55] Even private meetings would not be entirely safe. On one occasion, during a meeting with a group of Indians from various professions, one of the participants found a pretext to get Thurman out of the room and told him that the man sitting to his left, though an Indian, was a CID (Criminal Investigations Division) informant. One morning when the delegation was in Calcutta, and the delegation was one person short (someone was ill), someone came up to Thurman, inquiring, "Where is your fourth member? Our information is that there are four of you, but only three are getting off the train." But despite caution on the part of Indian sponsors and continuous surveillance by the British colonial police, in the end Thurman would not be hindered. There is a satisfaction that can come from having to work within narrow limits, knowing that your message will have to be oblique and implied, accessible only to those who have the power to discern beneath surface meanings, and that what you have to say will neither be overly obvious or painfully emphatic. This is how Thurman preferred to speak anyway. In the end, he said more or less whatever he wanted to.[56]

III

After the selection of Howard and Sue Bailey Thurman in April 1934, the India Committee still only had half a delegation. Picking their counterparts proved to be unexpectedly complicated. The committee considered many of the most promising and prominent young black student Christians of the era. Some of those contacted had prior commitments or found the prospects of spending half a year on the other side of the world daunting. In late May 1934, the committee asked Edward Carroll and Grace Towns Hamilton to join the delegation. Both would have distinguished careers. Carroll, a Methodist minister in Virginia, was in his midtwenties, and would go on to serve in a number of United Methodist pastorates until 1971—shortly after the United Methodists belatedly ended all internal segregation—when he would be named one of the denomination's first black bishops. Grace Towns Hamilton was in her late twenties and would become the executive director of the Atlanta branch of the National Urban League in 1943, remaining in the position until 1961, and in 1965 she would become the first African American woman elected to the Georgia legislature.[57]

But Hamilton's decision in January 1935 to withdraw from the delegation, feeling that she could not be apart from her four-year-old daughter for such an extended period, precipitated a crisis.[58] For various reasons, the committee was unable to name a replacement promptly, and they dithered until July when the selection was finally made. The fourth member of the delegation—presumably at the behest of her husband, Edward Carroll—would be Phenola Carroll, a twenty-four-year-old recent graduate from Morgan College in Maryland. Thurman was furious and dumbfounded.[59] He had wanted another candidate and had not been informed that Phenola Carroll was being considered before she was chosen. He did not think her qualified, or that she would have enough time to adequately prepare.[60] But the most crucial factor was that he felt outsiders would see both wives as little more than appendages to their husbands and would think they were chosen because of their spouses and not because they were the "four individuals who in the judgment of the Committee are the four persons best able to do this particular job."[61] Howard Thurman was convinced, with much justice, that Sue Bailey Thurman had been chosen for the delegation because she was the most qualified female available, but he was very sensitive to the appearance of nepotism. In late July Sue Bailey Thurman offered her resignation, and her husband's participation was teetering as well.[62] But by the summer of 1935 preparations had probably gone too far for the Thurmans to withdraw. The temporary replacement for his duties at Rankin Chapel had already been appointed, and after a year of contemplating going to Asia together, Howard did not want to go without Sue, and Sue did not want to stay home. So while the exact sequence of events is a bit difficult to trace in the existing correspondence, by August heads were cooler, calm had been restored, and the Thurmans remained delegation members in good standing.

There is no evidence that Thurman disliked Phenola or Edward Carroll, and the two couples would remain in touch (though they were not particularly close) for the remainder of their lives. In the end, the Thurmans and the Carrolls spent the better part of six months together, and there is not much reason to doubt Thurman's statement in his autobiography that by the end of the month-long voyage to Ceylon "we were a family and the purpose of our journey was clearly felt and thought through," and that at "no time was there serious conflict" between them.[63] But Phenola Carroll's selection continued to rankle. On December 20, 1935, Thurman relieved himself of his accumulated grievances by writing a cathartic blast to the India Committee, complaining of the high-handed way in which Phenola Carroll had been selected and of his dissatisfaction with her performance, especially her inability to speak on assigned topics for lectures. Thurman did not so much blame her as the India Committee that had delayed her selection until it was too late to afford her adequate preparation time.[64] In any event, the speaking burdens in Asia would be unequal and asymmetrical, and much would fall heavily on Thurman.[65]

One reason Thurman was so perturbed by the late addition of Phenola Carroll was the strenuous and unstinting efforts he and his wife had made to prepare for the work of the delegation. This was so despite the fact that Mordecai Wyatt Johnson was willing to grant Thurman only an unpaid sabbatical for the year he would be away. The unsalaried year would be, as Thurman later wrote, "an overwhelming hardship," particularly since he was still paying a loan of several thousand dollars incurred during the final illness of his first wife. Thurman was obliged to secure a loan on his life insurance to make the tour possible.[66] He would write in the spring of 1935 of the "sacredness" of the mission of the delegation and of its profound obligations to its various constituencies.[67] Thurman studied extensively for the tour, extending himself to be ready to speak on the sort of political and sociological themes that were not a part of his usual lecture and sermon repertoire, and informing himself as much as he could about contemporary developments in both the United States and South Asia. As he would write to fellow delegate Grace Towns Hamilton in October 1934:

> I am suggesting that as preparation for the work we will have to do there, that we spend most of the winter reading and studying in the following general fields; a detailed analysis of American culture, including the detailed history of two minorities, the American Negro and the American Indian; an analysis of the life and career of Jesus, historically considered, giving particular attention to the role of Christian minorities through the ages; a study of comparative religions, paying definite attention to Mohammedanism and Hinduism; an analysis of current, major social philosophies in our time, and their significance in the light of Christian ethics; a study of imperialism, both from the orthodox and the Marxian point of view, and finally, an examination of the major factors in Indian history.[68]

Thurman's preparations went beyond his elaborate reading program. To represent American blacks he tried to meet with as wide a spectrum of African American opinion as he could, from socialists like A. Philip Randolph to Robert Russa Moton, Booker T. Washington's recently retired successor at Tuskegee and still the standard bearer for (a somewhat modified version of) Washingtonian accommodationism.[69] He met with Indian students in the United States and with Indian scholars, arranged for the Indian anthropologist P. Kodanda Rao to travel from Yale University to Howard to discuss Indian matters with him.[70] (Two other meetings, discussed in the next chapter, were with two of Gandhi's associates, Madeleine Slade (Mirabehn) and Muriel Lester, in the United States on speaking tours.) For her part, Sue Bailey Thurman also undertook extensive preparations for the tour, making a special tour of Mexico in order to better represent the arts of the Americas to the Indians.[71]

As the date for the departure neared, the Thurmans had to resolve who would watch Anne Spencer (aged three) and Olive (aged seven) when Mom and Dad took a six-month break from parenting. After several schemes proved unviable, they decided to deposit both Thurman girls in Geneva, Switzerland, under the care and supervision of Thurman's sister Madaline. (Perhaps the locale had been suggested by Thurman's friend Willem Visser't Hooft.)[72] With the arrangements set, the five Thurmans—Howard, Sue, Madaline, Anne, and Olive—embarked on the *Ile de France* on September 21, 1935. They made a stormy crossing at the height of the hurricane season, and Thurman experienced one of those powerful storms he found so life-enhancing in which "the very roots of my being were exposed by the raw energy of the sea." Always a hearty eater, Thurman noted proudly in his autobiography that he never missed a meal on the trip, despite sometimes eating in an empty dining room while the other passengers were laid low by seasickness.[73] His sea legs were balanced, unfortunately, by the abject terror to which the storm reduced Anne and Olive.

But the ship eventually made its way to its port in Le Havre, and the Thurmans traveled to Geneva, where Madaline and the girls were properly ensconced in their accommodations and Thurman had the chance to confer with Visser't Hooft on India, from where he had recently returned. Eventually the Thurmans kissed their daughters good-bye and made their way to Marseilles, where they met up with the Carrolls and set sail for Ceylon. After a sultry crossing in the Mediterranean moonlight, the delegation made two ports of call, at Port Said in Egypt at the Mediterranean end of the Suez Canal and at Djibouti in French Somaliland.

Their published description of the latter stop, made almost to the day of the outbreak of the 1935 Italo-Ethiopian War between Italy, with its forces massed in the Italian colony of Eritrea, and Ethiopia—both neighboring on French Somaliland—seems strangely insouciant: "So fascinated were they [Sue Bailey Thurman and Phenola

Carroll] by the charming brass anklets and gay dark eyes of the damsel who accosted them in French with 'Danse, Mesdames?' that they forsook all and hurried back to the ship so as not to lose their hearts forever in Africa."[74] But (probably fortunately for the safety of all concerned) they did not linger, and the two couples continued their voyage, past the Horn of Africa, Arabia, and into the Indian Ocean. The trip had been planned to coincide with the end of the monsoon season in South Asia, and on October 21, as the S.S. *Chenonceaux* entered the old Dutch harbor in Colombo, the last traces of the high water and waves could still be seen. Thurman, who had seen the ocean meet the shore many, many times before, stood amidships taking in all the sounds, smells, and sights. The Pilgrimage of Friendship was about to commence.[75]

CHAPTER FOUR

The Negro Delegation in India

ONCE THURMAN AND THE other members of the Negro Delegation arrived in Colombo, the hard work for which they had prepared commenced almost immediately with daily rounds of lectures, sermons, meetings, interviews, meals, and high teas. The delegation spent about a fortnight in Ceylon, visiting all the major cities and taking in the major tourist attractions—one of the highlights was a visit to the Temple of the Tooth in Kandy, reputedly housing a molar of the Buddha.[1] Thurman had little to say on Ceylon's internal ethnic divisions, though he generally identified the people he met as either Sinhalese or Tamil. After their time in Ceylon, the delegation then crossed over into southern India, making their first extended stop at Trichinopoly (now Tiruchirapalli). They would stay in the region for about a month, visiting the Western Ghats and many cities on India's southwestern Malabar Coast, the area of the country where India's native Christian denominations were centered, traveling to major cities in the southeast, such as Madura and Alwaye, and spending a week in Madras (now Chennai). By December 20, after their stay in Masulipatam, they had finished their time in South Asia, and the delegation took their one break during the tour, spending a Christmas vacation in Darjeeling, near the Nepalese border. (Thurman, always zealous for peak experiences of natural sublimity, got up very early one morning, hiked in the darkness for several hours, and watched the sunrise on the foothills of Kinchinjunga, the third tallest mountain in the world. Suddenly the clouds parted, and for only a minute the peak of Mount Everest was visible in the distance. Thurman would write of the experience forty years later, "It remains for me a transcendent moment of sheer glory and beatitude, when time, space, and circumstance evaporated and when my naked spirit looked into the depths of what is forbidden for anyone to see. I would never, never be the same." Thurman would tease his wife forever after for sleeping in that morning and missing the glimpse of Everest.)[2]

After the vacation, they crossed the Bay of Bengal by boat to Rangoon, Burma, where they stayed a week. They returned by train, passing through what is now Bangladesh, on to Calcutta and other large cities in Western Bengal, before touring the major cities on the spine of North India in the heart of what had been the Mughal Empire: Benares, Allahabad, Cawnpore, Lucknow, Delhi, and Agra. The delegation then went on to the Punjab and the Northwest Frontier in what is now Pakistan, stopping in Lahore, Rawalpindi, and Peshawar (where they toured the Khyber Pass and peered into Afghanistan) before doubling back for a week in Bombay, the last major city on the tour. The tour then wound down, with the delegation returning in early March to Colombo from whence they started on their long trip home.

The delegation visited more than fifty cities during their tour. The tour centered on British Asia's Christian colleges, of which there were about forty, and they visited nearly all of them, along with sundry chapters of the YMCA and YWCA, churches and chapels of a variety of denominations, and public meetings of all sorts. It is not surprising, given the relentless pace of the tour, that all four of its members fell sick from time to time; Edward Carroll was unable to accompany the tour to Rangoon, and Phenola Carroll was indisposed from January 21 to the end of the tour with a case of scarlet fever. This led to a quarantine of the entire delegation at the end of January in Delhi, and the delegation canceled all of their appearances for a few days due to "illness and overwork."[3]

The delegation endured long, unrelenting days. The planned itinerary for November 11, 1935, in Madura, for instance, about the time Thurman had his first attack of nervous exhaustion, gives a sense of the daily pace. An informal gathering with members of the local Student Christian Movement at 8:00 A.M. was followed by a chapel service at 9:00 and visits to two local colleges (one Christian, one Hindu) at 10:00 and 10:45. After lunch with students and a midday rest period, there was a visit to a Hindu temple, then high tea with local prominent citizens, and another meeting with students at chapel, all before the day's finale, a large public meeting at a church and an 8:00 P.M. dinner. The delegation's dinners were typically quite extended affairs—leisurely, three-hour-long, multicourse displays of Indian hospitality.[4]

While the pace of the delegation's trip was tiring for all of its members, Thurman's responsibilities as chairman were considerable. He had to handle all the correspondence on arrangements and keep accounts of all expenses. In early February Thurman, near exhaustion, would write from Lahore: "We are now in the last month of schedule. I do not see how I can possibly last until March 1st but I can, I know. These are very very hard days for us all."[5]

The main job of the Negro Delegation was to talk, which they did at lectures, in sermons, at public addresses before crowds of up to four thousand (some of which were filmed), and at intimate gatherings and conversations with students. There were at least 265 speaking engagements in the 140 days the tour was in Asia, with Thurman speaking at 135 of the engagements, including all the large public addresses, in comparison to Sue Bailey Thurman, who spoke 69 times; Edward Carroll, 65; and Phenola Carroll, 23. These 265 engagements, as Thurman noted in the detailed schedule he prepared of the tour, did not count discussion groups, interviews, formal receptions, or time spent teaching choirs spirituals. Nor did it include unscheduled meetings, such as the interviews with Tagore and Gandhi.[6] As Thurman would later write of the tour's challenges, "You had to talk all day, making four one-hour lectures in the heat and all."[7]

We only have a partial list of the topics the delegates spoke on in Asia, and none of Thurman's texts are extant. There were lectures on "American Negro Achievements" and "Education of the Negro in America," on "Youth and Peace" and "The Tragedy of Dull-Mindedness" (one of Thurman's favorite sermon titles), along with lectures and presentations of the work of contemporary black poets. Sue Bailey Thurman often spoke on women's issues, giving lectures on "Negro Women" and "Women's Organizations" as well as "Internationalism through Music" and "Internationalism in the Beloved Community."[8]

There were two main topics of their lectures. As discussed in the last chapter, spirituals were probably the most common subject. Thurman delivered his lecture on "Deep River" and kindred spirituals at least ten times, along with at least an equal number of talks and demonstrations by Sue Bailey Thurman. Of the talks Thurman prepared especially for India, the one he delivered most frequently was a lecture he called "The Faith of the American Negro," and though we do not have an extant version in his own hand, it survives in several newspaper accounts.[9]

Despite its title, the talk was primarily political and historical; the "faith" in question was the confidence that enabled Negroes to survive and prosper after emancipation. Slaves had been brought to America without a common language and without a common purpose. During slavery, in the words of one newspaper account of Thurman's talk, they had "borne their sorrows with a quality of courage which belonged to men who were not bound with chains." Emancipation found blacks in a devastated South, and they found themselves "faced overnight with the practical problem of earning [their] food, guaranteeing for [themselves] economic security, and participating in ordinary American life." And from these unpromising roots much had been accomplished. The faith that enabled the Negro to endure had been a threefold faith, "the faith of the Negro in his own abilities," the "faith of the Negro in life itself," and the "faith of the Negro in God." Although much remained to be done, blacks in America had come a long way since 1865. Negroes were now accepted in many areas of American life, they were steadily breaking down professional barriers, and their counsel was valued in the highest echelons.

To judge from extant descriptions of the talk, which no doubt lack much of Thurman's original nuance, this was not, certainly by the standards of the 1960s or subsequently, a particularly strident indictment of the racism of American institutions. Although he gave ample weight to the forces that were arrayed against blacks, hindering and denying them success, Thurman's emphasis was on what blacks had created despite these handicaps. The vocabulary of the ideology of racial uplift that Thurman had been nurtured in was perhaps never fully extinguished in his mature writing, though by the mid-1930s he had certainly distanced himself from any naïve view that somehow accomplishment by a college-educated black elite had any particular utility for the trodden-upon black majority, a reality that he regularly reminded black college graduates in commencement addresses.[10] But Thurman and those similarly situated were justifiably proud of what they had accomplished in creating black institutions in the face of daunting difficulties. To focus too exclusively on the bleakness of America's racial landscape would have been to denigrate their own achievements or even the possibility of future change. For Thurman the "faith of the American Negro" was a belief in the possibility of transformation in the fortunes of American blacks on both an individual and a collective level. Though this would be something accomplished with white allies, and in part by entering (as full equals) white institutions, it was something that blacks would fundamentally have to do for themselves.

This was how the talk was received by its Indian audiences. Perhaps they were heartened by its essential optimism, its holding out the possibility that sweeping, epochal change was possibly closer than anyone dared hope. In the relative success of American blacks in the United States, Indians could see a refraction of their own circumstances, a confirmation of the fruits of nonviolent struggle. This was how a newspaper in Madras viewed "The Faith of the American Negro":

> The like of it has not been heard before. The thrill that the audience felt was not because of the articulation of their own deepest and unexpressed feelings. Such stirrings have been known before, as for example, when Mahatma Gandhi in his pre-Indian career came as the messenger of suffering Indians in South Africa. It was rather the response of hearts that felt their linking up with another race as the lecturer proceeded with

his interpretation of his people, defending them against false judgment, proclaiming the grit and character that was evolved under great stress, tracing the moods through which they have passed and expressing the bases of their confidence, while betraying no bitterness against their environment. It was no cold intellectual presentation of the incidents of a complex social history, but the soulful expression of the faith of the meek that rose conqueror over trials and suffering.[11]

Although Thurman did not emphasize racial conflict in his talks, many interpreted Thurman's lectures and sermons, and indeed, just the idea of the Negro delegation in India, as a racial challenge, an opening sally in what would be the global war against imperialism and white domination. T. J. George wrote Thurman in early 1936 that he thought "the great conflict in [the] future" will be "a question of white races against brown and black," and he praised the work of the Negro Delegation for giving ammunition for the "Asiatic" perspective.[12] At about the same time Thurman received a letter from a "Ch. John" praising the tour for giving insight into the "economic exploitation, political disenfranchisement, Educational inequalities, lynching" of the "imperialistic animals of the white Americans," who are just "one more example of patronizing oppressors preaching love. You will command respect . . . as few white men could."[13]

But if these Indian correspondents praised Thurman as a racial provocateur, some white listeners criticized him on the same ground. When he delivered "The Faith of the American Negro" in Lahore, one of those in the audience was Henry W. Luce (the father of Henry R. Luce of *Time* and *Life* fame) who had been a missionary in China for decades and was touring India. He was impressed by Thurman's talk, as he told him in a courteous letter. However, the talk left him thinking that Thurman was too exclusively blaming others for the problem of American Negroes and had spent insufficient time critiquing the internal problems of blacks. Moreover, Thurman had ignored the helping hand of well-intentioned whites and had argued that whites "had not lifted a finger to help," and that blacks "had attained all by their own inherent power." Luce argued that Thurman had forgotten the millions of whites who had fought and the many tens of thousands who had died to free the slaves, and Thurman's account of the slave trade had emphasized Christian culpability to the exclusion of the responsibilities of Muslims. He concluded that far from aiding racial harmony, Thurman's address "might . . . have the opposite effect." (Luce's letter struck a nerve with Thurman, and he printed it in its entirety in his autobiography, where he concluded that both he and Luce were "wrestling with the dilemmas created by the paradoxes in the American situation.")[14] Two very different audiences—one white and American, the other colored and Indian—heard Thurman's lecturing in India. They viewed talks like "The Faith of the American Negro," with its uncompromising demands for the full inclusion of blacks in American society, from the vantage of their own biases and found its message to be either bracingly or disturbingly radical.[15]

As the varied responses to "The Faith of the American Negro" indicate, all the talking Thurman did in India required, in turn, vast amounts of listening: to Indian students complaining of their own situation and their hatred of the British; with Indian Christians of all kinds, using Thurman as a mirror to explore and understand their own anomalous situation; with missionaries, explaining to Thurman their own challenges; to Hindus, Muslims, Buddhists, the learned and the unlettered, the powerful and the disinherited. For Thurman dialogue was essentially a religious task, an essential act of opening oneself and being receptive to the openness of others. And in the end, what Thurman most valued in his time in Asia was not what he said but what was said to him in conversations too numerous to be clearly remembered, each entering into the fabric of the trip, adding texture and nuance, making it a bit richer, denser, more complex. But a few conversations stood out, lingering long in his memory. We have already discussed one, with the anonymous lawyer in Ceylon. There were several others, two near Calcutta with Rabindranath Tagore and his close associate Kshiti Mohan Sen. And on the other side of the vast Indian subcontinent, near Bombay, the best-remembered episode of his time in Asia, his interview with Mahatma Gandhi.

II

Thurman had been an admirer of Rabindranath Tagore since his time at Rochester Theological Seminary, when he quoted him in one of his earliest published papers, and he saw him as a kindred soul, a spiritual searcher, a person bridging two worlds.[16] In 1936 Tagore, in his midseventies, was the most revered literary figure in India. In 1913 he became the first non-Western winner of the Nobel Prize in Literature (there would not be another until 1968) and would be admired in the West and lionized at home as the founding figure of the modern Bengali literary renaissance. Tagore was a protean figure whose literary oeuvre includes works in every major genre, a composer, a painter, an agricultural reformer, and an educator. In 1901 he opened a school at Santiniketan, near Calcutta, adding an institute of higher education, Visva-Bharati University, in 1921. It was different in form and academic expectation from Western schools and colleges; often classes had no examinations, and Tagore insisted that classes, except those requiring laboratories, be conducted out of doors, weather permitting. But though the school placed a considerable emphasis on Eastern learning (from China and Japan as well as India), it insisted on its ultimate compatibility with Western learning and science.[17] This was at a time when most British colleges in India, in the grasp of the dead, hoary hand of Thomas Babington Macaulay's notorious 1835 "Minute on Indian Education," still offered little or no instruction in native languages or literatures.[18]

The delegation would spend two days at Santiniketan, January 16 and 17, 1936. Howard Thurman lectured on "The Negro in American History" (a version of the "Faith of the American Negro"), and Sue Bailey Thurman lectured on the "History of Negro Music." The delegation had two meetings with Tagore, the first with a group of students sitting under a banyan tree, and the next day the Thurmans had a meeting with him in his house. Sue Bailey Thurman remembered Tagore looking every inch the Eastern sage: tall, with light-brown skin, long white hair, and a flowing, majestic beard—"He was a being of such rare beauty, so elegant of form and face—so redolent of the world's great seers who reflect the glory of a lighted mind!" She remembered Tagore reciting his poetry in English and Bengali to rapt listeners, speaking of the need for Indians to embrace the West on their own terms and the need for every people to find the universal messages in their own particular truths.[19]

But Thurman did not find in his discussions with Tagore the sort of give-and-take dialogue he most relished, and found him a profound but somewhat distant presence. He described the meeting in his auto-biography: "We took seats in front of his chair. He sat looking at us, but also through and beyond us, and then he would make some state-ment, as he focused his mind, his eyes, on our faces; then he would take off again. I felt his mind was going through cycles as if we were not even present. Then he would swing back from that orbit, settle in, take us into account again, and sweep out. It was not necessary to have an exchange of questions. It was as if we were there and being initiated into the secret working of a great mind and a giant spirit." It sounds as if the conversation was a bit one-sided, and perhaps a bit disappointing.[20]

But this was not the case with Thurman's other important meeting at Santiniketan, with Kshiti Mohan Sen, the head of its division of Oriental Studies. Indeed, in his autobiography Thurman writes that though he was very interested to see Tagore, his "chief concern" with his visit to Santiniketan was to have some time to meet with Sen.[21] Sen was a distinguished scholar of Hinduism and Indian religion. He and Tagore had been close associates at Santiniketan for decades, and he had worked with Tagore on many of his major philosophical works, such as *The Religion of Man* (1931).[22] Although most of Sen's works are in Bengali, his English language works include *Medieval Mysticism of India* (1930) and, subsequently, a standard introductory text, *Hinduism* (1961).[23]

Although Thurman for some reason had difficulties keeping Sen's name straight, he never forgot their meeting.[24] They spent the morn-ing sitting on the floor talking about Christianity and Hinduism. Al-though his grandson, the Nobel Prize–winning economist Amartya Sen, writes that Kshiti Mohan Sen's knowledge of English "was extremely limited," it presumably was better than Thurman's Bengali, and the linguistic difficulties perhaps contributed to an awkward beginning to their conversations.[25] Both men were tentative, touting their respective religious traditions, making their case against alternatives. When they broke for lunch, both men started to chuckle, and Thurman said he was a little embarrassed because both he and Sen had spent their morning's conversation "sparring for position—you from behind your Hindu breastwork, and I from behind my Christian embattlement." They both agreed to do better in the afternoon, and when they got together again, they did. Thurman described their discussion as

> the most primary, naked fusing of total religious experience with another human being of which I have ever been capable. It was as if we had stepped out of social, political, cultural frames of reference, and allowed two human beings to unite on a ground of reality that was unmarked by separateness and differences. This was a watershed experience of my life. We had become a part of each other even as we remained essentially individual. I was able to stand secure in my place and enter into his place without diminishing myself or threatening him.[26]

Thurman found in Sen what he had found in Rufus Jones, a kindred spirit. Sen, like Thurman, saw in practical mysticism the purest form of religion, a simple and direct communication with God, unhindered by creed, caste, or religious hierarchy. Sen dedicated his *Medieval Mystics of India* to "all those who have felt the Supreme Spirit in rare moments of self-realization and who seek life's fulfillment in a love that transcends limitations of creeds, customs, and race."[27] When Sen looked at Hinduism, he did not see a teeming multiplicity of mutually exclusive orthodoxies but a liberal religion in which believers were free to find their own path to God as part of a culturally inclusive, experientially based, religious pluralism.

Sen emphasized the historicity of Hinduism, its mutability and, in particular, its openness to other religious traditions, especially the fruitful interchanges between Hinduism and Islam, and he argued that Hinduism was at its peak after Islam "released the latent forces of India's religious life, and it was by her mystics that a synthesis was sought to be brought about between the conflicting elements of the two."[28] Hinduism provided its richness of religious expression; Islam brought its impatience with empty ritual and its deep commitment to an ethical monotheism. Moreover, for Sen the most admirable forms of Hinduism came from humble sources, artisans and itinerant mendicants, operating on the margins between Islamic Sufism and ecstatic Hindu worship; a religion of outcastes and pariahs indifferent if not openly hostile to the institutional and ritual dimensions of conventional religion. "Those who achieved and guided this synthesis were persons who, due to their birth in the so-called lower classes of society, were free from the bondage of scripture or of any institutional religion."[29]

Sen's Hinduism, finding its exemplars in humble weavers and cotton carders and in contemporary representatives of the mystical Hindu-Muslim fusion like the Bauls of Bengal, had much in common with Thurman's religion of an outcast, downtrodden, and politically marginal Jesus.[30] Thurman's Jesus, after meeting with Sen, became something of an honorary Hindu. Writing in 1938, Thurman would contrast the either-or nature of Christianity—exclusive, excluding, and anathematizing—with Hinduism, and he would conclude that Hinduism's "genius" seemed "to be synthesis-making. It possesses amazing powers of adjustment *and is profoundly elastic*" (Thurman's emphasis).[31] Although Thurman would always call himself a Christian, this would increasingly be more of a starting point than a destination, as he would wander, increasingly widely, in an interreligious search to realize the unity of God by transcending artificial cultural barriers. His meeting with Kshiti Mohan Sen was a crucial step in this journey.

III

But the most significant encounter Thurman had in India, both for himself and certainly in the eyes of posterity, was the meeting the Negro Delegation had in late February with Mahatma Gandhi. Gandhi and African American opinion had been long-distance admirers for many years, but this would be his first meeting with American blacks, and it would quietly reverberate throughout the subsequent history of the civil rights movement.[32] Gandhi first impinged on the consciousness of America's blacks in the years during and after World War I, after his return to India from South Africa in 1915. His campaigns of nonviolent protest seemed a way forward, an alternative to the unpalatable dichotomy of either foolhardy resistance or sullen acquiescence to racial oppression. Although some were of the opinion that a Gandhi in America would soon find himself lynched for his pains, the search was on for a black Gandhi and a way to translate Gandhiansm into a form that would be accessible for African Americans. By the early 1920s he was being hailed in the black press as a "messiah" and "saint"; in 1921 the *Chicago Defender* called him "the greatest man in the world today." (A few years later W. E. B. Du Bois would qualify this superlative only slightly, calling Gandhi "the greatest colored man in the world.")[33] The support and fascination with Gandhi transcended the usual divisions in black intellectual life; if Du Bois lauded Gandhi, so too did his bitter rival Marcus Garvey. Gandhi's actions regularly appeared in the pages of the journal Du Bois edited for the NAACP, the *Crisis*, and in 1929 Du Bois induced Gandhi to write a special statement "To the American Negro," telling his audience, among other things, that there was no dishonor in being slaves or descendents of slaves but only dishonor in being a slave owner.[34]

Almost from the start of his involvement with the Negro Delegation, Thurman had thoughts of meeting Gandhi, and he and others went to great efforts to try to arrange it. Muriel Lester, a prominent leader in the Fellowship of Reconciliation and director of Kingsley Hall, the well-known London settlement house, was so excited to hear about the Negro Delegation that she insisted Thurman travel cross-country (with the aerophobic Thurman traveling by train) from Washington, D.C., to Berkeley, California, at her expense, to meet with her for a few hours. "I am overjoyed to hear that you are going out with a few other Negroes to help the Indian people. I would like to talk to you about this, and oh! how I wish we could meet, if it was only for half an hour."[35] Lester knew Gandhi well, and had domiciled him at Kingsley Hall for several months in 1931 when he was in London for the Round Table Conference. Thurman met with Lester "in order to get a feel of the Indian spirit through her mind and words and heart,"[36] and she promised to get in touch with Gandhi about Thurman's forthcoming visit.

In early 1935 Thurman convinced Madeleine Slade, who had adopted the name Mirabehn, to visit Howard during a short American speaking tour. Slade, the daughter of a British admiral, had joined Gandhi's ashram and had become an important member of his personal entourage. Thurman wished to understand, in her own words, why she had given up so much to follow Gandhi, and he also thought it crucial that Slade get to meet with black Americans and convey to Gandhi the substance of the meeting. Slade made for a striking figure, tall and elegant in a simple sari, wearing sandals in a chilly Washington winter. She caused quite a stir at Howard, speaking on the characteristically Gandhian theme of "he who has more than he needs for efficient work is a thief."[37] After their meeting, she told him, "You must meet with Gandhiji while you are there," and promised to speak to him. Thurman mentioned both meetings in a short letter he wrote Gandhi on September 9, 1935, saying, "For years I have read about you" and "there are many things that I should like to talk through with you and covet the privilege very, very much."

To Thurman's delight, when he arrived in Colombo, among the other things waiting for him was the following postcard:

Wardha
6–10–35

Dear Friend,

I thank you for your letter of 9th Sept. just received. I shall be delighted to have you and your three friends whenever you can come before the end of this year. After that my movement will be uncertain though you will be welcome at this place whenever you come. Reverend Rallaram will be able to tell you

how simply we live here. If therefore we cannot provide western amenities of life, we will be making up for the deficiency by
the natural warmth of our affection.

Muriel [Lester] had prepared me to receive you here.

Yrs sinly -
MKGandhi

Arranging the meeting between Gandhi and the delegation proved
complex, and the details are somewhat difficult to sort out. Thurman claims in his autobiography that when the delegation reached
Bombay in February, they hadn't heard from Gandhi since his postcard in October.[38] This is belied by evidence that there were plans for
the delegation to spend their Christmas vacation at Gandhi's ashram at Wardha, which were canceled when Gandhi fell ill in early
December—a bout of high blood pressure that led him to cancel all of
his public engagements for well over a month.[39] When Gandhi recovered, subsequent plans were made for him to meet the delegation in
Delhi in early February, but this time it was the illness on the part of
the delegation—the collective exhaustion of all of its members—that
led to those plans falling through.[40] The delegation's time in Bombay
was, as usual, crowded with meetings, including a film (which alas,
no longer seems to be extant) of one of their meetings and squeezing
in time to hear pianist Teddy Weatherford. Weatherford was one of
the lions of the Chicago jazz scene in the 1920s—he recorded with
Louis Armstrong—and spent the latter years of his career as India's
preeminent jazz musician.[41]

But Thurman also worried about losing the opportunity to meet
with Gandhi, knowing that Bombay was the last stop on the tour
where a meeting would be practical. According to his autobiography,
on their second day in Bombay as Thurman was going to the post
office to telegraph to see if a meeting could be arranged, he spied a
man with a Gandhi cap. Thurman wrote, "Our eyes met as we passed,
though we said nothing. When I had gone about fifty feet something
just made me turn around to look back at him just as he turned
around to look back at me. He smiled; I smiled. We turned and came

toward each other and when we met he said, 'Are you, you?' And I said, 'Yes.' He said, 'Well, I have a letter for you from Gandhiji.'" It was another of the providential accidents that throughout his life Thurman found pregnant with deeper significance.

Gandhi's letter invited the delegation to meet him at Bardoli, a small town near Bombay where the Congress Party had an encampment and the site of a memorable campaign of satyagraha in 1928.[42] If other arrangements proved impossible, Gandhi offered to come to Bombay to meet with the delegation. Thurman promptly canceled all scheduled appearances and the delegation (minus Phenola Carroll, who was still recovering from scarlet fever) left to meet Gandhi, catching a train in the early morning hours of February 21. After a train trip of three hours, they arrived at Navsari Station at about four o'clock in the morning, where they were met by Mahadev Desai, Gandhi's personal secretary. They went to a mango grove, and while Sue Bailey Thurman and Edward Carroll rested in a bungalow, Howard Thurman and Desai spoke of Gandhi. Desai was also the recorder of the conversation the delegation had with Gandhi, which was published about a month later under the title "With Our Negro Guests" in the *Harijan*, a weekly newspaper that was a house organ for Gandhi and Gandhianism.[43] At daybreak, they traveled the twenty miles to Bardoli.

Gandhi often liked theological discussions in the early morning hours. Margaret Chatterjee has written that Gandhi "was very patient with those who wanted to draw him into theological discussion, but he often chose a very early hour for this, rationing the time to be allotted, and in his heart of hearts he believed there were better ways of spending the time."[44] But if anything, Gandhi's only problem with the Negro Delegation was that he felt there wasn't time enough to talk about all that he wanted to discuss. He greeted the delegation with great warmth, coming out of his tent to meet the car. Desai told Thurman that in his long experience, he did not remember Gandhi ever greeting visitors so warmly. They went in a tent and were invited to sit on the floor. Thurman related in his autobiography that "to my amazement, the first thing Gandhi did was to reach under his shawl and take out an old watch, saying, 'I apologize, but we must talk by the watch, because we have much to talk about and you have only three hours before you have to leave to take your train back to Bombay.'"[45] Gandhi started to ask questions. Thurman would say, "Never in my life have I been a part of that kind of examination: persistent, pragmatic, questions about American Negroes, about the course of slavery, and how we had survived it." According to Thurman, Gandhi asked him about "voting rights, lynching, discrimination, public school education, the churches and how they functioned. His questions covered the entire sweep of our experience in American society."[46]

Thurman gave Gandhi a brief overview of black history since Emancipation and talked about Booker T. Washington, W. E. B. Du Bois, and specifically mentioned to Gandhi Du Bois's most recent book, *Black Reconstruction*. Taking a page from that book, Thurman offered a rather Marxist analysis of Reconstruction and post-Reconstruction history, telling Gandhi that the Civil War destroyed the Southern aristocracy and "as soon as the armies of the occupation moved to the North the economic structure was paralyzed, leaving the whole structure in the hands of the poor Whites who smarted under the economic competition of the Negro."[47] Thurman explained the pernicious consequences of segregation in education and other areas of life, and he spoke of the history of Howard University, making a point of mentioning to Gandhi that Howard's president was among his most prominent African American supporters.[48]

Gandhi asked if the "prejudice against colour [was] growing or dying out," and Thurman gave a measured answer, saying it was difficult to say: "In one place things look much improved, whilst in another the outlook is still dark." Somewhat surprisingly, Thurman thought the greatest progress had been made in the South, where among many Southern white students "there is a disposition to improve upon the attitude of their forebears" and there was some small amelioration in general racial climate. However, he argued, the migrants to the North were dealing with the brunt of the Depression as well as the anger from whites worried about losing their jobs. "The economic question is acute everywhere, and in many of the industrial centers in [the]

Middle West the prejudice against the Negro shows itself in its ugliest form," he lamented, a theme he would take up again in a 1940 address in Chicago in which he argued that the situation in Chicago's ghetto was in some ways worse than conditions in the Jim Crow South.[49]

When Gandhi asked if interracial marriages were legally recognized, Edward Carroll said that more than half of the states had anti-miscegenation laws, and that in Virginia, where he was a pastor, he had to post a five-hundred-dollar bond to promise he would not solemnize any such union. Thurman, as he had in his 1926 thesis at Rochester Theological Seminary on the religious implications of pre-marital sex, saw the prohibition against intermarriage from a feminist perspective, explaining to Gandhi that the proscription of interracial marriage forced many black women into sexual bondage, and that "there has been a lot of intermixture of races as for 300 years or more the Negro woman has had no control over her body." (A possible subtext of this conversation—though it is not mentioned by either Desai or Thurman—is that there had been some consternation among African Americans at Gandhi's apparent criticism of intermarriage in a widely circulated 1930 summary of his teachings, and Gandhi perhaps wanted to dispel any doubts in this regard.)[50]

Then it was the delegation's turn to ask questions of Gandhi. One aspect of Gandhi's career that sometimes made American blacks uneasy was that during his years in South Africa native Africans had been excluded from his satyagraha campaigns. Sue Bailey Thurman, who consistently asked some of the more challenging questions, asked him about this, and Gandhi replied, "I purposely did not invite them. It would have endangered their cause. They would not have understood the technique of our struggle nor could they have seen the purpose or utility of non-violence." Whether or not this was fair on Gandhi's part, worries that satyagraha campaigns could easily get out of control—he often called off campaigns in India that turned violent—and his feeling that the gulf between Indians and Africans in South Africa made effective coordination impossible, were longstanding beliefs. In some ways the very reasons that convinced Gandhi he could not include blacks in his civil rights efforts in South Africa—

that satyagraha had to be specific to every national and racial group
and could not be imposed from without—made satyagraha all the
more attractive for American blacks seeking to create their own campaigns of civil disobedience.[51]

The conversation soon turned to a discussion of Islam, and why
it was a more congenial religion for many Africans than Christianity. Gandhi told Thurman, "The Moslem religion is the only religion
in the world in which no lines are drawn from within the religious
fellowship. Once you are in, you are all the way in. This is not true
in Christianity, it isn't true in Buddhism or Hinduism. If you had
become Moslem, even though you were a slave, in the faith you would
be equal to the master."[52]

Thurman concurred. He told Gandhi, "We are often told that but
for the Arabs there would have been no slavery. I do not believe it."
Gandhi agreed. "No it is not true at all. For the moment a slave ac-
cepts Islam he obtains equality with his master, and there are several
instances of this in history." This line of argument was quite fresh in
Thurman's mind, having been told no more than ten days before by
missionary Henry W. Luce in Lahore that rather than blame slavery
on the Christians, he might have said "it was largely Arab Muslims
that brought the slaves to the coast." (Thurman saw this as a species
of obfuscation to dilute the primary responsibility of Christians for
the Atlantic slave trade.) The conversation of religion continued, and
in the words of Mahadev Desai, "the whole discussion led to many a
question and cross-question during which the guests had an occasion
to see that Gandhiji's principle of equal respect for all religions was
no theoretical formula but a practical creed."

This was Thurman's creed as well. He had long made invidious
comparisons between the respective racial egalitarianism of Islam
and Christianity. He had never forgotten the encounter he had while
working as a youth minister in Roanoke, Virginia, in 1925, with a
Nigerian Muslim who told him that "Allah laughs aloud in his Mo-
hammedan heaven when he looks out upon the First Baptist Church,
colored, and First Baptist Church, white."[53] This view that Islam was
more racially enlightened than Christianity—a fairly common one

among black intellectuals of the era—was only strengthened by his time in India.[54] Thurman would write of attending a service for Eid al-Fitr (celebrating the end of Ramadan) in Calcutta: "the Maidan [a large public park] was filled with thousands of Mussilmen [sic] assembled for the preparation of breaking a fast. There were the rich and the poor, the educated and the uneducated, those who stood high and those who stood low in the community—they were all there, side by side, without distinction. Only one who has lived my life can know the thrill that a spectacle of that sort gives."[55]

Thurman did note that Muslims were less friendly to him than Hindus, and he attributed this to the fact that perhaps "as Christians we seem to be greater traitors to Mohammedanism due to our African background than to Hinduism." He also noted that Muslim women were less likely to be present in public venues than Hindu women, and when they were, far more likely to be partially or totally veiled. While Thurman had little patience for Christian evangelists in India, he seems to have had a greater tolerance for Muslim proselytizers. "The fact that every Mussilman [sic] whom I met seemed to me to be a missionary out to make converts for his faith gave me great respect for them," perhaps because he saw Islam as a religion authentic to India, or because the Hindu reluctance to make converts for their faith conveyed the underlying implication that outsiders really weren't worthy of becoming Hindus. In any event, Thurman appreciated Islam for its directness and the commitment it inspired in its adherents, and even the assumption of its superiority to other religions was refreshing, a constant reminder of the emptiness of the pretensions of Christianity to the same status.[56] In all, Thurman came to share the views of Rabindranath Tagore, Kshiti Mohan Sen, and Mahatma Gandhi that there was something incredibly vital and precious about India's genuinely multicultural and multireligious civilization, one in which Christianity had a distinctly marginal presence.

The conversation then turned, in the words of Desai, to "the main thing that had drawn the distinguished members to Gandhiji," his philosophy of ahimsa (nonviolence) and satyagraha (civil disobedience campaigns). "Is non-violence from your point of view a form of direct action?" Thurman asked. "It is not one form," Gandhi replied, "it is the only form." Nonviolence, Gandhi said, does not exist without an active expression of it, and indeed, "one cannot be passively non-violent."

Gandhi went on to lament that the term had been widely mis-understood. *Ahimsa* was a Sanskrit word with deep resonance in all of South Asia's ancient karmic religions, Buddhism, Hinduism, and (especially) Jainism, in which ahimsa stood for a commitment to re-frain from harming living things.[57] He felt there was no good English language equivalent for *ahimsa*, so he created the term *nonviolence* (the earliest usage in the *Oxford English Dictionary*, citing Gandhi, is from 1920), but told Thurman that he regretted the fact that his coinage started with the "negative particle 'non.'" On the contrary, Gandhi in-sisted nonviolence was "a force which is more positive than electricity" and subtler and more pervasive than the ether.

Gandhi went on to expound his theory of nonviolence to the del-egation. "We are surrounded in life by strife and bloodshed, life living upon life." But "some great seer [unnamed by Gandhi, perhaps Jesus or Buddha], who ages ago penetrated the centre of truth said: It was not through strife and violence, but through non-violence that man can fulfill his destiny and his duty to his fellow creatures." He continued: "At the center of non-violence is a force which is self-acting." "Ahimsa," Gandhi told the visiting Christians, meant "'love' in the Pauline sense, yet something more," presumably referring to the famous passage in 1 Corinthians, "Faith, hope, and love abides, these three, but the great-est of these is love." (Although the passage Gandhi referred to was Thurman's favorite passage from the corpus of the Pauline epistles, the two men agreed that the religion of Paul was a fateful detour from the authentic religion of Jesus. Gandhi had written in 1928, "I draw a great distinction between the Sermon on the Mount and the Letters of Paul. They are a graft on Christ's teaching, his own gloss apart from Christ's experience.")[58]

But *love*, even in its Pauline sense, was liable to be too easily mis-understood, either as too narrowly focused on a love of God, or, more troubling to Gandhi with his profoundly puritanical attitudes toward sexuality, almost impossible to purge of its connotations of carnality. So, Gandhi concluded, he was forced to define *ahimsa* negatively: "But it does not express a negative force, but a force superior to all the forces put together. One person who can express Ahimsa in life exercises a force superior to all the forces of brutality."

For Gandhi nonviolence was not really an idea at all. It was, as he told the delegation repeatedly, a force, a physical reality, a metaphysical substrate that underlined and defined all reality, the deeper truth behind the dross and flux of the world, the truth beneath and beyond the seeming brutality that apparently confined both human life and the world of nature to endless cycles of gratuitous violence. It was a force that individuals could accumulate and concentrate. Ahimsa was a force, as Gandhi indicated, "the force," in the constitution of the universe.[59]

Thurman, always at his religious core a nature mystic, a romantic vitalist in the mode of Olive Schreiner, was very sympathetic to Gandhi's broader point that the ultimate truth, whether it was labeled God or ahimsa, was at once natural and supernatural, profoundly alive but not limited to any specific living thing. "If the source of life is alive, then it follows that life itself is alive," Thurman would write, somewhat cryptically but characteristically, in 1944. What he meant by this was that there was an underlying moral order in the universe. "The cosmos is the kind of order that sustains and supports the demands that the relationships between men and between man and God be one of harmony [and] integration."[60] Gandhi's ahimsa was a close relative of Thurman's increasingly unconventional notion of God.

As the conversation continued, Gandhi and Thurman, discovering their deep religious affinities, continued to discuss the metaphysics of nonviolence. Worldly possessions, Gandhi told Thurman, stood in the way of mastery of ahimsa: "It possesses nothing, therefore it possesses everything." And Gandhi explained another paradox: while ahimsa was completely egalitarian, open to all—"if there was any exclusiveness about it, I should reject it at once"—because of the difficulty of the path, mastery was granted to few. Thurman's question of whether it was possible for a single human being to embody ahimsa provoked the following dialogue:

GANDHI: It is possible. Perhaps your question is more universal than you mean. Isn't it possible, you mean to ask, for one single Indian for instance to resist the exploitation of 300 million Indians? Or do you mean the onslaught of the whole world against a single individual personally?

THURMAN: Yes, that is one half of the question. I wanted to know if one man can hold the whole violence at bay?

GANDHI: If he cannot, you must take it that he is not a true representative of Ahimsa.

The conversation had turned to one of the peculiarities of Gandhian nonviolence. As in many spiritual practices, there was a combination of great humility and unbounded arrogance in Gandhi's notion of ahimsa. For it was Gandhi's profound belief that all it required was one person, one who truly mastered nonviolence, to end British imperialism and that such a person could embody and realize the hopes of hundreds of millions of people. Needless to say, Gandhi thought he might be that person, and he came very close to realizing this goal. A major reason for his frequent fasts was his belief that through his asceticism he would become a stronger vessel of ahimsa. Judith Brown has written of the 1924 fast he undertook after an outbreak of Muslim-Hindu rioting. "He blamed himself for the violence around him, believing that if he had been perfectly non-violent this would not have happened. . . . He was convinced that the soul's strength grew in proportion to that which a man disciplined his flesh."[61] Gandhi was of course a canny manipulator of the press and a very shrewd politician, but an underlying motivation for nearly all of his actions was the accumulation of soul force.

For Gandhi, satyagraha was at its core a careful, personal spiritual discipline. One individual's commitment to ahimsa could change a continent because it could be shared and copied. But it would have to be imitated and emulated precisely or not at all. In a part of the conversation Thurman remembered but has no parallel in Desai's transcription, Thurman asked Gandhi why the independence movement had so far failed in its efforts to rid the country of the British. Gandhi answered that the effectiveness of ahimsa "depends upon the degree to which the masses of people are able to embrace such a notion and have it become a working part of their total experience. It cannot be the unique property of the leaders; it has to be rooted in mass ascent and creative push." Gandhi told him, Thurman would write, that when he "first began our movement it failed, and it will continue to fail until it is embraced by the masses of the people."

Gandhi went on to say that the problem with the Indian masses is that they did not have enough "vitality" to embrace ahimsa, and Thurman records that "it struck me with a tremendous wallop that I had never associated ethics and morality with physical vitality. It was a new notion trying to penetrate my mind." Gandhi went on to explain what he meant by vitality. First, it simply meant physical strength. The masses were hungry, and the pains in their stomachs and the need for survival made any attention to higher ideals impossible. And then it meant a sense of self-respect. This was why it was so important to redevelop native industries like weaving and improve agricultural resources so as not to rely on imported clothing or foodstuffs. Gandhi also told Thurman that the Indian masses had not lost their self-respect due to "the presence of the conqueror in our midst" but because of their toleration of injustices within, especially the institution of untouchability.

Gandhi's notion of vitality, even if it hit Thurman with a "wallop," was one, in a somewhat different guise, thoroughly familiar to him—namely, that oppression tends to rob people of their self-respect and their moral self-awareness, and that until this is repaired, those who seek to change this will find no adequate redress. So Thurman had argued in several works before coming to India, most importantly in "Good News for the Underprivileged." There he asserted that continual fear of violence by those at the bottom of society "disorganizes the individual from within. It strikes continually at the basic ground of his self-estimate, and by so doing makes it impossible for him to live creatively and to function."[62]

As a consequence, both Thurman and Gandhi saw the impetus for movements for social change arising less from mass politics than from a handful of persons who had realized the proper techniques for self-mastery and could, by their example, show others the way. Any effort based on hatred, resentment, or exclusion and out of a desire for revenge and a mere turning of the tables will always fail or will be a hollow victory, and in the end changing nothing. Thurman told his protégé James Farmer in 1943, at a time when Farmer was beginning to blaze his own trail as a leader of nonviolent protest, that "I was very much interested in the fact that Mr. Gandhi told me that such civil disobedience broke down in India because the masses of the people were not able to sustain so lofty a creative idea over a time interval of sufficient duration to be practically effective. They were unable so to do, not because they were lacking in courage or in willingness, but rather in vitality."[63] Both Thurman and Gandhi believed that without the quest for personal spiritual development, genuine social change becomes impossible.

As they continued to discuss nonviolence, Thurman asked Gandhi "how to train individuals or communities in this difficult art." Gandhi, in his answer, spoke of the Christian notion of the kingdom of heaven (probably by way of Tolstoy's *The Kingdom of God Is Within You*, a work that had a deep impact on him early in life) to explicate his profoundly Indian idea of the reality of nonviolence. Eventually, as the karma of our lives leads to our rebirth on a higher level, as societies themselves are transformed and reincarnated in new guises, the goal will be reached:

> There is no royal road, except through living the creed in your own life which must be a living sermon. Of course the expressions in one's own life presupposes great study, tremendous perseverance, and thorough cleansing of one's self of all the impurities. If for the mastering of the physical sciences you

have to devote a whole life-time, how many lifetimes may be needed for mastering the greatest spiritual force that mankind has known? But why worry even if it means several lifetimes. For this is the only permanent thing in life, if this is the only thing that counts, then whatever effort you bestow on mastering it is well spent. Seek ye first the Kingdom of Heaven and everything else shall be added to you. The Kingdom of Heaven is Ahimsa.

Sue Bailey Thurman, perhaps getting a little weary of the airy philosophical discussion between her husband and Gandhi, tried to bring the discussion of nonviolence down to a more practical plane: "How am I to act," she asked Gandhi, "supposing my own brother was lynched before my very eyes?" In response Gandhi said, "Supposing I was a Negro, and my sister was ravished by a White or lynched by a whole community, what would be my duty? I ask myself." His answer was that "there is such a thing self-immolation." This is as difficult a concept as it sounds, a willed burning, if not of oneself, of one's bridges, of one's familiar contacts and connections, of any ties that bind in any way to the perpetuation of evil, done with the knowledge that without the complicity of the oppressed, oppression will never succeed. "I must not wish ill to these [the whites who lynched or raped those in my community], but neither must I cooperate with them, and I refuse to cooperate with even my brother Negroes who tolerate the wrong. This is the self-immolation I mean."

Self-immolation was a hard and frightening doctrine, the logical conclusion of Gandhi's convictions extended to what many saw as illogical extremes. The following year Gandhi would tell Thurman's colleagues and good friends Benjamin Mays and Channing Tobias (in India for a World Student Christian Federation conference) that the resistance of the Ethiopians to the Italian invasion would have been much more effective if "they had retired from the field and allowed themselves to be slaughtered."[64] And in 1938, writing shortly after Kristallnacht, he controversially counseled German Jews that "suffering undergone voluntarily will bring . . . an inner strength and joy."[65] "One's faith," Gandhi told the delegation in 1936, "must remain undimmed whilst life ebbs out minute by minute."

When Gandhi sensed that Thurman and the Negro Delegation seemed a bit quizzical about the doctrine of self-immolation, he emphasized that he was speaking of an ideal, which could only be imperfectly approached. "I am a very poor specimen of the practice of non-violence, and my answer may not convince you. But I am striving very hard, and even if I do not succeed fully in this life, my faith will not diminish."

If he was not entirely convinced, Gandhi's notion of self-immolation made a considerable impact on Thurman. As Gandhi pointed out, it was inextricably connected to the ratcheting, ever higher, of noncooperation with oppression, whatever the costs. This was one of the bases of his nationalism, that systematic noncooperation was creating space for national renewal, swaraj (self-reliance), and independence in India. Gandhi was a nationalist, creating a movement for Indians and consciously trying to exclude British influences and culture. Nationalism, per se, never had much appeal for Thurman. What worked for the disinherited majority in India could not be borrowed for a disinherited minority in America. If blacks in America could and must do much on their own, they ultimately needed allies in order to succeed. Blacks would not expel whites from the United States. The solution to America's racial woes had to be an interracial one. (It is one of the ironies of the civil rights movement that black nationalists who took up Gandhi's call for national separation and independence, like Malcolm X, usually did so by explicitly rejecting Gandhian nonviolence.)

What Thurman appreciated in the idea of self-immolation was the linking of religious self-examination with a personal investigation of how an individual, every individual, is complicit in the evil that surrounds and envelops them, and that spiritual growth requires the severing of those ties strand by strand. Everyone was complicit in Jim Crow, white or black, whether by exercising or profiting from their dominance over others, or through their indifference or acquiescence. The goal of nonviolence was to consciously complicate one's life, trying to make oneself, as Gandhi told Thurman, a living sermon. Start by refusing to make small compromises with evil, and work your way up to the larger ones. In the end, when no further compromise is possible, you have to be willing to die for your beliefs, call it self-immolation, crucifixion, or some other name. Without this ultimate commitment to what Gandhi would have called truth, beliefs were nothing more than easy words and empty posturing. This conviction would become Thurman's and would form the basis of his theology of social change.

IV

The time grew near for the conversation to end. The Negro Delegation had appointments in Bombay they had to keep. But both sides wanted the conversation to continue. "We want you to come to America," Sue Bailey Thurman said to Gandhi. "Not for White America, but for the Negroes, we have many a problem that cries for solution, and we need you badly." But Gandhi said that he couldn't come, not when the work in India was so unfinished and not when Gandhi had so many doubts, not about the rightness of the cause or his message but whether he was its real messenger. "How I wish I could [come]" he told the delegation, but he couldn't do so before he gave "a demonstration here of all that I have been saying. I must make good the message here before I bring it to you. I do not say that I am defeated, but I still have to perfect myself. You may be sure that the moment I feel the call within me I shall not hesitate."[66] Thurman said that American blacks were ready for the message. "Much of the peculiar background of our own life in America is our own interpretation of the Christian religion. When one goes through the pages of the hundreds of Negro spirituals, striking things are brought to my mind which remind me of all you have told us today."

There were parting gifts. Gandhi gave Sue Bailey Thurman a basket of tropical fruit. Howard Thurman then asked Gandhi if he could have a piece of cloth that Gandhi himself had spun. Several months later Desai sent Thurman a swathe from Gandhi's own loom. It would remain for the rest of his life one of his most precious and treasured possessions. And the Negro Delegation sang two spirituals. In the *Harijan*, Mahadev Desai suggested this was at Thurman's initiative: "Mrs. Thurman is a soulful singer, and Dr. Thurman would not think of going away without leaving us with something to treasure in our memory." In his autobiography Thurman suggests that the spiritual singing was at Gandhi's behest. "Will you sing one of your songs for me? Will you sing, 'Were You There When They Crucified My Lord?'"[67] With Sue Bailey Thurman in the lead, and Howard Thurman and Eddie Carroll on background vocals, they sang that spiritual as well as "We Are Climbing Jacob's Ladder," which for Desai "gave expression to the deep-seated hope and aspiration in the breast of every oppressed community to climb higher and higher until the goal was won."

Thurman says that while they were singing Gandhi and his associates bowed their heads in prayer; their singing was followed by an extended silence and then a few spoken words of prayer. Gandhi had thought that "Were You There When They Crucified My Lord?" provided "the root experience of the entire human race under the spread of the healing wings of suffering."[68] At the end of this long silence Gandhi offered his final comments, which would become the best-known excerpt from the interview, a prophecy and a benediction. "Well," said Gandhi, bidding good-bye to them, "if it comes true it may be through the Negroes that the unadulterated message of non-violence will be delivered to the world."[69]

In his autobiography, however, Thurman provides a different ending to the conversation. Gandhi had disliked Christian missionaries since his boyhood in Gujarat, with their talk of "saving souls," their assumption that everyone else lived in darkness and that Asian converts must not only accept a new God but also turn their back on their heritage.[70] Although he had come to appreciate the finer aspects of Christianity—especially the radical pacifist strain that led from Garrison and Thoreau to Tolstoy—he had never overcome his basic conviction that Christianity in India, with its Western baggage, was in the end an excrescence. He had found in Thurman a Christian who agreed with him. He told Thurman that the biggest obstacle to the spread of Christianity in India is "Christianity as it is practiced, as it has been identified with Western civilization and colonialism. This is the greatest enemy Jesus Christ has in my country—not Hinduism, or Buddhism, or any of the indigenous religions—but Christianity itself."[71] However the conversation ended, Thurman and the other members of the Negro Delegation left Gandhi knowing that in some sense they had been transfigured by his presence.

Thurman's meeting with Gandhi was published in March 1936 in the *Harijan*, and it soon was disseminated beyond the fairly restricted circulation (in the United States, at least) of Gandhi's weekly. As early as April 1936, Thurman would receive a letter from a white female admirer (from a small town in Montana, of all out-of-the-way places), telling him that she had "simply wept as I read" it. She wrote that she was proud of his spiritual gifts and his openness to the spiritual gifts of others, and was "richly deeply proud of you—proud of you as I have not been proud of my fellow Americans for a long time."[72] Gandhi's parting comment would become a catchphrase within the civil rights movement, his blessing and benediction on what God had wrought in America. In early 1957 in Atlanta, at the end of the founding meeting of what would become the Southern Christian Leadership Conference, its two leaders, Bayard Rustin and Martin Luther King Jr.—tired, exhausted, exhilarated, satisfied—sat talking. Do you remember, Rustin asked King, what Gandhi told Howard Thurman in India, many years ago? and quoted Gandhi's words.[73] The force of ahimsa was with them.

Inconveniently for the requirements of a neat and well-made narrative, Thurman's supreme moment of vision in India, his confirmatory and concluding epiphany, occurred a few weeks before he met Gandhi. But in many ways the meeting with Gandhi simply confirmed what he had already learned from India. The delegation was speaking in Peshawar (in what is now Pakistan) and spending a morning sightseeing, visiting the fabled Khyber Pass, the legendary route from Afghanistan through the high mountains of the Hindu Kush through which much of European and Middle Eastern civilization had entered the Indian subcontinent.

The area around Peshawar and the Khyber Pass is, at this writing, probably the most dangerous place on earth. It is the home of the Taliban and Al-Qaeda, and since the destruction of New York City's World Trade Center on September 11, 2001, ground zero for the conflict between an imperial United States and militant Islam. It was not all that much safer when the Negro Delegation came through in early 1936. In the middle of India's Northwest Frontier Province, it was home to a number of Pashtun tribes that had never been truly pacified or incorporated into British India. It had been the site of many of Rudyard Kipling's best stories of imperial derring-do on horseback, though by 1936 the British were using RAF bombers to attack the tribesmen.[74]

But that morning in early February Thurman was not concerned with the chronic political instability in the region. He was looking into Afghanistan as a camel train passed, bringing goods to the bazaars of North India. He felt he was moving back in time. "Here was the gateway through which Roman and Mogul conquerors had come in other days bringing with them goods, new concepts, and the violence of armed might." At once, "all that we had seen in and felt in India seemed to be miraculously brought into focus." America, with its ethnic, racial, and religious diversities, in some ways had a lot in common with India. But America's Christianity, its dominant religion, was blinkered and creedal, rigid with subdivision upon subdivision, a series of barriers and obstacles in the way of those seeking a common religious ground from worshiping together. By contrast India seemed to celebrate a more or less harmonious, multiethnic, multireligious diversity. Thurman closed his 1938 report to the India Committee, his longest statement on the trip, with the following comment: India "seemed to be God-intoxicated. Despite all the superficialities and leeches that are present in all developed religions, more than any other place I have ever known India seems capable of grasping completely a religion that inspires overwhelming personal sacrifices and complete ethical and moral devotion."[75]

The worst of the divisions in American religion and American society as a whole were those of race. Everywhere the delegation went in Asia, in almost every city, the same question was asked though in different ways: "Why is the church powerless against the color bar?" The answers of the delegates were necessarily defensive, because in all of North America there was not a single instance of a church with a completely interracial membership.

This, Thurman resolved, would have to change. He had recently read of an unprecedented event, an attempt to create an interracial religious fellowship in Philadelphia that would meet regularly.[76] Perhaps this was the vanguard of a different type of Christianity. Certainly, new churches had to be created, practicing new forms of worship in congregations far removed from the artificial and all too self-conscious interracialism that often prevailed when whites and blacks were exhorted to worship together. They would have to be genuine communities, like those in India—plastic and evolving, proudly heterogeneous, with their own culture, sensitive and adjusting to the needs of their members. It was not enough to create a new setting for Christian worship; it would have to be a fundamentally new type of Christianity: one stripped of dogmatism, universal in its scope and sympathies; one united humanity worshiping the one and undivided God. Like ahimsa, religion was a force, one powerful enough—if harnessed correctly—to pull down the walls of Jim Crow person by person, congregation by congregation, city by city, state by state until an entire nation would be utterly transformed. Thurman saw clearly what he must do next. "We knew that we must test whether a religious fellowship could be developed in America that was capable of cutting across all racial barriers, with a carry-over into the common life, a fellowship that would alter the behavior patterns of those involved. It became imperative now to find out if experiences of spiritual unity among people could be more compelling than the experiences which divide them."[77]

This is the most profound lesson Thurman learned from India. And after returning to the United States, after eight years of pondering the message, in 1944 Thurman left Howard University to become co-pastor of the Church for the Fellowship of All Peoples in San Francisco, one of the first religious bodies in the United States expressly created as an interracial congregation.

But social change is not always so high-minded, and sometimes it is conveyed in a language that might make a Gandhi or a Tagore blush. British Asia was undergoing what would be a largely nonviolent transformation that by 1936 had in large measure rendered the British overlords superfluous long before they finally departed. They retained their ability to coerce and to use military force but had lost the ability to control the hearts and the minds and the bodies and the lives of the Asians they governed. In a 1957 article, Thurman would relate another Indian epiphany, less exalted and refined perhaps than his experience at the Khyber Pass but just as powerful:

> As I sat in a train compartment in Calcutta, a little Indian porter staggered into the compartment with a trunk on his head and two heavy pieces of luggage in his hands. He put them down and then with great effort established them securely in the luggage rack. A British colonel was waiting. When the porter finished, the colonel gave him a coin. He looked at the coin, and then looked into the face of the colonel, and tossed the coin back so that it struck the colonel on the nose. Immediately the colonel struck the Indian across the shoulders with his bamboo stick. The Indian snatched the stick from his hand, broke it on his bony knees, and threw it out of the train window. The train started moving and the porter jumped out of the train and ran along side pouring out expletives which I could not understand but I could feel. All the way to his destination, the colonel kept muttering to himself; the only thing that I could hear was a repetition of the phrase, "it's time for me to retire and leave this blank country." The force of revolution was at work.[78]

A nonviolent revolution does not destroy its opponents. Either they are changed or, cowed and chastened, they slink from the scene, utterly beside the point. That is what happened in India. Look around you and listen carefully, Thurman was telling his listeners, beyond the immediate clamor of the violent reaction to the civil rights movement, and what you can see and hear is Jim Crow, slowly if noisily becoming irrelevant, slinking away, crawling off, and dying.

CHAPTER FIVE

What Thurman Learned from India

ON SUNDAY MORNING, AUGUST 13, 1942, Howard Thurman met with a reporter, Peter Dana, from the *Pittsburgh Courier*, one of the nation's most influential black newspapers. Thurman was staying at the Theresa Hotel in Harlem on his way back to Washington and Howard University from speaking engagements in New England. India was on his mind, as had been so often the case since his time in South Asia in 1935 and 1936. He had especially been thinking about it the previous week, since Gandhi and the Indian Congress Party had initiated their "Quit India" campaign, which called for immediate Indian independence. British authorities responded by promptly arresting Gandhi and the rest of the Congress Party leadership, and they would remain incarcerated for the remainder of the war. Thurman was outraged. "There aren't enough jails in all India," he told Dana, "to imprison the spirit of present day India that articulates itself in Gandhi and Nehru." The "imperialist stubbornness of Britain" had already reduced their claims of fighting for democracy to a "moral absurdity." As he would occasionally do during the war, Thurman muted his deep pacifist doubts about the entire enterprise to express a general sympathy with the Allies' professed war aims and argued that there was no way for this war to end, other than "the freedom of all people and their equality under the law." One cannot wage a war for freedom with Britain's foot on the neck of the Indian people.[1]

Dana took stock of the "modest, stocky, black man, with resonant voice and smiling countenance" he was talking to. He was, he told his readers, one of the best-known of contemporary speakers and thinkers in American colleges and universities, but not sufficiently known to the general public. Nonetheless, he wrote that Thurman had "probably moved more cynical men and intellectual women than any other speaker of his generation." Thurman was a mystic, but "a mystic with a practical turn of mind, with a thorough understanding of the economics and politics of the modern world," and was "easily one of the most brilliant and profound men in America." In sum, Thurman represented a "Christian likeness of many of the best qualities of Gandhi and Nehru." Indeed, Thurman was "one of the few black men in this country around whom a great, conscious movement of Negroes could be built, not unlike the great Indian movement with which Gandhi and Nehru are associated."[2]

At the time Dana wrote his article, the black press had been casting envious glances at Gandhi and India for more than two decades; if Gandhi could create and summon a great nonviolent movement in India for freedom and citizenship, tying the British in knots, why couldn't American blacks create their own version, advancing their interests, confounding their tormentors? As of yet, this movement had no champion. Still there was much talk and the stirrings of action by A. Philip Randolph, head of the March on Washington Movement, members of the Fellowship of Reconciliation, and other troublers of America's racial waters.

And of course, from this ferment, there would indeed arise a great Gandhian movement led by African Americans. Thurman would not be its leader. (The man who would lead it, and who probably had already met Thurman, was enjoying the last days of his summer vacation before starting his freshman year at Booker T. Washington High School in Atlanta.) Leading the movement would not have been a role congenial to Thurman or his talents, which did not lie in the nitty-gritty of political strategizing, and his natural reserve would have been a poor fit with the public demands on the titular head of a great political movement. In any event, there is no shame in not being Martin Luther King Jr. But what is most striking in Dana's article in the *Pittsburgh Courier* is that, in the summer of 1942, there were many who thought that Thurman was the sort of person around whom a great political movement of American Negroes might coalesce.

II

When Thurman returned from India in the spring of 1936, he remained much in the grip of his experiences in Asia, and in trying to explain them to others, he sought to understand them better himself. The lessons he offered were many and varied. His conviction about the inadequacy of existing political, social, and religious institutions was reinforced, as was his understanding and sympathy for radical nonviolence, for which he had a deeper insight into its possibilities and pitfalls. The similarities and differences between India and America fascinated him. Thurman returned to America with a passion and mission to redress injustice. His politics had never before been, or subsequently would be, as militant or as featured in his religious discourse as in the decade after his return from India. The impact of the Great Depression and the looming cataclysm of World War II contributed to Thurman's sense of urgency. But India, and what Thurman had learned there, was never far from his mind.

One of the lessons Thurman learned was a sense of the worldwide nature of the oppression of people of color and the connections between racism at home and imperialism overseas. This was not a new idea, and it was one that black intellectuals of the 1930s were beginning to explore in depth—his good friend Ralph Bunche in *A World View of Race* (1936) had just written eloquently on this very topic.[3] Thurman's opposition to imperialism was of long standing. He wrote in 1925 of "certain governments that have raped the continent [Africa] and its people through so many bloody years."[4] But Thurman now understood this viscerally. He wrote Max Yergan in early 1937 in astonishing words for a man born in the Deep South at the height of the Jim Crow era: "The only thing I can say in passing is that I did not know what it was to wrestle with hate until my experience in that country [India]. I may add that I am not thinking of anything that was directed at me as a person but the complete futility that is present in the mind when one sees what it is that Imperialism truly involves."[5] Thurman's growing friendship with Max Yergan was indicative of his radical turn of mind in 1937. Yergan, a black American YMCA field secretary, whom Thurman had known and known about for years, had achieved fame in the years following World War I by organizing and inspiring blacks in South Africa. In 1936 he left both the Y movement and official Christianity, arguing that religion was of little utility in organizing for radical social change, too eager to seek consensus with those in power. Writing to a friend in March of that year, Thurman allowed that Yergan was "less sentimental about the functional significance of Christianity" than he had previously been, but nonetheless, in Thurman's opinion, "what he has to say is of inestimable worth to all of us committed to the far-reaching ends of the Kingdom of God." As Thurman knew well, Max Yergan's radically unsentimental view of American Christianity and its overseas missionary work had taken him to the borders of Communism.[6]

Thurman did not travel the same path, but in the 1930s and 1940s he was definitely a person of the left. His main political allegiances during the 1930s can probably best be described as nondogmatic, non-Marxist socialism. Socialist Party leader Eugene V. Debs had been a hero since Thurman's earliest days.[7] Whether or not Thurman was a member in the 1930s—his reticence on this makes definitive statements impossible—a number of his friends and associates, such as Patrick Malin, Francis Henson, Ralph Harlow, and Reinhold Niebuhr, were formally or informally associated with the Socialist Party.[8] Thurman was never a Communist, or even particularly close to the party, but like nearly all black intellectuals in the 1930s, he was intrigued by Communism and respected the forthrightness of the party's condemnation of racial inequality. However, the Communist Party was far too authoritarian and dogmatic (to say nothing of being too dismissive of pacifism and religion) to be of more than passing interest to Thurman, and he would keep himself (and later, the Fellowship Church) at a respectful distance from the party.[9] But whatever its roots and its precise ideological complexion, there is no denying the radicalness of his critique of capitalism and imperialism in the late 1930s.

Thurman's social thought during this period is best observed in his lecture series The Significance of Jesus, delivered in Ontario in the

summer of 1937. This is the most extended and probably the most important of all of his writings during the 1930s, examining from a number of different aspects the life of Jesus and its social consequences,
from his birth to his crucifixion. This writing also shows most clearly
the influence of Reinhold Niebuhr—always "Reinie" to Thurman—a
friend for many years.[10] If Thurman never accepted Niebuhr's critique
of pacifism or his forays into what he called (somewhat misleadingly)
neo-orthodoxy, he shared Niebuhr's radical critique of the Social
Gospel offered in his thunderclap of a magnum opus, *Moral Man
and Immoral Society* (1932). Thurman knew it well, and he knew that
Niebuhr thought the standard Social Gospel nowhere more platitu-
dinous than on matters of racial oppression. (Thurman had written
in a 1935 talk, "Can We Be Christians Today?" "The Kingdom of God
will never come by a moral appeal to people who must always live in
an immoral society.")[11]

In 1932, with Thurman providing the benediction, Niebuhr had
delivered the commencement address to graduates of Morehouse
and Spelman colleges, telling them of the limitation of the Social
Gospel. Instead of Christian idealism, "dreaming that all men are
brothers," what was needed was "political realism [and] social intelli-
gence." "Power makes selfishness," and as a result he doubted whether
"most white people will ever be unselfish." Because social power is
shared and not individual, appeals to the conscience may be "nice and
sweet" but inefficacious, since the "devils of hatred, greed and racial
outrages arise from collective man." The response must be appropriate in kind.[12] Perhaps Thurman was thinking of Niebuhr's address
when in the second of his Significance of Jesus lectures he argued
that there was a fundamental difference between changing individual
morality and changing the moral fabric of society as a whole. Offering an interpretation of the third temptation of Jesus, Thurman has
Satan tell Jesus, God may have created humankind, but "I made the
relationships between men." Thurman argued Satan's truth exposes
the fallacy of "orthodox religion" that all that is needed to bring about
the "Kingdom of God" is to save souls. When people find themselves
"caught in a framework of relationships evil in design, . . . their very

good deeds themselves developed into instrumentalities for evil," "it is not enough to save the souls of men: the relationships that exist between men must be saved also."[13]

To change "the relationships between men," to transform the skein of enmeshed obligations and debts that tie individuals to one another, was an essentially religious task, in part because it mired one in the sordid specificities of one's own existence, unable to glimpse anything higher. Two years later, in his lecture series Mysticism and Social Change, using Rufus Jones's distinction between affirmation and negation mystics, Thurman would argue that the affirmation mystic is not interested in social action because of "any particular political or economic theory" or "from the point of view of humanitarianism or humanism," as important as they are; rather, it is because "he knows society as he knows it ensnares the human spirit in a maze of particulars so that the One cannot be sensed nor the good realized."[14]

To accomplish this task, Thurman argued in the third of his Significance of Jesus lectures that it would be necessary to abolish private property. All possessions were species of self-love, "a kind of activity having as its purpose the maintenance and furtherance of one's own life," and from this "fundamental passion that urges the individual to guarantee and to perpetuate himself, his family, his group or class" come all the evils of society, the force behind "all imperialism, back of all exploitation." Everything else only functions as means to this end. When the factory owner loves his factory as himself, he would "feel quite justified in importing gunmen or thugs to kill defenseless strikers in a factory." This is how contemporary America worked: "Property becomes sacred only when it has already become private, and when property becomes sacred, personality becomes secular."[15]

Most Christians, Thurman argued, know this, but they are afraid of its implications. It requires the believer to place "one's property at the mercy of the welfare of those who have no property rights," and it demands, should the need arise, a "willingness to renounce all personal claims to possession." This is a hard road to follow, and most deceive themselves into thinking that by restraining their appetites, by giving alms and supporting charities, they are fulfilling this obligation. But this is self-deception. Those who take their obligations in this regard seriously will come to the conclusion that they must put themselves "squarely against the possession of all personal property and to recognize it as a thing making for evil in the world and to work in all ways for legislation and for public opinion that would make private property impossible."[16]

Thurman's utopia is more Gandhian than Marxist. He suggested that property be allotted on the simple Gandhian maxim that "he who has more than he needs is a thief." For Thurman, private property implicates the holder in networks of hidden frameworks of dominance and complicates and obfuscates people's lives. And when the propertied try to maximize their wealth and then use the state to protect it, the result, he would argue elsewhere, is fascism, which in its American variant was built on the two pillars of racism and opposition to unions.[17] Thurman's conception of a world freed of private property in The Significance of Jesus is Niebuhrian in its anticapitalism and its disdain of half measures and partial solutions, and at the same time is a powerfully Gandhian vision of people giving away their property to regain their souls and to find the world.

But if there was to be a social revolution, for Thurman it had to be a democratic revolution, one realized through the principles of American democracy, or what he thought the principles of democracy should actually be. His social radicalism was joined to a fierce, essentially Jefferson belief—Thurman greatly admired Jefferson—in realizing the equality of all people through maximizing democratic values. One of the lectures Thurman gave fairly frequently after his return from Asia (primarily at black colleges, perhaps because he wanted to speak more freely about race) was "What We May Learn from India," which as the title indicates was a report of impressions and reflections from his recent trip. He opened by discussing the limitations of Christianity in India, quoting Gandhi to the effect that "the greatest enemy that the religion of Jesus has in India is Christianity." He then went on to relate various instances of color prejudice he encountered in India, primarily directed not against him but by the British toward native Indians. He was struck again and again by the impotency of Christianity to remedy this or offer any sort of critique that would not seem hopelessly hypocritical. (He related, as he often did in these years, the story of his encounter with the lawyer in Ceylon.) "Christianity is powerless to make any inroads on the question of color prejudice in India," he concluded, "because of the way it has made peace with race and color prejudice in the West."[18]

However, when it came to the possibility of positive social change, and he compared the prospects of overcoming imperialism in India against those of challenging racism in the United States, on the whole Thurman thought the prospects were somewhat brighter at home. Indians, living in a country controlled by a "white conqueror" in a "land which he has stolen" had "no political ideal in an imperialistic regime on which he may bring the Britisher or European to the bar of moral justice." In the United States, on the other hand, there was an avowed if generally not honored commitment to "practices that are democratic in their genius and before which undemocratic practices can be condemned as antithetical and immoral." Unlike India, where the conqueror and the conquered worshiped different gods, in America, almost all are committed, in theory at least, "to the same Christian ideal of brotherliness" that condemns acts that fail to meet this standard as "sinful and unchristian." Blacks in America had avenues, means of redress, simply not available to Hindus and Muslims in India.

Thurman further argued that if British imperialists had been quite successful in prying apart Indians by religion, language, caste, and political status, racism in America generally had the opposite effect; the history of race relations since emancipation and the rigorous application of the "one drop rule" had the effect of minimizing internal differences among people of African descent. "From the point of view of white supremacy and control in America," argued Thurman, this was "the master blunder in strategy." This was also one of the rare occasions on which the very dark-skinned Thurman discussed the vexed question of color preference within African American life, pointing to the Anglo-Indians, people of mixed British and Indian ancestry. They were widely hired in the Raj as low-level functionaries in the colonial service, and generally identified with their superiors. Thurman offered them up as an example of what happened when the ruling race was successful in creating a mulatto caste, and he warned against certain unnamed "Negro intellectuals" who seemed bent upon creating a similar caste in the United States. In any event, Thurman's message to his American audience was clear. The task of overcoming racial subordination in India and America was in many ways very similar and called for similar tactics. But because of a common religion and a common political culture, black Americans perhaps had certain advantages, or at least alternative routes to equality, that Indians lacked. The challenge, he concluded, was having the courage and cleverness to utilize them.[19]

Thurman made the same point in a different way in a lecture that concentrated on the United States and was one of his very few forays into extended sociological commentary. In 1940 he spoke to a Chicago meeting of the National Conference of Christians and Jews on "The Negro and the City." After accounting for all the hardships blacks in Chicago had faced and were still confronting in the wake of the Great Migration, he came to the conclusion that "the Negro in the northern city is not a citizen and his position is a perpetual threat and constant disgrace to democracy." (That the Negro in the South was not a citizen was a truth that Thurman did not think worth debating.) Whatever the legal realities and technicalities, he argued, there really is no such thing as second-class citizenship.[20]

For Thurman, the hallmark of real citizenship was less defined by rights than the ability to assume duties and obligations. "Responsibility, a free initiative, the sense of the future, these are the things that make for civic character, that make real citizens. These are denied the Negro." Without the responsibilities of real citizenship (and the concomitant lack of control over one's own life and destiny), it is impossible to be fully mature. And without the duties of citizenship being universally available, it was impossible for anyone, either those with it or those without it, to claim they lived in a true democracy. Thurman went on to address how wartime needs can disturb the status quo. During World War I promises were made to blacks to gain their assent to the war—"persona was conferred upon him by the dominant social group—he was made to feel that he counted—that the future of American democracy was dependent upon him." It was a lie, of course, as black soldiers and others found out after the war ended when there was a decided effort by many whites to force blacks to relinquish whatever relatively nugatory gains had been earned. The result was the Red Summer of 1919, and Thurman, in one of very few instances in which he spoke approvingly of violent protest, described the rioting as "a sign of life, of an awakening citizenship." He gave the analogy of a person with a foot or limb long numb that suddenly throbs back into life with intense pain, its owner glad to have feeling restored, however much it might hurt.[21]

For Thurman, one of the ironies of American democracy was that while underprivileged minorities can and must fight for their rights, they will fully achieve them while forced to live their lives within the ambit of segregated institutions, and they can only leave segregated institutions with the approval of the dominant majority. "An individual has persona or personhood conferred upon him by a social group that has definite statuses to which he belongs." All the organizations that conferred status on blacks were themselves segregated and even the best of them (like Howard University) carried with them a badge of inferiority. One way forward was to create interracial institutions. Like many black intellectuals in the 1930s and 1940s, Thurman singled out the role of minorities in some of the CIO unions as a model: to join a union as a full and equal member was to immediately attain a new civic status.[22] But true equality would not be achieved "until churches, schools, governing boards of all kinds, political, secular, and religious, guarantee the Negroes' [sic] right as a citizen to belong and participate in the common life." Negroes must be given "responsibility and the incentive to exercise a free initiative," he concluded, "if life ultimately is to be sane and secure for us all."

Thurman's 1940 talk looked back to the Great War as an even greater one was looming. Thurman felt, once again, that if war came to America it would only heighten the ambiguous status of blacks within American democracy. He would write in 1943 that "the diseases in the body politic become much more acute in the minds of less privileged persons such as Negroes. As these diseases are exposed to the searching diagnosis of the meaning of democracy, the gulf between the dream as uttered and the idea as practiced is wide, abysmal, and deep."[23]

The previous year he told an audience at the North Carolina College for Negroes in Durham (now North Carolina Central University), in a talk entitled "Cultural and Spiritual Responsibilities of a Minority Population," that "there is a vast difference [between] democracy and the American way of life." He continued on, saying that racial minorities have "a unique opportunity to maintain the sensitiveness essential to the democratic way of living." Racial minorities are "the first people to be sensitive to the loss of democratic principles of life. We must constantly be calling to these ideas." For in the end racial minorities "shall be largely responsible for the soul of America. We are called at this moment of crisis in our nation's history."[24]

III

If Thurman was one of the most prominent African American exponents of nonviolence as a means for social change in the years before, during, and after World War II, there is an essential paradox about his role, one touched on by Peter Dana in his article on Thurman in the *Pittsburgh Courier* in 1942; namely, that he "is not sufficiently known to the general public."[25] The lack of knowledge about Thurman has continued. He remains relatively obscure to the general public and even the educated public. The reasons for this are manifold. He did not become the leader of a great political movement. If Thurman's work is known, it is among students of the black church or liberal Christianity and it is for his later work, the books that he began to publish in the late 1940s. One important reason why Thurman's distinctive thinking in the 1930s and early 1940s has never been well known is that it was not easily accessible in print. Most who knew of Thurman did not read him; they heard him or studied with him or consulted with him. Thurman's way of getting out his message was primarily oral.

During the late 1930s and early 1940s Thurman published very little, and much of that obscurely. "The Significance of Jesus" appeared only in a small Canadian mimeograph edition, while the circulation of "Mysticism and Social Change" was limited to the bulletin of a Midwestern theological seminary. Neither was reprinted in Thurman's lifetime. Until he moved to San Francisco in 1944 to be co-pastor of the Fellowship Church, he had published no books, although six followed in the next nine years. He claimed in 1959, "Until I came to San Francisco I had little interest in writing."[26] This is something of an exaggeration—he labored hard to publish "The Significance of Jesus" in the late 1930s with a major publisher, to no avail.[27] A review of his first book, *The Greatest of These*, a collection of prose poems published in late 1944, opened, "Howard Thurman is one of those uniquely gifted spirits of our time about whom we say: 'Why doesn't he publish more?' We almost never see anything from his hand." (The reviewer, like many, had his favorite Thurman moment, an "unforgettable" conference some years before when Thurman offered a hilltop meditation addressing the setting sun.)[28]

His published books, perhaps somewhat tempered by Cold War realities, do not adequately capture the radicalness of his positions in the late 1930s and 1940s. To hear Thurman from this earlier period, we must try to do just that—listen. And we will find that the way he said it was as impressive to his audience as what he had to say, and both the message and the medium contributed equally to the power of what he was trying to convey.

The 1930s and 1940s were perhaps the last time in American history when public speaking and oratory were still forms of mass communication. Certainly it is impossible to imagine anyone today becoming well known through speaking engagements alone without significant exposure in print or electronic media, as did Thurman. Although by the 1930s the days of the lyceums and the Chautauqua circuit were rapidly fading in the era of electronic broadcasting, lecturing was still one of the best ways of disseminating a message. This was especially true for the religious left, an audience with an almost inexhaustible appetite for listening to speakers. Joseph Kip Kosek, historian of the Fellowship of Reconciliation (FOR), has written of the penchant of its leaders for speech making and how for many it "became not only the antidote to violence, but also a substitute for armed combat, a benign way of exercising power in the world."[29] This was true for Thurman as well, and unlike the white leaders of FOR, he had other rather obvious agendas as well, especially when, as was so often the case, he spoke before predominantly white audiences.

Howard Thurman had a lot to say, and he loved to say it, but there was an element of compulsiveness to his speaking tours and engagements that hints at other things as well, psychological urges that he perhaps only imperfectly understood. He had been greatly in demand as a speaker from his earliest days in seminary, and this would only expand as his career unfolded. It is clear that Thurman gained a great satisfaction from his speaking engagements, and even seemed to like (generally) the constant travel, which after an early disastrous attempt at learning to drive was limited almost entirely to trains.[30] To read Thurman's correspondence is to reenter the vanished world of Pullman coaches and overnight berths, of mastering the complexities of oversized train schedules as well as trying to cope with the byzantine inconsistencies and capriciousness of Jim Crow. Train travel, at least, gave him a chance to rest, to withdraw into himself with the latest mystery novel and a favorite book of poetry in hand, between engagements.[31] (In 1944 he would list "reading poetry" along with "making noise on my clarinet" as his only hobbies.)[32] Thurman found public speaking utterly draining and, at the same time, something he couldn't live without.

When he returned from Asia in the spring of 1936, after his exhausting four months of speaking in India, he immediately jumped into a fevered round of new speaking engagements, accepting as many dates as time, other obligations, and his physical constitution permitted, in part to make up for the lost income from his unpaid sabbatical in 1935–36. (One of those obligations was teaching at Howard, which he would resume in the fall with a new title, dean of chapel, only the third university chaplain, and the first at a black college, to be so honored.)[33] He would write in May 1937 that he had "been on the go day and night since my return from India" and had traveled at least fifteen thousand miles, accepting engagements on both coasts and many places between.[34] All this travel tottered Thurman's somewhat fragile psychological state; almost two years of nonstop motion precipitated a mild nervous breakdown, and his physician ordered a complete rest.

It is impossible to give a complete enumeration of Thurman's speaking engagements between his return from India and his going to the Fellowship Church in 1944, but it was extremely extensive, with many dozens of engagements a year, often with several in a single day in different cities. (This is where his knowledge of train schedules was essential.) There were regular annual stops: the black YMCA and YWCA conference at Kings Mountain, North Carolina; the Holy Week services at the St. Antoine's YMCA in Detroit (where by 1935 there already was a Howard Thurman fan club); Student Christian Conferences at Asilomar in Northern California; and a series of regular stops at colleges, churches, and preparatory schools where close friends, black and white, headed the chapel. To these he added as many of the numerous requests for his time and presence as he could arrange.[35] For G. James Fleming, who wrote a laudatory article about Thurman in the NAACP's magazine the *Crisis* in August 1939, "Preacher at Large to Universities," his countless speaking engagements at colleges, especially at white colleges, where he was an "interracial minister plenipotentiary," was perhaps the most distinctive aspect of his ministry.[36] For Fleming, Thurman's position as dean of chapel at Howard was "only a beginning, his campus really takes in all parts of the US and Canada and sometimes more distant lands. The flock starts with his own people but includes men and women of all races and colors and nationalities." The article tells of Thurman's appearances at more than one hundred different white colleges, often returning for many engagements. Noting it was already a cliché, Fleming claimed that "in most of the engagements filled by Howard Thurman, he is 'the only Negro' or 'the First Negro' (with apologies for these overused terms). In every case he wins friends for the Negro race and for the cause of greater social justice for all mankind and for a 'broader, vitalizing democracy' in America." For Fleming, Thurman was not only a preacher but also "a philosopher, mystic, interpreter, student, preacher, and very human person all in one. And if he were not very human and understanding, if he could not draw very near to young college people, all other things would count for very little."[37]

The "first Negro" cliché aside, like few black lecturers before him, Thurman was as welcome and as comfortable speaking to white audiences as black audiences. Probably no black minister of his time was as comfortable or spoke as extensively and frequently before white audiences, as he crossed and recrossed the racial divide on an almost weekly basis. In this he was a pioneer and a very conscious model for later black ministers, such as Martin Luther King Jr., who similarly tried to cultivate both a white and a black audience.[38] In a typical comment, Marshall Talley, a leader in the National Baptist Convention, wrote Thurman describing a 1941 talk where "numbers of white people were almost thrown into hysterics as they commented with me upon your marvelous delivery and the profound philosophy of your utterances."[39]

But if blacks were proud of Thurman's facility in speaking to whites, it also made them somewhat uneasy. Fleming went on to assure his readers that Thurman was "every inch a Negro," and that whatever he speaks about, "sooner or later, those who come into contact with him try to find his solution for the problem of races [sic], want to know what is his prescription for interracial amity, and a hundred other things." For Fleming, if Thurman was deep and philosophical, he didn't let his listeners off with airy abstractions or empty words of racial harmony. While Thurman "dwells on the mountain top—or has his eye toward the mountain top where men like Kagawa, Tagore, Gandhi, and John Dewey dwell—he does not fight windmills or beat the air. He can call a spade a spade; he does not try to explain away the wrongs about him with nice nothings, although he is never hateful, he often 'takes up the cudgels for his race and can be militant and caustic.'"[40]

Hurdling racial barriers as deftly as did Thurman requires keenness and sure-footedness in order to avoid pandering, telling racially specific audiences what they want to hear and not telling them what they don't want to hear. Thurman did not have two different styles for white and black audiences; there is no indication that he would sometimes adopt a more "down home" style for black audiences and a more elevated tone for whites (something that Martin Luther King Jr. would be criticized for). The comments about his style before all groups are remarkably similar—elevated, dense, allusive, difficult to grasp, and yet somehow immensely attractive. The *Atlanta Daily World* in 1932 reported a typical appearance of Thurman before a black audience: "Rev. Howard Thurman rose to a vast pinnacle last Monday noon. With the characteristic mysticism and philosophy that pervades his innumerable addresses and public contributions whenever he appears on a public program, Reverend Mr. Thurman held his audience spellbound and awed."[41] James Farmer has a succinct description of Thurman's preaching at Howard in the late 1930s: "When Thurman occupied the university pulpit, Rankin Memorial Chapel was packed. Though few but theologians and philosophers comprehended what he was saying, everyone else thought if only they *had* understood it would have been wonderful, so mesmerizing was his resonant voice and so captivating was the artistry of his delivery. Those who did grasp the meaning of his sermons were even more ecstatic."[42]

And yet, Thurman's appearances before white and black audiences were not identical. Before blacks he often identified with the audience in a way that would have been impossible before whites, as in his 1938 lecture at the black college Tennessee A&I when he offered the observation that "I have never in my life seen an educated Negro who was not discouraged unless I was looking at someone this morning."[43] At Morehouse College in 1936 he praised Gandhi's belief that "India ought to be solely Indian and completely self-contained" and his efforts to remove the stigma from the untouchables, arguing that American blacks should heed the same lesson. "We rise or we fall by our attachment for or our detachment from the masses of the Negroes," he said in appealing to the college-educated group to show its solidarity with the underprivileged masses. Thurman concluded that "this same sense of racial solidarity, a confidence in life and a sense of humor that sees through circumstances, these three values have enabled the Negro to survive in an environment in which virtually every assumption is against survival."[44]

He would never speak this way before a white audience, and generally avoided speaking directly on race relations before whites. This was in part because he was convinced of its futility, like a tiresome scolding that one had already heard and ignored once too often. But Thurman also felt there was an element of condescension in these invitations, as if the only subject he and other very accomplished black intellectuals were fit to speak about was the race question, while the rest of the store of human knowledge was entirely reserved for whites. His replies to invitations to speak on race could be curt, as was this response to a request to speak at Haverford College in 1934 (the curtness perhaps amplified because he knew from experience that Haverford did not admit blacks): "I am not a sociologist and am not qualified to make a scientific presentation of all that is involved. I know what I think and what I feel and why I think it. To express this is to waste my time and other people's time. Very few individuals change their racial attitudes on the basis of an address however powerful it may be."[45] When praised by a black official of the Urban League for his measured appearance before a predominantly white audience, for not going into the "rantings and excoriations" on the race question that were typical on such occasion, Thurman was very pleased. He responded that it had been "a long time since I have received a letter with which I was in more complete accord." He went on to say that he did not "accept invitations to discuss the race question; not because I do not think that the race question needs to be discussed, but I am determined to make my contribution along the lines of my preparation and my chosen field of activity. I cannot do this if I become merely a propagandist or a sociologist."[46] Thurman's goal in speaking before whites was to assert his full equality with the audience. As he would write elsewhere, "If a man can feel sorry for you, he can very easily absolve himself from dealing with you as an equal."[47] The last thing he wanted from white audiences was sympathy or pity.

Yet, he couldn't avoid race entirely, and didn't really want to either, and he certainly didn't want to imply to white audiences that there was nothing more to say or think about on this subject. But, just as he had in India, he communicated his message through indirection. As he noted to a correspondent in 1940, when speaking before a white audience his appearance on a white campus was "about race" before he opened his mouth, because "I am definitely Negroid in type any address that I give to a predominantly white audience has more bearing on race relations than my words."[48] That is, in some ways it was a wasted opportunity to speak only about what the audience thought he should speak about. If he handled the speech properly, a white audience would have more questions about the status of blacks in American society than if he were to give a sociological lecture on that topic. Thurman's dark brown skin was his starting point and not his destination. As he wrote in 1937, in his sermons his "point of interest is religion interpreted against the background of my own life and the life of my group in America. I am very much interested in some of the problems that arise in the experience of people who attempt to be Christian in a society that is essentially un-Christian."[49] In the end, to focus on race was to limit his subject to one instance of the universal human tendency to have dominant and subordinate races; to focus on race was to treat it as a problem that could be solved in isolation from a host of other social ills (such as militarism or the rights of labor) that were impeding American democracy. Hobby horses were always dangerous, as he would preach in 1938: "This is always the problem of reformation: To put all of one's emphasis upon one particular thing and when that thing is achieved and the Kingdom of God has not come, then the reformer sits in the twilight of his idols."[50] And so Thurman would speak about race before white audiences, but on his own terms, and in his own way.

Probably the main reason Thurman was reluctant to speak about race was a more general reluctance to be didactic or to impart instruction. The goal was to inspire, to let his hearers find their own meanings and causes in his words, to find their own life stories in his anecdotes about his own experience. Everyone who has written on the subject has noted the unique and distinctive spell that Thurman was able to create in his preaching. It drew on several homiletic traditions, yet beholden to none. If he was raised and formed in the black church, his preaching had little in common with the rhythmic cadence often seen as characteristic of the black preacher. From childhood he was at-tracted to the speaking style of educated black preachers, such as Mor-decai Wyatt Johnson. (He had also listened intently to distinguished white preachers. In his autobiography he mentions that during the summer of 1922 while in New York City, he would go every Sunday to the Fifth Avenue Presbyterian Church to hear Hugh Black, a famous Scottish preacher and professor at Union Theological Seminary.)[51] As he would write in 1940, "The basic requirements for effective speak-ing are two. First, a consciousness of having something to say, and second, the ability to use the English language clearly, intelligently, and correctly."[52] But Thurman neither engaged in stem-winding ora-tory nor was coolly analytical, and he offered neither pomposity nor a faux cozy informality. If there is one quality Thurman sought in his preaching, it is perhaps best characterized as poetic. He wrote a cor-respondent in 1940, "I quote poetry in my addresses often because a good poem summarizes very often effectively in short compass what it would take many prosaic utterances to do."[53] Whether quoting poetry or not, Thurman eschewed the prosaic.

It was the ability to achieve a sense of intimacy even before large audiences, the sense that he was speaking to each person directly, that regularly awed his hearers. The 1939 article in the *Crisis* noted that "there are many people who will cancel everything to go hear Howard Thurman speak; his language is beautiful, his ideals and points of view intriguing. Most of all, people are overwhelmed by his silences, and marvel at how eloquent he can be without ever shouting or 'orat-ing,' and his ability to get to rock-bottom issues."[54] Music, poetry, and silence are the words that come up again and again in describing Thurman's preaching style. James Earl Massey has made the inspired suggestion that Thurman's preaching reminded him of the late music of Beethoven with its enigmatic themes, silences, and unexpected syn-copations and modulations, giving the listener the feeling that some-how time had been suspended, that Thurman was "almost forcing one to become introspective."[55]

Part of the power of Thurman's sermonic style in the late 1930s was the listener's sense of sharing in Thurman's struggle to expound and express his inner thoughts and religious life, the artlessness of personal confession related with consummate artfulness. For Thurman, the core of religion was the personal experience of the divine and the difficulty and the essential importance of sharing this experience with others. This is well captured by Evilio Grillo, a high school student of Cuban background befriended by the Thurmans in the late 1930s, who describes Thurman preaching in Rankin Chapel, and it is worth reprinting at length:

> He spoke with a transfixing eloquence. He had an awe-inspiring command of the English language. He was understood by most people, for his sermons expressed feeling eloquently, were lucid, and above all, were poetic. He managed always to involve his audiences as he wove, with his expressive face, piercing eyes, and gracefully moving arms and body, a passage in a sermon that had vital meaning for him. He would struggle almost painfully as he introduced a theme, insisting that his auditors struggle with him for understanding. Once assured that the congregation was fully his, he poured forth with a waterfall of language, beautiful, ethereal, profoundly moving.
>
> He was a large, very dark man, a powerful, inviting presence. He moved his whole body with a light arresting grace, that complemented fully the beauty of his language and the music of his speech. His deep, melodic voice surrounded and enveloped the congregation, held by the sheer power of his presentation. While he projected himself as the deeply spiritual man that he was, his every sermon was also an exercise in virtuoso theater.[56]

Thurman used his gift for projecting his intimacy in his teaching. Eschewing textbooks and routines, he would, describing his teaching at Morehouse and Spelman in the late 1920s and early 1930s, take a basic concept "such as the relation between the universal and the particular, or the timeless and the temporal," and he would challenge one student to work through its definitions and implications, sometimes spending an entire class period on one student. James Farmer has a memorable portrait of the spiritual intensity Thurman brought to his teaching at Howard in the late 1930s. "When this extraordinary man walked into a social ethics class, a silence born of awe reigned. It always seemed as if we had dragged him away from private meditation." Having gained the rapt attention of his class, he then offered an observation with no right or wrong answers and proceeded Socratically, letting the students speak, saying little himself, because as Farmer writes, "it was Thurman's belief that answers must come from within, from the bit of God in each of us."[57]

Even teaching a small seminar class might have been too crowded. Thurman's ideal audience was one (or two), in which the power and intimacy of intense dialogue could be developed to its fullest. All other forms of personal interaction and teaching experiences were, at their best, imitations. From this, Thurman learned how to speak in a way that to his listeners, regardless of the size of the crowd, seemed like he was speaking to them personally, addressing their own concerns and articulating their private spiritual dilemmas. From his undergraduate days and years in seminary, Thurman attracted many who wished to share with him their confidences, their own stories, their secrets. Mentorship is even more ephemeral than sermonic performance; there is generally no public record at all, and its participants discreetly silent. An article from 1941 describes Thurman the spiritual counselor in action, probably with white college students:

> June—a summer conference of the Student Christian Movement—under a tree besides the lake or on the front steps of a tent or cabin. They have been there for two hours already and others who have appointments have been sensitive enough to let them alone, as though some inner voice spoke. In the end, the two (or three, four, or more) get up and slowly walk away and those who know feel the hand of God has touched another student's life through the voice and sensitive spirit of Howard Thurman.[58]

The same article reported that Thurman was working on a book— alas, never to be published, or never, as far as we can tell, to get beyond his personal to-do list—that would have drawn "from his years of work with thousands of students."[59] Thurman's ability to connect to individuals in the most private aspects of their lives was a crucial aspect of his ministry. His message, whatever else he happened to be speaking about, was always the need to root our shared and social interactions in our own interiority, and how our public actions, if they are to be authentic, must be based on our deepest, most private, and most hidden and difficult-to-examine parts. The only things worth saying start in silence.

IV

Let us then listen to Thurman preach in the late 1930s by examining two sermons he gave, a few days apart, to predominantly white audiences at the end of 1937 and beginning of 1938. Even if he was not mentioned by name, the message and example of Gandhi hovered over both talks. On December 28, 1937, Thurman spoke on the assigned topic of "The Sources of Power for Christian Action" before a Methodist Student Conference in St. Louis. He left after his address to travel to Miami University in Oxford, Ohio, where he spoke to the annual conference of the National Assemblies of Student Christian Associations. At both conferences he was the only black speaker. The two conferences overlapped, and Thurman found himself in a quandary, though a compromise was eventually worked out so that he split his time between the two. Thurman was expressly asked to speak before the Methodist convention because of the complexity of their racial politics, amid fears that the impending reunion of Northern and Southern Methodists would be at the expense of black Methodists, which is indeed what came to pass. Those who invited Thurman to speak thought it important for the "Negro leadership of this particular student conference [to] be of the very best caliber that our country affords" and that "the Negro speakers not be limited, as so often was the case, to speak on race relations." It was the sort of invitation Thurman couldn't refuse.[60]

But the status of blacks at the Methodist conference was even more complicated than the organizers had allowed. They had made an agreement with the conference hotel, in still rigidly segregated St. Louis, that though blacks could participate in the deliberations, they would not be allowed to eat or lodge at the hotel. Thurman was unaware of this when he disembarked from the train and was met by a delegation from the conference who escorted him to the hotel, where he had his breakfast. When they returned to the dining room for lunch after Thurman gave his morning address, the delegation was told by the manager that while they had allowed Thurman to have breakfast, they couldn't allow him to have lunch as well. For Thurman there was nothing more unjust about Jim Crow than its capriciousness, its myriad local variations, and how it made every black subject to the whim of its enforcers. The hotel manager offered to feed him lunch in the room of one of the white guests. Thurman told his hosts that this was unacceptable, and left the hotel, angry and frustrated.

But Thurman still had an obligation to give his evening address and returned to the hotel in the late afternoon, after spending several hours wandering the streets of St. Louis, enraged, silently nursing his grievances. When the time came for Thurman to deliver his talk, he didn't deliver a tirade or an impassioned attack on the evils of Jim Crow. But he didn't ignore what had happened earlier in the day either. He spoke on his assigned topic, "The Sources of Power of Christian Action." The only deviation from the scheduled talk occurred at the beginning when he calmly told the audience what had happened earlier in the day and how their church had made all those present, wittingly or unwittingly, complicit in the actions of the hotel management. "The time will come," Thurman said, "when you are in the same position as the men who made this commitment to your behalf. When that time comes I want you to remember this experience."[61]

He then turned to his prepared comments. His argument was similar to the one he offered in the last part of the Significance of Jesus series and to the argument he would make a few days later in Oxford, Ohio. He started, as he did so often in the late 1930s, with the dilemmas of a person trying to live a Christian life in a society that perverted all Christian ideals:

The Christian sees that society is organized on other than principles of kinship and brotherhood. He sees that the strong do live by bleeding the weak. He sees that fear and dishonesty run the entire frantic gamut of our culture and our daily living. He sees institutions dedicated to high and holy ends, finding themselves as literal instruments of violence and exploitation in the world. He sees before his very eyes the degradation of ideals, of reverence and respect for life and personality. He sees himself functioning in a state that has given itself over to cheap political conniving and skullduggery. He sees his own government arming for protection against enemies, visible and invisible, and a large share of his own funds going to support engines of war against which, as a Christian, he is dedicated to struggle.[62]

Any Christian action worthy of the name had to begin with personal piety for which there could be no substitute or simulacrum, Thurman told his audience. What this means is that "as a Christian I must see to it that what I condemn in society, I do not permit to grow and flower in me." But this was just the beginning, in part because it was ultimately impossible to live a fully moral life in the midst of evil, and that "even if my heart is pure, my motives are above reproach and, as far as my personal action is concerned, it is unequivocal and positive—this is not enough." It is easy to be moral about things that are distant, that do not affect the "areas of their security." People cannot live in a society of which they disapprove without "some measure of compromise." But the moral person reduces the area of their personal compromise, while the immoral person lets it increase. In the end, Thurman said, speaking for everyman and everywoman, "I share the guilt of my age, of my society, of my race." One cannot lead a moral life while surrounded by immorality without trying to change it, and therefore it was necessary to "exhaust all possible means that do no conflict with my ends for bringing about the kind of society in which it is possible for men in large groups, without external limitations, to experience the good life."[63]

But how to do this? Thurman's insight into the ineffectuality of individual moral goodness in an evil society formed the backdrop for the rest of the discussion in "The Sources of Power of Christian Action," and the solutions he offered were firmly grounded in non-violence. The first option for Christian action that Thurman discussed is what he called "moral suasion," an attempt "to awaken individuals to some kind of definite consciousness as to what is the meaning of their action." (Or, as he defined it a few days later in Oxford, Ohio, moral suasion is an effort "to make articulate in my fellow man a sense of the significance of his own actions" and thereby try "to woo him into a sense of sinfulness and into a sense of sonship.")[64] By moral suasion, Thurman meant the usual ethical appeal of the Social Gospel and any other approach that basically relied on the goodwill of those in power. Thurman probably had in mind the efforts of traditional black organizations, such as the NAACP and the National Urban League, to advance the cause of black equality through lobbying, legal redress, and other more or less polite methods of advocacy.

The problem with moral suasion was that it depends on the benevolence of those one is trying to persuade, and the general high level of "moral atrophy" will often render this inefficacious. Moral suasion, Thurman would argue a few days later, can only work if there are "hooks on which to hang it," and generally the other party "has taken out all the screws" so there is nothing to latch on to, to grasp or grapple with.[65] One cannot always wait for the consciences of those in power to slowly awake from their slumbers. "To wait for moral pressure to work its perfect work may be too late. The oppressed may be annihilated meanwhile." When it comes to moral suasion, one must always, Thurman counseled, be "essentially and intensely realistic," be shrewd, and be prepared for failure.

But if (and when) moral suasion fails, something Thurman called "shock" or the "shock method" must be tried. He told his audience in St. Louis that shock could be accomplished by "organizing a boycott, by organizing non-cooperation, by engineering non-violent strikes." This was necessary because people in power "do not voluntarily, my friends, relinquish their hold on their place without being uprooted," either by something from without or by "volcanic eruption from within." By use of Thurman's shock method, one can try to "tear men free from their alignments to the evil way, to free them so that they may be given an immediate sense of acute insecurity." When this happens, he would say in Ohio, "for one breathless moment or for one breathless week he becomes the brother in experience with the insecure and the weak." Only when people are stripped of their false sense of security, their untroubled complacency about their own goodness and the basic decency of their society, can they begin to respond to the evil around them. Social change had to be snatched from those who hold the levers of power.[66]

Thurman was not afraid to use the language of coercion in describing the shock method. His good friend Reinhold Niebuhr, for one, argued that Gandhianism and other species of radical nonviolence were just alternative forms of coercion, all the more pernicious because they claimed they were something higher, above the sordid world of interests. Some pacifists, uneasy with the implied compulsion in the use of tactics such as boycotts and sit-ins, would have agreed.[67] Thurman struggled with Niebuhr's argument, and in his 1939 lecture series *Mysticism and Social Change*, he worried whether militant nonviolent social action, boycotts, and threats of noncooperation, such that will "shock the oppressor into a state of upheaval and insecurity," were in their own ways implicitly coercive. But simply waiting for moral suasion to work was pointless. If there was implicit intimidation in the use of the shock treatment, then it was of a different order than the "threat, coercion, overt violence" it will be met with from the dominant society. The challenge for those who employed the nonviolence of the shock method was to resist the temptation to respond in kind, because "violence hardens the egocentric will of men and gives to unrestrained self-regarding impulses the widest possible range." In the end, Thurman would argue, like moral suasion, the shock method is a very limited response to evil, with definite boundaries that one cannot go beyond. Evil will ultimately destroy itself because the seeds of its self-destruction are inherent within it, even while "the ultimate end of life is somehow even now being worked out through the long weary stages in the revelation of God in the progress of history." One must have the faith and confidence and insight to know that "working and waiting are two separate activities of the human spirit but he who works for the new day in that act waits for its coming which can be achieved by God and God alone."[68]

This cumulative, patient (what Gandhi might call karmic) approach to history meant that beyond the shock method, there was one other response to evil that every genuine Christian must consider and must keep in reserve, argued Thurman. If one's daily compromises with evil become too much to endure, if one feels society is closing in and contaminating "the center of one's conviction," losing one's moral coherence is not an option. When "I have exhausted all means available to me," he would say in Ohio, "when I have exhausted everything, it becomes necessary for me to register, with all of my passionate endeavor, my complete disapproval of an evil world, by offering my life as the sacrifice supreme because it is logic of all that I have been doing."[69] This, argued Thurman in his Significance of Jesus lecture series, is the true meaning of Jesus's cross. "Without morbidity, without a martyr complex he chose rather to be destroyed than to relinquish his right to be true to his deepest self." Jesus became, Thurman said, "a savior" in his death, not because he died for our sins but because he didn't flinch or turn from his destiny.[70] In St. Louis he said, "As for me, I believe it is better to be killed than to kill, and that the spirit of God will help an individual decide which is the best moment for martyrdom, so that martyrdom will be an act of the profoundest redemptive significance rather than death, merely."

But how does one get or find the power for such a commitment? The ultimate source is God, and "only an infinite resource can meet an infinite need," something that can "absorb all the limitations of one's life, limitations of thought, limitations of action." One can reach God in several ways, most directly (and for most people, most easily) through prayer. Thurman's God was not an external moral arbiter, a promulgator of commandments from on high, but a means to searching self-examination: "I must have a guarantor of my deeds, a guarantor of my values in the clear lucid light in which I can see myself as I am, stripped bare of all pretenses, of all subterfuge, all artificiality. And once I have seen it, I know what it is I seek and I know what it is that society needs." "A man's life becomes meaningful," he said in St. Louis, "and whole to the extent that he is willing to stake everything on a conviction that what he does when he is most himself has the approval and the imprimatur of the Highest."[71]

But if the challenge to evil must start within the private recesses of one's conscience and relationship to God, any effective challenge will require collaborators, colleagues, comrades. They are needed for spiritual as well as practical reasons. The sole individual, a voice crying in the wilderness, is likely to be beset by the enormity and loneliness of the task at hand. "Christians projecting themselves into an unchristian society, working to transform it, are likely to be overwhelmed by a majority opinion which negates the things for which they stand." Like many on the Christian pacifist left, Thurman had little use for mass politics or mass movements and instead emphasized the leaven, the small bands of dedicated followers of nonviolent resistance who by the strength of their beliefs would be able to bend great historical forces to their will. If one source of the belief in the power of small-scale transformation came from the apostles and the call of discipleship, another was certainly Gandhi's ashrams. Thurman praised to his St. Louis audience the importance of finding a "sense of communion with a select group of like-minded seekers and achievers of the good life for themselves and their age."[72] This would become an increasingly popular sentiment among the pacifist left. In the same year as Thurman's address in St. Louis, Richard Gregg, probably the most significant American interpreter of Gandhi in the 1930s, in *Training for Peace* advocated the creation of small pacifist cells with five to twelve members that would study and carefully prepare for nonviolent resistance. Thurman's talk was an early example of what one wry observer during the war would call "Kristigraha."[73]

Thurman ended the formal part of his talk in St. Louis speaking of the necessity for each person to listen intently to his or her own spirit, to "the still small voice of God, without which nothing has meaning quite." After his talk, his obligation not quite finished, Thurman took several questions from the audience. One questioner, troubled by something he had said, asked him to clarify his understanding of the relationship between Jesus and God. Thurman was forthright in his answer: "There are times in my own experience when I must have what is to me a sense, not of the presence of Jesus Christ, important as that is, but a sense of the presence of God himself. And in my mind and my own experience, those two things are not necessarily identical. I simply speak for myself." In the Significance of Jesus series, Thurman had elaborated on this. If Jesus was God, then when he prayed to God, feigning ignorance of what was about to happen to him, Jesus was engaging in mere "playacting, or shadowboxing." The prayer life of Jesus was the clinching argument against the conventional trinitarianism and the "tendency to make Jesus and God identical." Thurman was a believer in God and not in Jesus, and if Thurman approached God through Christianity, it was not in any traditional understanding the Christian God.[74] The final questioner asked how it was possible that people could give their moral approval to things that they knew to be immoral. Thurman said he had no good answer but only knew that this is what people consistently did. The less something directly affects us, Thurman said, the more religious and moral we tend to be in evaluating it. The closer something gets to home, to our self-interests, the more immoral and irreligious we become. And if you become comfortable in this position, before long "you discover that, well, really the thing is not that bad. . . . We find ourselves putting the imprimatur of our character on the bad things that do not seem so bad. Or we imagine that we are withholding our approval of evil, as if this was enough." To the extent that Jim Crow becomes comfortable and customary, Thurman believed, something, whether black or white, you think you can successfully navigate, you have become part of the problem. If you think you are taking advantage of evil, it is taking advantage of you.

This was the last thing Thurman said to his audience, and with this comment he took his leave of the Methodist conference and the city of St. Louis. Without saying anything specific on race or civil rights, save his opening comments on his treatment earlier in the day, few in the audience in St. Louis could have doubted that they had just heard a searing sermon on racial injustice and the necessity to make the necessary sacrifices to combat it, up to and including one's own life.

After the incident in the dining room, Thurman had spent the day in St. Louis in a state of considerable agitation. He was, in the best of times, a deeply sensitive man, subject to cavernous depressions and profound mood swings. He never developed the thick skin needed to deflect such incidents from the core of his personality, and racial slights could make him physically ill, as happened this day. He would write the conference sponsors several weeks later, after receiving an apology for the episode, that "I am very sorry that the incident took place because recovery from such things is most difficult." Thurman had delivered the sermon, he later wrote, with a "very very terrible headache," and the fact "that I did not have lunch aggravated my feeling." He left without saying good-bye to his hosts. He found a Negro restaurant for dinner, and then went to the railroad station and waited until the Pullman car opened at 9:00 P.M. Although the train did not leave until midnight, Thurman was in his bed by 9:30, seeking the restoration he so often found on trains. A few came to offer support, such as Harold Case, a Methodist minister from Kansas who later as president of Boston University hired Thurman as dean of chapel in 1953. But one suspects that he was most interested in getting the day's events behind him and falling into a deep and restful sleep.[75]

When Thurman awoke he was in Ohio at Miami University in Oxford. He would be one of the main speakers at the National Assemblies of Student Christian Associations. This was a very large conference with more than 1,350 delegates and representatives from forty-three states and more than three hundred colleges, universities, and seminaries. The conference organizers wanted the speakers to weigh in, in a distinctively Christian fashion, on the leading issues of the day—war or peace, industrial harmony or strife, discrimination or racial equality. As the call to the conference expressed it, "What does it mean to be Christian in a world such as this? . . . What are the personal and social implications of a religion based on the ethics of Jesus?"[76]

Thurman spoke twice at Oxford. Perhaps because of the complications of his St. Louis engagement, he had made little advanced preparation. He would write conference organizer A. Roland Elliott, "A large part of the material which I used had to be worked out as I proceeded."[77] His first talk, "Man and the World of Nature," was decades ahead of its time, a pronouncement of a religious ecology and on the environmental and spiritual consequences of viewing nature as something only fit for human domination, which he argued was at the heart of all human brutality.[78]

Thurman's other talk at the conference in Oxford, Ohio, was "Christian, Who Calls Me Christian?" It followed the same general outline of his talk in St. Louis on how a Christian could live a Christian life in an outwardly Christian country that everywhere was dedicated to the obliteration of Christian values. "If I let flower in my own heart what I condemn in society and in my fellow man, 'Christian, Who Calls Me Christian?'" (This catchphrase, long a favorite of Thurman's, came back several times during the address.)[79] The "great task is the redemption of the human spirit from evil." It can be destroyed only by the "strength that comes from a great cause, and a man's loyalty to it." This can ennoble "our most ordinary task," providing the "freedom of mind that comes with a great commitment." With this, said Thurman in a wonderful phrase, comes the "orderly recklessness" that can rob "a man of the fear of death." It was, he allowed, "difficult for an intellectual to experience this thing." But it was necessary, because "the kingdom of evil must be held by fanatics." Its opposite, its antidote, was not a cautious, prudential, rationalism but a commitment rooted in an emotional, nonrational, and essentially religious impulse. Without it, one would be so overwhelmed by doubts as to be reduced to inaction or would endeavor to gain protection from one's doubts through foolish bravado or lashing out in acts of violence. Freedom from fear—"fear of failure, fear of death, fear of being misunderstood, fear that I am mistaken in the thing that I am undertaking, fear that all my life long I might live for a cause only to find at the end that the cause is wrong"—cannot be found through rational means.[80]

It was when one was in the grasp of such a passion for social change that "in moments of profound meditation [one becomes] sometimes for one transcendental moment only a central part of the purposes of life." And when one, in those circumstances, hears "the still, small voice of God," the journey toward the necessary personal and social transformation becomes filled "with a music all of its own, and even the stars in their courses and all the wooded world of nature will participate in the triumphant music of my heart." When one helps bring about social transformation, one experiences the unity of all things and the unity of all things in God. And, Thurman said in closing, "This is the joy, the utter bliss that comes from doing God's work in redeeming society from evil." If you are unable or unwilling to try to experience this, then, "Christian, Who Calls Me Christian?"

"Christian, Who Calls Me Christian?" is Thurman at his most powerful and urgent. One who was there wrote in 1941, "Thirteen hundred of us from all over the map sat in hushed silence as we reached out for his words and sought contact with his soul.'Christian, Who Calls Me Christian?' was the topic, and many of us went away wondering just why anyone should call us Christian."[81] Thurman received many similar comments. One woman wrote, "We think your closing address on Friday evening was one of the unforgettable events of the conference and we wish you to know how much it inspired us all."[82] A delegate from Columbia University wanted Thurman to know that he and his friends "all agreed that you are one of the most dramatic speakers they have ever listened to."[83] The president of Hiram College, writing to Thurman to invite him to speak at his Ohio college, gushed, "If you were a man given to vanity, you would be made unduly vain by the praises which our Hiram delegates to the Miami convention are singing. So far as I can make out from their reports the convention was very largely Howard Thurman and each individually has been to ask me if I will not try to get you to visit the campus."[84]

Perhaps the highest praise Thurman received was from his old friend George "Shorty" Collins who, back in the 1920s while he was still an undergraduate at Morehouse, had introduced Thurman to both pacifism and the works of Olive Schreiner. But their paths had not crossed for a number of years before Collins heard Thurman speak at Oxford: "I had wondered, as we all do, what might have happened to your ideas and to your spirit, in view of all the situations through which we have gone. It meant much to me that you have gone on growing in the direction which I had thought and hoped you would. You are one of the prophets of the day."[85] Thurman's good friend Allan Hunter, a Congregationalist minister in Los Angeles, would have agreed. In 1935 he was writing a book on five modern religious prophets, all pacifists and towering religious figures of the day—Albert Schweitzer, Muriel Lester, Mahatma Gandhi, and the prominent Japanese Christian pacifist Toyohiko Kagawa— and asked Thurman to be the fifth and final subject of the book.[86]

Perhaps Thurman was not a prophet. (He certainly didn't think he was.) But he was a powerful interpreter and translator of the message of Gandhi and helped bring his ideas to an American, and an African American, audience. He was hardly alone. The 1930s were a decade when notions of radical nonviolence were percolating throughout the pacifist and Christian left, from well-known leaders of opinion to the humble and anonymous, such as the Sunday school teacher in Indianola, Mississippi, who told anthropologist Hortense Powdermaker in the early 1930s that if blacks hate whites they just poison themselves, and that Gandhi had the right idea and "has Christ in him. . . . It is through love that we will conquer."[87] Amid this ferment, Howard Thurman was a key figure. The seeds planted by Thurman would soon bear fruit, and in the 1940s the first campaigns of nonviolent resistance would begin—slowly, ineluctably, the long, hard process of cracking and shattering Jim Crow. Few did more than Thurman to advance Gandhi's message or did more to help realize Gandhi's famous words of parting to him: "It may be through the Negroes that the unadulterated message of nonviolence will be delivered to the world." In the 1940s Thurman would transform his own life to put this into practice.

CHAPTER SIX

Thurman's War and the Creation of the Fellowship Church

KARL MARX ONCE FAMOUSLY observed that all great world-historic events occur twice, first as tragedy and second as farce. This, alas, does not apply to world wars. If the First World War was a tragedy, the second was a tragedy so deep and dark as to defy comprehension. For Thurman, as with everyone of his generation, the two world wars were the two great global touchstones of his lifetime, both very similar, both very different, both shaping him profoundly. If the First World War exploded almost overnight, the coming of the Second World War unfolded with an agonizing slowness. Thurman had been too young to fight in the First World War. He was a member of the generation that shuddered when it thought of the horribleness wrought between 1914 and 1918 and pledged itself to never let anything like it happen again. But of course it did happen again, and Thurman had been a near witness to the first spark, glancing by the Italo-Ethiopian War of 1935 as he made his passage to Asia as a member of the Pilgrimage of Friendship, and looked at the prospect of that conflict with foreboding, writing Muriel Lester in September 1935, "How terrible it is that we have moved few steps in advance of where we were in 1914. In fact, it seems to me that hatred and bitterness are moving rapidly to the surface of life in so many relationships that have worn thin since the beginning of the depression." Never, he concluded, had there been a time when "the peace and love testimony of individuals was so critically needful."[1]

Thurman would continue to offer his peace testimony in the years to come. In a sermon of June 1937, "Keep Awake," he spoke of "the threat of war that is increasingly imminent with the passing days" and how preventing this required a personal commitment "more impor-

tant than the fact of life or death, something which becomes for you
the call of God."[2] The following year he condemned the murder in aer-
ial bombardments of "thousands and thousands of defenseless men,
women and children" in places as far flung as China, Spain, and India
(where during his stay there a few years earlier he undoubtedly heard
of the ongoing campaign of the RAF against Waziristan tribesmen).[3]
When asked in the summer of 1937 whether—like many black intellectuals of the time—he approved of Japan's invasion of China as an
example of a nonwhite nation standing up to the Western powers, he
acknowledged that while "his pride is with Japan," he was wisely "opposed fundamentally to imperialism, whether the imperialist be black,
yellow, white, or any other color," and that "as a pacifist, I am opposed
to the whole sordid struggle going on between China and Japan."[4]

He also opposed the domestic manifestations of the spirit of militarism, which he felt long before the consequences of the attack on
Pearl Harbor had pervaded American society. In the fall of 1940 as
cochair (with his longtime friend Frank Wilson) of the Fellowship of
Religious Workers in Negro Colleges and Universities, an organization of chaplains at black colleges, he linked the "advance of military
despotism in Europe and Asia" to the "subtle encroachments of the
anti-democratic spirit in our own land," both raising questions about
"the preservation of essential human liberties and the protection of
the integrity of human personality."[5] He even applied his antiwar principles to the greatest and most tragic challenge for pacifists in these
years, the unspeakable evil of the Nazi persecution of the Jews. His
old friend and ardent pacifist Allan Hunter wrote him in March 1939
reminding him of a conversation with "the girl engaged to a communist, who kept pushing you after church in the manse on the issue of
what a Jew should do about the Nazis. What you suggested there—
that one can somehow maintain the integrity of one's spirit on the
third level of refusing to hate—lingers with us."[6]

Thurman's pacifism went beyond words. He became a vice chairman of the Fellowship of Reconciliation (FOR), by far the highest-
ranking black in the organization, in the fall of 1940.[7] A.J. Muste,
the energetic cochair of FOR, would often call on him during the

war years for special tasks, such as trying to relieve tensions in wartime Detroit.[8] In the spring of 1940, with talk in the air of reinstating
the draft (as happened later in the year), Thurman spent much time
lobbying the National Baptist Convention (the main black Baptist
denomination) to officially recognize a conscientious objector regis-
try for its members.[9] This was a very personal matter for Thurman.
When in 1942, as every male under age forty-five was obliged to do, he
registered for the draft, he did so as a conscientious objector, eschewing the safety of a ministerial deferment.[10]

But to employ a useful distinction of Joseph Kip Kosek, if Thurman's commitment to nonviolence never wavered, his public avowal
of pacifism became more equivocal.[11] While Thurman would continue
to criticize militarism and its consequences in his sermons, he never
publicly condemned the war or those who chose to fight in it, whether
voluntarily or after their conscription. This seems to have been less a
consequence of any changed attitudes to the war, or to war in general,
and more the social and domestic consequences and ramifications of
the Second World War.

Central to his thinking was his sense that the war, either positively
or negatively, would have an immense impact on the status of American blacks, and that as a result he couldn't place himself entirely outside or above it. As he wrote A. J. Muste, "I know that war is not only
futile but is thoroughly and completely evil and diabolical." But on
the other side of the dilemma for Thurman was that "Negro men
and women need so much more counseling during these times than
ordinarily." He was sure that "the thousands of Negro men who will
be taken into camp should not be deserted by other Negroes like me."
His word as university chaplain might make a difference. "Often our
very presence will stay the hands of brutality and cruelty on the part
of white men who are in position of authority over them [black sol-
diers] and whose normally weak scruples as to treatment are almost
thoroughly routed by the customary moral disintegration opened by
war." In the end, he concluded to Muste, "what my duty is as a Christian is sometimes very obscure."[12]

But if the meaning of the war was obscure, it utterly absorbed Thurman's energies, enveloping him, he related at the end of 1941, "every waking moment."[13] Two years later he wrote the war so dominates "the horizon of men's thoughts that everything that is not directly related to the crisis situation seems irrelevant and without significance."[14] There was nothing unrelated to the war, certainly not the status of American blacks; and many hoped that the nature of the mobilization for the war and the political and social upheavals it brought would in some ways shake the foundations of Jim Crow. There were positive portents. The Fair Employment Practices Commission (FEPC), created in July 1941, had as its mandate the elimination of discrimination in defense-related industries and was the first significant federal intervention in civil rights since the end of Reconstruction. This came about because of increased black visibility and political power in the North. In 1945 New York became the first state to outlaw discrimination in employment and education. Other Northern states soon followed. These actions were accompanied by a flood of words from the federal and state governments and in books and on the radio addressing aspects of "the Negro problem" and the hope and promise of its postwar amelioration.

But the other wartime reality was that enforcement of the new legislation was limited; whatever the promises of a better postwar future were, black soldiers were still serving in a Jim Crow military, and a few minor cracks aside, the edifice of racial discrimination remained very much intact. For all these reasons, positive and negative, Thurman took his responsibility to Howard University soldiers very seriously. He would write in his 1943 annual report as dean of chapel at Howard that "my correspondence with men in the camps is voluminous, I have tried to maintain personal contact with all the fellows who advised me as to their mailing address."[15] In his correspondence with soldiers, Thurman offered his personal encouragement without endorsing the broader military enterprise. He wrote in 1943 to a former student who was the only black commissioned officer in his unit of his "unique responsibility." Thurman hoped "you are able to give to the men the kind of guidance, counsel, and inspiration that will make it possible for them to go through this experience without complete moral and spiritual bankruptcy."[16]

The status and treatment of black soldiers were matters of his utmost concern. In 1943 he congratulated a white correspondent who started a USO unit for blacks at a Kansas army base, telling her "you are working away to make a breathing space possible for Negro soldiers who have no power at the moment to help themselves," and that "even now, we can win the military victory on the battlefield of the world, and lose the war at home."[17] When a correspondent challenged the military prowess of black soldiers, Thurman sprung to their defense, denying categorically the emotional instability of Negro men under fire at the front. "Little by little, the significance of Negroes for the armed forces on sea, in the air and on land is being realized, and I dare say, that before the war is over they will be in all the armed forces. It is the only democratic thing to do."[18]

But on the whole Thurman thought race relations were deteriorating in wartime America. This was in part because the war, official professions aside, was often seen in starkly racial terms. As he would write in 1943, "The fact that we were attacked by Japan has aggravated greatly the tension between the races. I am not suggesting that the war between Japan and the United States is a race war, but certainly many people have thought of it in terms of a non-white race 'daring' to attack a white race. This has given excellent justification for the expression of the prejudices against non-white peoples just under the surface of the American consciousness."[19] Thurman was deeply shocked by the Japanese internments. As Greg Robinson has shown, the Christian left were among the few vocal opponents of the internments as they unfolded, and Thurman's own involvement included visiting at least two internment camps and working to arrange the transfer of Japanese American students to Howard.[20] When Thurman moved to San Francisco in the summer of 1944, he found himself living and working in a hollowed-out former Japanese neighborhood, one of several West Coast ground zeros of the internment. As he would later write:

It was not infrequent that one saw billboard caricatures of the Japanese: grotesque faces, huge buck teeth, large dark-rimmed thick-lensed eyeglasses. The point was, in effect, to read the Japanese out of the human race; they were construed as mon-

sters and as such stood in immediate candidacy for destruction. They were so defined as to be placed in a category to
which ordinary decent behavior did not apply. . . . It was open
season for their potential extermination.[21]

It was all too easy for this murderous rage against the Japanese to be
turned against other racial minorities, especially blacks. If the war was
creating massive demographic shifts in the South and encouraging
blacks to be more assertive, it was at the same time fostering a fierce
pushback by whites who wanted blacks to return to their accustomed
places. By 1943 Thurman was writing of "an increasing determination
and grimness on the part of white Americans. It seems perfectly clear
to them that Negroes everywhere are getting out of their place. The
argument runs like this: 'Negroes do not know what to do with their
new sense of significance. They are flippant, arrogant, bigoted, over-
bearing. Therefore, they must be curbed, held in check so that when
the war is over they may drop quickly back into their prewar secondary citizen status.'"[22] In his extensive travels throughout the country
he had seen or heard tell of numerous instances of black challenges to
the racial status quo and the white response. He would write a correspondent at the end of the summer of 1942 that he had "traveled some
thirteen or fourteen thousand miles since early June, and the picture
is the same everywhere—sporadic outbursts of violence, meanness,
murder, bloodshed, and a great paralysis in the presence of it all."[23]

What was to be done? If the war provided a tenuous opening to
blacks and the advancement of racial equality, it also, like all wars, was
unleashing untold stores of hatred, resentment, and naked brutality.
How to gain something positive for racial minorities during the hor-
ror of the war, and then how to protect them against what Thurman
was sure would be the inevitable postwar reaction? Thurman's most
personal answer came in a 1942 letter to a man he almost certainly
never met, a conscientious objector named Kay Beach, then serving in
a Civilian Public Service camp (a sort of CCC camp with barbed wire
and armed guards for COs willing to serve the country in nonmili-
tary capacities). Beach had written him, questioning Thurman on the

ethics of black nonviolence and whether black protests for their civil rights would turn violent, which Beach thought would be a tragedy.

The problem with black nonviolence, Thurman responded, was that for most blacks the essential step forward to political awareness was a refusal to be intimidated, since "for many years Negroes for various reasons have tended to be far too docile. Their docility has been confused with an alleged meekness and cowardliness."[24] While this was not true, "so deep is the resentment of many Negroes to this overall picture that the technique of non-violent action is regarded by them as being an expression of cowardice." Violence and aggression all too often became the measure of the strength of one's commitment to challenging Jim Crow. The trick was to "maintain in non-violent *action* an increment of courage that would be disassociated from the so called 'hat in the hand' attitude."[25]

Politically active blacks often started from a profound mistrust of whites and skepticism toward those bearing good intentions. Well-intentioned whites all too often saw blacks as little more than unfinished and raw vessels for their sympathy. The need for whites and blacks to work together was precisely to overcome the abstractness of race relations lived in separate segregated worlds. Writing to Beach, Thurman expressed enthusiasm for "any attempt on the part of interracial units to combine directly non-violent action and a program of constructive adjustment in group relations. . . . It seems to me that one of the important solutions is to be found in the work of small groups in communities all over the United States demonstrating courageous, peaceful action, carefully planned and carefully executed."[26]

Thurman had made similar arguments before, in his two lecture series, The Significance of Jesus and Mysticism and Social Change, though as we have noted, the circulation of these lectures was extremely limited. He offered a recapitulation in his important article "The Will to Segregation" in *Fellowship*, the journal of the Fellowship of Reconciliation, in August 1943. If *Fellowship* was hardly a mass-circulation publication, he could not have found a more important or receptive audience for his argument. Thurman was hardly the only Christian pacifist who was uncertain about how to respond to the war. The members of FOR knew all too well that the war was popular at home, and many erstwhile allies were now firmly in the camp of war supporters. The pacifist stance of the moral equivalence of the combatants, which had been so effective in the First World War, now struck most (including many in FOR) as somehow grotesque. The pacifist ranks had been dramatically thinned, and most important of all, their peace witness was now reduced to an infinitesimal political impact. In all, it was "the dark night of the pacifist soul."[27] Without abandoning their opposition to war, many searched for a way to contest their irrelevance, to find other arenas for their nonviolence, moral equivalents of pacifism. The fight for racial equality was an obvious alternative, and this became an increasingly important part of Christian pacifism during the war years. This was of course not an entirely new idea, and as we have discussed, since the late 1920s Thurman had been making the argument that pacifism was as much about domestic violence at home as militarism abroad, and that radical nonviolence had no greater task than to challenge and confront racial oppression. By the early 1940s the peace movement was beginning to catch up to Howard Thurman.[28]

Thurman's article in *Fellowship* described "the Will to Segregation" as the "American technique for the control of the Negro minority." Segregation was for Thurman a malign psychological force, hovering over black and white America alike, realized and concretized in particular individuals and institutions, the product of myriad individual acts to enforce or acquiesce in the rules of racial inequality. But it was important to remember that segregation was, at its core, a will to dominate, and it could be challenged, and defeated, only by a will of equal strength and fervor. If this was done adequately, all of its laws, ordinances, judicial and extrajudicial means of enforcement would simply vanish and slip away. The way to break segregation's will was to attack it at its most vulnerable point, its individual supporters and (perhaps even more important) its casual abetters, which could be accomplished through the shock technique discussed earlier. The goal was not a moral appeal to the segregators but an effort to rip people from their complicity and complacency with evil. Only in this way would people in power relinquish "their hold on their place. It is not until something becomes movable in the situation that men are spiritually prepared to apply Christian idealism to un-ideal and un-christian situations." This was, as much as anything Thurman would ever write, a call to nonviolent battle, to the barricades of Jim Crow. "Action of this kind requires great discipline of mind, emotions and body to the end that forces may not be released that will do complete violence both to one's ideals and to one's purpose. All must be done with the full consciousness of the Divine Scrutiny."[29]

II

By 1943 Thurman was not only speaking and writing about the need for a great nonviolent struggle against racism, he also had mentored and shaped a number of figures who were beginning to take leadership roles in the fight. Like all successful mentoring, the learning flowed both ways: Thurman gained much from his protégés, and in the end their deeds would have a major impact on his words.

Although he is little remembered today, Prentice Thomas was a significant figure in the struggle for racial and economic justice in the late 1930s and early 1940s. A Texas native, Thomas was Thurman's student at Howard's School of Religion before staying on at Howard for a law degree, graduating in 1937. Thurman recommended him for a leadership position at an interracial cooperative farm in the Mississippi Delta sponsored by Christian socialists, which faced considerable internal and external opposition, predicting that he "will be heard from some day as a lawyer and a champion of the rise of the disinherited."[30] Thomas subsequently worked with the interracial Southern Tenant Farmers Union, another organization associated with the Socialist Party. This, like the cooperative farm, was dangerous work. But as a Quaker and a pacifist (and a conscientious objector during the war), he was a resolute practitioner of nonviolence. He achieved his greatest prominence, starting in 1942, during a stint as an assistant to his fellow Howard Law grad Thurgood Marshall at the NAACP Legal Defense Fund in New York City during the war, where he was involved in a wide range of legal cases, from price-gouging in Harlem to death-row defenses. Alas, his time in New York City did not have a happy outcome, because as Risa Goluboff has written, "it soon became clear that the NAACP's developing agenda did not match Thomas's more left-leaning and agricultural bias."[31] (A major conference on agricultural labor that Thomas had planned was angrily canceled by the NAACP's executive director Walter White.) Thomas resigned in 1943 and returned to the relative obscurity of a Kentucky law practice. One of the main sources of his political and spiritual energy was the teachings of Howard Thurman. As Thomas wrote his mentor in 1937, when he was regularly risking his life for the Southern Tenant Farmers Union, "Give me seventeen years of life and study, and perhaps you will see some more of *your own* philosophy materialize in my work."[32]

Thurman was also a spiritual and political mentor to many who never formally studied with him, such as Bill Sutherland and Pauli Murray. In June 1941 he received a letter from Bill Sutherland, reminding Thurman "of a night long ago at Bates College, when I kept you up until one o'clock philosophizing and such." Sutherland was writing Thurman about his dilemma whether to focus his energies on pacifism or the struggle for racial equality. If in the short term pacifism won (he was a conscientious objector during the war who served time for draft resistance), the latter cause would be his life's work. In 1953 he emigrated to the Gold Coast (later Ghana) and would remain in Africa for many decades, a pacifist, Pan-Africanist, and supporter of African liberation.[33]

By the time Pauli Murray entered Howard Law School in 1941, she already had created a significant career for herself as a fighter for racial equality and experienced several bruising confrontations with Jim Crow, which included time in a Petersburg, Virginia, jail for refusing to obey the local transportation laws and work with the Workers Defense League. She had mused about starting and heading an "American satyagraha movement." She would have many opportunities at Howard to continue the fight, and in early 1944 became the leader of student protests against nearby Washington area restaurants that refused to serve blacks. The demonstrations attracted considerable local attention, and Mordecai Wyatt Johnson, out of fear that Howard might get into hot water with its conservative, segregationist congressional funders, ordered Murray and the protesters to desist. Murray appealed to Thurman, who gave the deeply religious Murray (she would later become an Episcopal priest) some much needed spiritual counsel. He intervened with Johnson, and the demonstrations continued. Murray remembers Thurman telling her during the crisis that "a characteristic of evil is that we never fully destroy it. When we beat it down in one place, it pops up in another."[34] The two would remain close.

Thurman communicated the same lesson of the ubiquity and tenacity of evil, and the relentlessness needed to defeat it, to James Farmer, his most prominent protégé, who as leader of the Congress of Racial Equality (CORE) was one of the civil rights movement's "big four" during its 1960s heyday. Like Prentice Thomas, Farmer came to the Howard School of Religion from Texas, entering as a student in 1938, and almost immediately fell under the spell of the "incomparable Howard Thurman." Farmer's description of Thurman's pedagogy helps us understand how he could be such an effective teacher for budding social activists. After a slow entrance into the class—"he would look over the heads of those in class, into space, for what seemed minutes," he would then offer in his "slow, laborious manner" a provocative thesis and wait for the class to respond. The example Farmer chose was a favorite of Thurman's: that "we are what we do—in spite of reservations." Thurman said little, waiting for the students to find their own answers. And the responses came. Was Thurman talking about soldiers killing in wartime? Or accepting an assigned status of inferiority, such as sitting in the balcony of a Jim Crow theater? The lesson that the oppressed, if they don't challenge it, become complicit in their own oppression, and that any program of spiritual nonviolence starts with oneself and works outward, is one that Farmer took to heart.[35]

Thurman introduced Farmer to the works and thought of Gandhi, and under his influence Farmer embraced pacifism and became a conscientious objector. Thurman also directed Farmer's master's thesis, "A

Critical Analysis of the Historical Interrelationship Between Religion and Racism."[36] This was a favorite topic of Thurman's, and Farmer's argument followed Thurman's critique of evangelical Protestantism, arguing that the "spiritual arrogance" of belonging to the God's chosen elect and God's chosen race was essentially the same. Farmer held that Calvinist theology, with its relentless dichotomizing the world into spiritual haves and have-nots, provided the underlying justification of the slave trade and the presumption of African inferiority. Thurman was impressed by the thesis and urged Farmer to publish it. In the meantime, Farmer, on Thurman's recommendation, was hired by FOR as a part-time student secretary in Washington.[37]

Shortly after graduating Howard in 1941, Farmer became a full-time field secretary for FOR in Chicago. In early 1942 in an article in *Fellowship*, "The Race Logic of Pacifism," Farmer outlined a program for nonviolent resistance to segregation, arguing much as Thurman would that the war had both exacerbated racial tension and presented an opportunity for racial minorities, one that could only be taken advantage of through nonviolent direct action, undertaken on an interracial basis. Echoing Thurman's emphasis on the person, Farmer wrote that pacifists had to refuse to cooperate with "all those social practices which wreak havoc with personality and despoil the human community."[38]

Farmer put those ideas into practice when in May 1942 the Chicago FOR group and allies organized what he called the "first organized civil rights sit-in in American history," successfully desegregating a restaurant in the Hyde Park neighborhood.[39] Farmer's conception of nonviolence was broader than many in FOR wanted, because it acknowledged the coercive nature of direct action, condoning the use of police to oblige recalcitrant property owners to obey existing civil rights laws (thereby giving sanction to the use of force implicit in all police actions), and also because, while wanting the movement to be rigorously nonviolent, Farmer did not want to limit membership to pacifists only. For all these reasons, FOR thought it wise for the new Committee (later Congress) for Racial Equality to be connected to but institutionally distinct from the parent organization.[40]

Over the next several decades CORE would have various ups and downs, but through James Farmer it would probably come as close to realizing Thurman's political and religious ideals as any organization could: broadly pacifist in its sympathies but focused on racial discrimination in America; inspired by religious conviction without being overtly religious; concentrating its efforts on grassroots direct action; committed to interracialism as one of its founding principles; of the left but not overtly sympathetic to Communism. Thurman wrote Farmer in early 1943, "Non-violent civil disobedience is a technique that presupposes very definite discipline. It is an act of the will arising out of a profound spiritual conviction, which by its very nature is devoid either of ill-will, contempt, or cowardice." For Thurman radical nonviolence was always at its core a spiritual discipline, a way of transforming evil without becoming infected by "fear, revenge or hate."[41] Thurman imparted this high-minded conception of social change to those he came into contact with, including Prentice Thomas, Bill Sutherland, Pauli Murray, James Farmer, and many others, planting seeds for the civil rights revolution to come.

For Thurman, the pioneers of the civil rights revolution were the "apostles of sensitiveness," a popular catchphrase with Thurman in the mid-1940s, which he used in several addresses of the period (most significantly in an eponymous sermon he gave in 1946 at the Cathedral of St. John the Divine in New York City under the auspices of the Interracial Fellowship of Greater New York) and as the title of one of his books. The apostles of sensitiveness were individuals who took it upon themselves to transform society, the harbingers and forerunners of a new social order; their sensitivity a keen awareness of others and profound empathy for the hopes, fears, and dreams of people not like them. They knew that society was mutable and that the social order was not fixed. "To be overcome with paralysis, fear and indecision in the presence of crusted intolerance, and injustice however deeply entrenched, is to say 'No' to life and affirm that the contradictions of one's experiences are in themselves ultimate. This is to deny the sense of alternative, to reject the Holy Spirit of God, to turn one's back upon life." Operating in small groups, they will create the basis for the world to come. "Whatever the world of the future will be like depends in no small part upon the spear-head that will be provided by those who have worked out in a thousand social laboratories, techniques and methods for implementing those ideas which are so seriously threatened at home and abroad."[42]

The apostles of sensitiveness must not allow themselves to become cowed or intimidated, Thurman argued. "They must resist every attempt to place false and misleading labels on them such as red, subversive, divisive. This is a very clever device inspired by fear, bigotry, intolerance."[43] Since racial minorities were those most likely to be the casualties of the degradation of the democratic ideal, they were likely to be recruits out of proportion to their numbers. Whatever their background, the apostles of sensitiveness would have to be the "nerve endings for the body politic," jangling the country out of its complacencies, creating enough pain to force it to pay attention to its injuries and sores. The apostles of sensitiveness would be the outsiders, the marginalized, the underprivileged, the disinherited, and those who have established special links to them; they would be the apostles of an American campaign of radical nonviolence.

III

Thurman often noted the irony of Christians taking the lead in the fight against Jim Crow, the products of a church that was, for all intents and purposes, entirely segregated and more racially separate than America's schools, places of entertainment, public transportation, or workplaces. For Christians who professed allegiance to racial equality, what task could be more pressing than the racial integration of the church? As Thurman asked in his August 1943 article "The Will to Segregation," what does it mean "when over and over again we give the sanction of our religion and the weight of our practice to those subtle anti-christian practices expressed in segregated churches and even in segregated graveyards! Can we expect more of the state, of the body politic, of industry than we expect of the church? How can we teach love from behind the great high walls of separateness?" What was

needed in the church was a "radical internal reorganization of policy
and of structural change." What was needed was a way to tap and draw
on the great positive forces within the church currently kept at bay.
"My contention is that if the 'will to segregate' is relaxed in the church
then the resources of mind and spirit and power that are already in
the church can begin working formally and informally on the radical
changes that are necessary if the church is to become Christian."[44]
One of the basic problems of the Christian church for Thurman was,
as he would later write, that from its founding it had been committed
to a revolutionary ethic but "deluded itself into thinking its revolutionary ethic can be implemented in less than revolutionary terms."[45]
Thurman's solution, his revolution, was simple. The church had to
become fully interracial, and this process had to start somewhere. A
segregated church could not be a force to integrate the society outside
its doors. As we have seen, Thurman had been thinking about this
for many years, since his epiphany at the Khyber Pass in early 1936
when he knew he had to test "whether a religious fellowship could be
developed in America that was capable of cutting across racial barriers," whether "the experiences of spiritual unity among people could
be more compelling than the experiences that divide them."[46] This
was, he would write in 1945, "a dream which has haunted me for ten
years."[47] But there was no existing congregation in the United States
that remotely met Thurman's requirements, certainly not his home
congregation, Rankin Chapel at Howard, which, as he wrote, had of
course a "well-nigh complete homogeneity as to race." The closest was
the Fellowship Church in Philadelphia, sponsored by the Committee on Race Relations of the Society of Friends. This was not quite
a church—it met only once a month, alternating between white and
black venues—but it was one of the first efforts at establishing a regular, interracial worship service in the United States.[48] This had been
an inspiration of the Khyber Pass epiphany; Thurman would preach
at the Fellowship Church frequently in the late 1930s and early 1940s,
and he was clearly impressed by what it had achieved. He urged the
church to become full time, every Sunday, and he evidently pledged
in that case to become its full-time minister. Marjorie Penney would

write him in October 1942, "Believe me, if and when the Fellowship Church becomes more than a series of services, we shall be seriously thinking of what you said regarding your interest in it."[49]

It was only during the war that the interracial church movement, like so many of America's racial experiments, really got its start. From Detroit to Pasadena, churches of various sorts (some meeting every Sunday, some not) started to call themselves interracial.[50] And in various cities—New York, Newark, Chicago, and San Francisco—interracial, urban, Christian, Gandhian cooperatives sprouted, all short-lived, all dedicated to Gandhian principles of service to the downtrodden. Their members lived simply, dedicated themselves to their spiritual callings and to assisting the local minority communities.[51] The Fellowship Church was the product of a combination of these efforts to revive and reshape American Christianity. One Gandhian cooperative in San Francisco, followers of the principles of Thurman's friend Muriel Lester, was known as the Sakai group, so-called because of their residence in a house formerly owned by the Sakai family before their wartime expulsion with other Japanese families from San Francisco. The Sakai group was a group of women committed to working with the surrounding neighborhood, which was in the process of rapidly becoming a black neighborhood because the former Japantown was one of the few areas in the city that welcomed black residents. The small prewar black community in San Francisco underwent a sixfold growth during the war years with most newcomers attracted by work in the defense industries and local shipyards. The burgeoning increase in the black population led to the usual social dislocations, and the Sakai group was just one of many efforts to develop programs to assist them. But the basic insight of the Sakai group, which became the basis for the Fellowship Church, was that nothing was more important to the newcomers than basic fellowship and worshiping with them as equals. Sometime in 1943, they felt the need to establish something more substantial than the informal religious gatherings they had been conducting. To this end they contacted Alfred Fisk, a socialist, pacifist, and local Presbyterian minister and professor of philosophy, probably through mutual contacts at the Fellowship of Reconciliation.[52]

Fisk thought that starting an interracial church was a wonderful idea. Wanting a recommendation for a black co-pastor, he contacted A. J. Muste, who in turn contacted Thurman. In mid-October 1943 Thurman received a letter from Muste telling him of the embryonic interracial church project in San Francisco. Thurman's first thought was his good friend Herbert King, then in need of a job, but King was not interested. Fisk, in his first letter to Thurman, said he wanted to create a church that would not be "in any sense run by whites for Negroes. It should be *of* and *by* and *for* both groups."[53] Thurman liked those Lincolnian prepositions and wrote back that the idea for the new church was "the most significant single step that institutional Christianity is taking in the direction of a really new order for America."[54] Fisk pressed Thurman on his possible interest in becoming co-pastor, and Thurman did not require much persuasion. By mid-November he agreed to try to obtain a leave of absence from Howard to co-pastor the church. One reason was that he was getting restless at Howard and had been quietly exploring other employment options as a pulpit minister (including the prominent Olivet Baptist Church in Chicago) and at black colleges (including his alma mater, Morehouse). But these possibilities, however attractive, remained securely behind the color line, and if they would have been personally satisfying, they would have done nothing to directly challenge or breach the separate black and white universes of religion and education.[55] From the outset he would write of the San Francisco church, "There was kindling in my mind the *possibility* that this may be *the* opportunity toward which my life had been moving."[56]

There were many skeptics, including his wife, Sue Bailey Thurman, who at first was not at all enthusiastic about the move.[57] Mordecai Wyatt Johnson gave Thurman permission for an unpaid leave of absence, but the venture struck him as rather quixotic.[58] Many of Thurman's friends and colleagues were dismayed by his plans to leave Howard, which as he wrote Fisk in March 1944 "came as a distinct shock to the student body as a whole and to many of the faculty. Serious pressures are already being exerted in an effort to force a reconsideration but to no avail."[59] Some were upset that Thurman would be cutting himself from his role as mentor and teacher to a rising generation of black divinity students. Thurman would write that those of his friends who were "most critical of my leaving the East at this desperate time have called almost dramatic attention to the fact that I have no right to tie myself down to preach to a handful of people."[60] (His services at Howard's Rankin Chapel drew upwards of five hundred people, and the San Francisco church in the beginning had an average Sunday attendance of about forty.) The new church, which always had somewhat shaky finances, could pay him only about half of what he earned at Howard, and for the privilege he would have to uproot his somewhat reluctant family and transport them across the continent. In the decision to move to San Francisco there was a recklessness, a staking of his future on an uncertain outcome, that seems out of character with his usual caution. It would be an enormous sacrifice for Thurman and his family, but they would do whatever was needed to make the venture a success. If, as he wrote Fisk, "there is any validity in our claim that God sustains His Kingdom in the world," then they had to assume the "risks involved in our bold venture and we must be prepared to take our share of them."[61] The Fellowship Church was Thurman's leap of faith for a new type of American Christianity.

After extensive preparation by Fisk, the Sakai group, and the other early members, the Fellowship Church held its first services on December 12, 1943, with sixty-six in attendance, about one-third of whom were blacks. The attendance was down to thirty-six the following week.[62] Beginnings, Thurman and Fisk reminded one another, are often inauspicious. The two men took their co-pastorship very seriously and consulted one another on all matters of importance. Much of the story of the Fellowship Church's first months is contained in the remarkable correspondence between the two men, from October 1943 through June 1944 when Thurman was still in Washington. (It is a minor historical irony that once Thurman arrived in San Francisco and the two men could speak directly this marvelous record of the church ceases.)[63]

The Fellowship Church would have more than the usual share of birth pains. From the beginning the two co-pastors knew the church's first home was a stopgap, and Fisk explored any number of possible alternatives (some of which did not want to rent their facilities to a racially mixed organization) without resolution. There were questions about how to conduct services and activities such as the church's Sunday and summer schools, with Fisk's ideas being somewhat more traditional than other centers within the congregation, such as the Sakai group with whom he did not get along.[64]

But the most heated disagreements in the early months of the church (and for the historian, the most interesting) involved Fisk's disputes with the fiery assistant pastor who served the church from February 1944 until Thurman's arrival in July, Albert Cleage Jr. Cleage was at the beginning of a controversial career that, by the late 1960s when he served as minister of the Shrine of the Black Madonna in Detroit, would make him one of the best-known black nationalists in the country. The two men clashed over pastoral duties (Fisk thought Cleage had shirked his responsibilities to the congregation), and they clashed over politics. Cleage was not yet the black nationalist he would become (though he was already being called a "Negro nationalist"), but this meant something different for Cleage than it would a quarter century later. At the time, he supported the idea of an interracial church, and interracialism in general, though he was already intensely focused on a political ministry and on racial matters and had little patience for the more facile talk of fellowship and brotherhood. The breaking point between him and Fisk was a forum at the church on discriminatory practices by the American Federation of Labor (AFL) craft unions in the Bay Area shipyards. The event was dominated by representatives of left-wing Congress of Industrial Organizations (CIO) unions close to the Communist Party. Fisk certainly supported the fight against workplace discrimination, but he did not want the church to be identified with the Communists. Fisk and the San Francisco Presbytery considered relieving Cleage of his duties. Thurman, uneasily observing the unfolding of these events from Washington, helped arrange a shaky truce that kept Cleage in San Francisco until shortly before Thurman's arrival.[65]

What was perhaps most significant about the Fisk-Cleage dispute for Thurman was what it said about the complexity and potential risks of politics within the Fellowship Church. Thurman knew that many people were active in the church primarily because of its political orientation. He also knew of the popularity of Communism with progressives, white and black, in the Bay Area, but he steered the church away from a connection with the Communist Party.[66] The church would remain quite political (though nonpartisan), supporting antidiscrimination legislation such as a state version of the Fair Employment Practices Commission, but not beholden to any particular party or ideology. Thurman wondered whether "our church, born essentially in the womb of a social issue, would have great difficulty maintaining a spiritual center," and there was no denying that at times the "social issue" became so acute that it "required tremendous care to vouchsafe the religious genius."[67] Thurman's challenge was to keep the spiritual and the political in balance and to make the church at once "a genuine source of religious experience and life for a group of interested and committed people" and "a clearing place for all kinds of activities in which racial groups may cooperate on the basis of a community of need and interest."[68]

Establishing this balance was Thurman's most pressing task when he arrived in California in July 1944. Many church members would have been happy if the Fellowship Church operated by placing a thin religious veneer on what was basically a social endeavor. Thurman felt what was needed was a formal commitment, a statement of principles. While he generally shied away from any creedal affirmation, Thurman felt the experimental and unprecedented nature of the Fellowship Church and the evident divisions within the church made it necessary. The dominant feeling of the board was that a formal commitment would be a mistake and that it would splinter the church and reveal and enhance its underlying heterogeneity. But Thurman persisted, in large part because he felt as a new church, lacking the usual common ties that bring people to worship together, they needed some way of affirming their interconnection, that "some kind of verbal platform upon which to stand" was needed lest "all authentic growth would be cut off."[69]

The first version of the "Commitment," adopted in the fall of 1944, pledged its signers to participate "in the union of men and women of varying national, cultural, and racial heritage, in church communion" through membership and "the strength of corporate worship" in the Fellowship Church. It would go through at least three published versions, which tended, in each restatement, to take the church farther and farther from a traditional Christian conception of a church. For the first version's joining in "the unfolding of the ideal of Christian fellowship" would be substituted in the second by an affirmation of the "growing understanding of all men as sons of God." Seeking "a vital interpretation of the highest manifestation of God—Jesus Christ—in all my relationships" became, in a later version, searching for a vital experience of God "as revealed in Jesus of Nazareth and other great religious spirits whose fellowship with God was the foundation of their fellowship with man."[70]

The second version of the Commitment received a lot of national attention, and some thought the change from "Jesus Christ" to "Jesus of Nazareth" was "not an improvement."[71] On the other hand, one prominent liberal minister thought that failing to mention any religious figure other than Jesus was "disastrously limiting."[72] This had not been the intention of the church, and this was emended in the third version of the Commitment, adopted in 1949, which sought the "vital experience of God as revealed in Jesus of Nazareth and other great religious spirits." The God of the Fellowship Church, Thurman would often write, was a God that was "neither male nor female, black nor white, Protestant nor Catholic nor Buddhist nor Hindu."[73]

Defining and maintaining the interracial character of the Fellowship Church would be a constant struggle. In his first letter to Thurman, Fisk said that the new church would have to be interracial in all of its aspects: "the boards of the church, the choir, the Sunday School and its staff will all be of mixed character."[74] But both men knew that for the congregation to be genuinely interracial it would require constant vigilance. The essential paradox of encouraging interracial activities was that the only way to achieve (in Thurman's terms) a genuine "relaxation" of racial separateness and lack of self-consciousness about interracial contacts was, in the beginning, to pay strict attention to racial balances and prevent domination by one race or the other. Thurman would write in 1947, "From our observation we knew of no single institution that had been able to do this without introducing artificial controls, such as for instance, a mechanical equalization of participation from various groups."[75] In time these artificial controls would be limited, but the paradox remained; the relaxation of the will to segregate required constant vigilance.

There was another complexity of interracialism, perhaps captured in the old observation that a neighborhood whose population was evenly divided racially would be called "black" by whites and "mixed" by blacks. For many, *interracial* was a polite codeword for *black*. Nothing annoyed Thurman more. Thurman was determined that the church not be supported by any of the traditional foundations dedicated to black causes, such as the Rosenwald Foundation, and would later write that the perception of the Fellowship Church as an "object of charity" from philanthropic whites would be fatal, lest the church be crippled by the "disease that has dogged the vitality and health of the Christian enterprise, . . . the deadly disease of condescension." If you treat someone as an object of your pity or charity, "he can easily absolve himself from dealing with you in any sense as an equal."[76] If there was one thing the Fellowship Church absolutely would not do, it would be to uplift the Negro.

This issue was confronted directly in the summer of 1944 when Thurman, to the surprise and objection of most of the congregation, insisted that the church move from its current location at the center of the growing black population in San Francisco, lest in a short time the congregation become completely black or disappear entirely. Many in the congregation argued that locating the church in its current setting was the very intent of the entire project, which was precisely to serve that very neighborhood, and complained that Thurman was an ivory tower intellectual, disconnected from his own people, and willing to sacrifice them to abstract notions of racial justice.[77] Nonetheless, Thurman was adamant that sacrifices, sometimes counterintuitive sacrifices, had to be made to insure the interracial character of the church, lest it be ripped apart by the usual sociological forces that assigned to almost every American institution, religious or secular, a dominant racial identity. He did not want the church in its early development to become primarily involved in community settlement activities for he felt this would make the church a kind of "dumping ground" for uplift and sacrificial helpfulness that "is often terribly degrading to the personalities of all the people involved."[78] Thurman won the argument, and the church would move in the fall, exchanging buildings with the former Filipino Methodist Church two blocks beyond the racial dividing line; for Thurman the move made all the difference. Building interracialism was sometimes rife with paradoxes.

One additional reason why Thurman was reluctant to have the church be seen as a black church was because that would only reinforce the parochial American bias that race came in only two varieties, and would lose the advantage of a location in San Francisco, a city Thurman claimed housed "sixty-three different national and cultural background groups." The church was deeply committed to multicultural (what in the 1940s was generally called intercultural) activities. Its summer school, of which Thurman was especially proud, largely consisted of introducing the children to the various ethnicities in the San Francisco area. The church choir and visiting performers regularly presented concerts of music from different ethnic cultures. During the years Thurman was minister of the Fellowship Church, it would have assistant pastors of Asian, Mexican, and African American backgrounds (as well as a female assistant pastor). The ultimate goal of all the intercultural activities of the church was to see if they could broaden children and others' "knowledge of other people in America without the negative aspects of the missionary enterprise" in order to meet on "the basis of absolute equality, without any hint of superiority, deference, or condescension."[79] If this could happen anywhere in America, thought Thurman, it would be at the Fellowship Church.

Thurman's dogged commitment to interracialism was an important factor in the decision, in the summer of 1945, to sever the congregation's connection to the Presbyterian Church. The support of the Presbyterian Church had been utterly crucial to the start of Fellowship Church. Thurman appreciated it, and he did not feel the tie to be too burdensome. While Thurman himself never had any interest in denomination or denominationalism (and his association with organized Baptism had always been exiguous at best), he thought it important that, at least at first, the Fellowship Church not be perceived as an outsider or outlier but in the heart of American Protestantism, which meant that some denominational affiliation was useful.[80] But in the summer of 1945, the Board of National Missions of the United Presbyterian Church in the U.S.A., wrote that the church should make its primary function serving the immediate community in which it was located (that is, become a mission church to the black community) and should consider itself only incidentally interracial.[81] This was Thurman's greatest fear. The time had come for a split from the Presbyterians, whatever the effects on the bottom line, which would be considerable. After extensive discussion, the vote was held on August 1, 1945, and overwhelmingly supported an independent status as a nondenominational congregation, which really had been Thurman's intentions all along. Thurman remembers the moment of the split as one of "panic—quiet, muted, glowing panic."[82]

The decision to break with the Presbyterian church in the summer of 1945 had an impact on two important events the following year. First, in the spring of 1946 when pressed by Howard University to either return full time or resign, he chose the latter course. He had hoped to work out a deal whereby he could split his time between the coasts, but this proved impossible. Many (like Benjamin Mays) were shocked to hear that Thurman had severed all his ties to Howard.[83] He would write a friend several weeks after his decision that "it goes without saying that this was the most crucial decision of my life, because it means burning bridges behind and sailing forth in the open independence of the sea."[84] However, as he wrote his former Howard colleague William Stuart Nelson, "I feel a deep urgency and an exhilaration in the choice."[85]

Several months later Alfred Fisk decided to end his association with the Fellowship Church. The main reason he gave in a letter to Thurman was the lack of an adequate Sunday school for his son, but it is clear that to the extent this figured into his decision, it was merely the latest of a series of accumulating differences with the direction of the church, and perhaps a growing sense that Thurman's charisma had made Fisk extraneous.[86] From Thurman's perspective, Fisk's leaving was probably unavoidable, and probably for the best. As Thurman wrote a friend in 1945, the significance of the interracial co-pastorship was primarily symbolic, dramatizing the importance of the undertaking, but it was difficult to work out in practice, since it is difficult to have two equal centers of authority in any organization. In the end he concluded, "The church should outgrow the co-pastor arrangement as early as possible. Obviously, such an arrangement is artificial."[87] Fisk's leaving the church made official what had been the reality for a while: the pastor of the Fellowship Church was Howard Thurman.

Increasingly the Fellowship Church was a reflection of Thurman's own theological priorities and predilections. As he had done at Howard, he experimented with the liturgy, introducing liturgical dance into worship services as well as medieval chanting or the sound of a Chinese flute. He also continued his practice, at Christmas time, of having living and illuminated representations of the Renaissance paintings of the Madonna, with the Madonna represented by women of different nationalities. He developed special meditation services resembling Quaker meetings, where the congregation would sit in silence contemplating either their own thoughts or a special reading Thurman had prepared. The church also had a small meditation room that contained a painting of Gandhi (by Thurman), a statue of the Buddha, some Hebrew prayer books, and sacred texts from a variety of faiths.[88]

If Thurman's purpose was to encourage a direct, experiential religion and connection to God, it also had a strong intellectual component. The most important way in which he imparted information was through his sermons and study groups. With Thurman greatly reducing his number of outside engagements, he was now able to deliver sermon series, which were connected talks on common themes, such as the Sermon on the Mount, "The Dilemma of the Liberal," the Hebrew prophets, or a series of thirteen sermons on the figures included in Sheldon Cheney's *Men Who Have Walked with God*, a history of mysticism from the Buddha and Plotinus to twentieth-century American mystics. At its best, worship in the Fellowship Church explored the many roads to God, the private and public, the intellectual and emotional, different paths to a single goal. As Thurman would write a friend in 1948, "I wish you might visit the church sometime and have the sense of wholeness that comes from participating in the fellowship of God as a human spirit without age, sex, race, or denomination. There is something cleansing about ridding oneself of barriers that separate one from one's fellows."[89]

IV

Thurman's success at the Fellowship Church was deeply satisfying. The growth of the congregation was real, though hardly spectacular, with an average by the early 1950s of slightly more than two hundred in attendance on a typical Sunday. But the Fellowship Church was always intended to be something greater than itself, a model and an exemplar, a spark and a catalyst of what Thurman hoped would be a broader interracial church movement of national scope. Thurman had written Fisk in May 1944 that "I am trying to give the widest possible spread to the knowledge concerning the venture because it will help a climate in which this sort of thing can take place effectively in other parts of the country."[90] Fisk had felt the same way, writing in August 1945, "We think of ourselves as part of a wide movement permeating the Church life of the nation."[91] Thurman would write and speak of the Fellowship Church and the interracial church ideal often and offer advice to ministers from Portland, Oregon, to Newark, New Jersey, interested in starting similar efforts in their own cities.[92] He would often write of his determination to make this his lifework, stating in May 1946, "It seems clear to me that for the next 10 or 15 years I should give my life to the Fellowship Church Movement in this country."[93] Thurman was convinced that the interracial church movement would be "my opportunity to have a national leadership at this point. I do not seek such a thing but the degree to which the job fulfills its promise, to that degree will national leadership in this area of religious life be mandatory."[94]

Led by the Fellowship Church, there was a flurry of interracial church foundings in the immediate postwar period. A survey from 1947 found eight interracial congregations of different sorts, with Northern California, for reasons that are not entirely clear, as home to half of them. (In 1945, George Edmund Haynes of the Federal Council of Churches would describe the Bay Area as "a vast interracial experiment station.")[95] Thurman had grave doubts about franchising the Fellowship Church. It would be a great temptation, he would write, when starting a new venture like the Fellowship Church, to try to replicate its success, "to multiply ourselves on the basis of program and commitment and thereby become another denomination."[96] The last thing Thurman wanted to do was to add to the divisions within the Christian church: a nondenominational church becoming just another denomination. Every interracial church would have to be distinct and separate. The impact of the Fellowship Church, Thurman felt, would be through the working of the spirit, by being admired and emulated by others, rather than explicitly duplicating itself. In the end, the best way, and really the only way, to create an integrated Christianity in America would be for local churches everywhere, quietly and without fanfare, to open their doors and pews to people of all races and make the reality of an interracial congregation a fact of utter unremarkableness.[97] If Gandhi believed that one person sufficiently dedicated to the pursuit of the spiritual values of nonviolence could change a continent, Thurman, in a similar way, felt that if the Fellowship Church accumulated enough soul force, this would by itself be enough to transform American religion. Thurman would found only one Fellowship Church, and this would have to be enough.

Perhaps the most delicate question raised by the Fellowship Church and the interracial church movement it spawned was what would happen to existing race-specific churches. Thurman's answer was one of studied ambiguity. In his 1943 essay "The Will to Segregation," Thurman did not speculate in any detail on what the transformed church might look like but suggested that it would not "mean that there are no congregations that are all Negro, or that are all white, but freedom of choice, which is basically a sense of alternatives, will be available to any persons without regard to the faithful perpetuation of the pattern of segregation upon which the Christian church in America is constructed." But many in the interracial church movement would have agreed with Langston Hughes, who visited the interracial churches in San Francisco in the spring of 1944: "These churches here by the Golden Gate seek to apply true Christian ethics to American democracy. They are what I have always thought all churches should be. Since there is no white or colored heaven, white or colored hell, no Jim Crow in eternity as far as I know, I do not see why all peoples should not worship together here on earth."[98] In 1950 Benjamin Mays predicted that "there will be no Negro church in the year 2000 and there will be no white churches. There will exist only Christian churches."[99] For Thurman's part he made clear that, writing in 1959, "the Negro has a rich and redemptive heritage which must not be lost in an effort to become an integrated religious fellowship." Still, he closed *Footprints of a Dream*, his history of the church, with the hope that the church he had founded in San Francisco would help create "a common meeting place in which there would be no Negro church and no white church, but the church of God—that is the task we must work to finish."[100] In the end, for Thurman, the goal of an interracial church movement would permit the creation of a different kind of black church as a part of a new Christianity that did not assign a primary importance to racial difference.

But the promise of the Fellowship Church and that of the interracial church movement was never matched by the reality. The Fellowship Church never really found a way to reach out to the urban poor and always had a predominantly middle-class membership with more whites than blacks.[101] Thurman addressed some of the broader reasons for the failure of the growth of the interracial church movement in the closing pages of *Footprints of a Dream*. Urban geography worked against it, as all cities in the 1950s became increasingly segregated, with whites and blacks living at ever greater spatial removes from one another. Thurman had worked hard to place the Fellowship Church in a neighborhood situation that both whites and blacks would find comfortable, but such locations would become ever more elusive. The church was proving to be the most recalcitrant of all institutions to integrate; whites did not see the need and blacks were reluctant to give up what they had. As the civil rights movement developed, it would become clear that the black church as it was currently constituted, far from being an obstacle to civil rights, would be one of its greatest strengths, and this would include the evangelical and Pentecostal wings of the black church as well as the liberal churches Thurman favored. In the end, Jim Crow would be smashed and routed without Sunday mornings becoming appreciably less segregated. In 1946, W. E. B. Du Bois suggested, after visiting the Fellowship Church and other West Coast interracial churches, that it was a useful development, but he felt that, in the end, religion would be the last American institution to breach the color divide. Perhaps Du Bois was right.[102]

On the other hand, as Alfred Broussard has suggested, it is unfair to fault Thurman and the Fellowship Church for single-handedly failing to eradicate racial discrimination in the church.[103] If a truly interracial church still seems to be a gleam on the far horizon, the mixture of races in Christian worship is not quite the oddity it was in 1944. And perhaps Thurman's other goals in creating the Fellowship Church, reorienting American religion toward a spirituality of radical egalitarianism in race, gender, creed, and belief, have been in part realized in progressive faith communities across North America. Utopias need to be judged by different, less immediate, and more flexible standards. The transformation in American Christianity, in American spirituality, that Thurman sought in the Fellowship Church is still unfolding.

Although Thurman dearly loved the Fellowship Church—it would remain the favorite of all his positions, the only time in his adult life he was really his own boss and had a more or less free hand in shaping his ministry—he moved on, with regret. Throughout his time at the Fellowship Church he spent at least a month, usually in January, back East, preaching as often as three times a day, making up for lost income and keeping up old ties. The East and the world of mainstream higher education, now willing to consider hiring black faculty, beckoned. In 1953 he accepted an offer from Boston University to become dean of chapel, the first black to hold this position at a predominantly white university. Certainly one of his reasons for the move was that he missed mentoring students and worried that by preaching to the same group of people week in and week out, he was not operating "with the maximum possibility of contagion."[104] He remained at Boston University until he retired in 1965 and returned to San Francisco, which would be his home for the rest of his life. Until his death in 1981 he would be mentor and inspiration for several generations of young ministers, from James Lawson to Jesse Jackson. He would continue to elaborate his ideas in his preaching, in his teaching, in seminars, and in books, which were published in increasing profusion. His distinctive spiritual message was elaborated in new ways, including the distribution of tapes of his sermons, which would become a major focus of the Howard Thurman Educational Trust, established in 1965 on his retirement.

It was in this last phase of his life that Thurman would publish most of the works for which he is best remembered: *Jesus and the Disinherited* (1949), *The Creative Encounter* (1955), *The Inward Journey* (1961), *Disciplines of the Spirit* (1963), *The Search for Common Ground* (1971), and *With Head and Heart* (1979), his autobiography. But it was earlier, in the 1930s and 1940s, that he had his biggest influence on the course of the civil rights movement. Never again did he have access to a rising generation of young black progressive Christian activists as he had during the Howard years. By the 1950s, the great Gandhian movement he had helped nurture had come into its own, and the leadership roles would be filled by others. He was content to give advice, to preach, teach, and write a series of quietly influential works focusing on the personal dimensions of spirituality. Only in 1965 would he publish a work directly concerned with civil rights, *The Luminous Darkness*. But by the time it appeared, Thurman's unwavering commitment to integration and interracial cooperation (and his undisguised disdain for black nationalism) made him seem, to many, a man a bit out of touch with his times, and perhaps in some way he was. What made Thurman so valuable as a mentor and model for the nascent civil rights movement in the 1930s and 1940s was that he embraced his own contradictions, seeking the unity of God amid the bitter fractures and divisions of humanity; seeking an intensely spiritual and mystic religion, not as a refuge from the insistent responsibilities of the search for a better world, but as a way to realize it. And he embraced contradictions, in himself and in those around him, because he knew that they were not ultimate.

Martin Luther King Jr. and Jesus and the Disinherited

JESUS AND THE DISINHERITED (1949) is Howard Thurman's most popular and influential book. This is not surprising. As Jonathan Rieder has noted, if some of Thurman's books feel oracular, with "the gossamer feel of reverie, the wispy distance of trance," not *Jesus and the Disinherited*. It seems different, composed of different stuff, more blunt and candid. It has, Rieder suggests, "an earthier quality," one "in keeping with its concern with social oppression. Despite the vibrancy of the humanistic vision, the racial awareness is always present."[1] Of all of Thurman's books (his autobiography obviously excepted), *Jesus and the Disinherited* is the one most rooted in his own life situation, concerned with what it meant to be a black man growing up in the Deep South in the early decades of the twentieth century. In its very focus on himself, his own people, and their suffering, it becomes his most succinct and powerful statement of his belief that Christianity, properly practiced, permits no essential distinction between races, classes, the powerful and the powerless, or even different religions.

None of Thurman's books had a longer period of gestation. The roots of *Jesus and the Disinherited* lie in Thurman's hatred of Atlanta. Although he lived there twice, as an undergraduate and as a faculty member in the late 1920s and early 1930s, Thurman never liked the city. He always found it a haunted place, full of white menace and belligerence. During his undergraduate years at Morehouse from 1919 to 1923 he turned to the Fellowship of Reconciliation and pacifism to appease his unease, his sense of living under a constant, implicit threat of violence. This feeling hadn't changed by the time of his second stint in Atlanta, as a faculty member at Spelman and Morehouse from 1928 to 1932. In 1930 an organization that called itself the American Fascisti Order of the Black Shirts regularly paraded down Peachtree Street with signs such as "Niggers, Back to the Cotton Fields—City Jobs are for White Folks," and then there was the murder of Morehouse undergraduate Dennis Hubert in June 1930, supposedly for insulting a white woman. This was the beginning of a reign of terror, which saw the house of the murdered man's father burned to the ground and the attempted abduction of Thurman's friend and Morehouse colleague Charles Hubert, uncle to the dead man, by a group of masked men. Blacks at Morehouse and in the local community sat up late with shotguns (which as blacks they were not legally allowed to own) waiting for the nightriders. Morehouse president John Hope would comment on the incident, "Must all the colored youth of Atlanta, of Georgia, forever go about in terror of their lives?"[2]

It was in this general atmosphere, while he was teaching a course on "The Life of Christ" at Spelman, that Thurman explored with students "the mind of Jesus as found in the Gospels."[3] He and the young women in the class found themselves "on a personal quest for a sense of our own worth, using the life of Jesus as example. The racial climate was so oppressive and affected us all so intimately that analogies between His life as a Jew in a Roman world and our own were obvious."[4] Thurman was thoroughly familiar with the current scholarship on the life of Jesus by University of Chicago professor Shirley Jackson Case and others treating Jesus as a historical figure, emphasizing his status as a Jew and the very uncomfortable status of all Jews in first century CE Palestine, beset by doubts, ground beneath the boot heels of Roman imperialism.[5] The studies of the historical Jesus offered contemporary blacks cold comfort. The rising political tension in Palestine culminated in a revolt that would fail disastrously, saw the destruction of the temple, and would destroy Jewish rule in Palestine and come within a hairbreadth of ending Judaism all together. Anger at one's oppressors, if allowed to imprudently flare, was more likely to devastate the oppressed than the intended targets.

Thurman had known oppression well enough and intimately enough not to sentimentalize it or valorize it. He had written in

1929 of the "sense of helplessness and despair" that was one of the most common responses to oppression, along with fear and hatred and their constant disguise, deception. To look at the Jews in first century CE Palestine was to see a society that, from the contradictory and complementary impulses to fear the Romans, hate the Romans, and then in some way be like the Romans and beat them at their own game, was pulling itself apart and destroying itself. It was into the midst of this society at this time of crisis that Jesus was born.

We do not know when Thurman first spoke publicly outside of his classes at Spelman of the parallels between the situation faced by Jesus in first-century Palestine and those between blacks in Atlanta and elsewhere in twentieth-century America, but by February 1932, while he was still employed at Morehouse and Spelman, he gave a lecture to a packed auditorium in Atlanta titled "The Kind of Religion the Negro Needs in Times Like These." A brief published account of the talk stated that Thurman had noted that "the religion espoused by the 'lowly Nazarene'" had received "much of its significance from the fact that its exponent was a member of a despised circumscribed minority group." Thurman's talk led to "a lively discussion fired at the speaker from all parts of the house."[6]

Thurman offered another version of the same talk later that year, "The Message of Religion to Underprivileged People," to the City Wide Young People's Forum in Baltimore. In the surviving newspaper account of his talk, Thurman's main point was that "the tragedy of the race was that the idea of his being the world's underdog was sinking into his soul." This was the message of "the press, magazines, schools, and even the church," all "conspiring in one grand course to make us think we are nothing."[7] He was even more pointed in another version of the talk several years later, before a meeting of the NAACP in Washington, D.C., saying that a Christianity presided over by a "white Christ, flaxen-haired angels, and black imps" ingrained this feeling of inferiority. Christianity's most basic commandment was that every person learn to be "honest and sincere" with him- and herself and with others, while every black person knew that "if we were sincere and honest, we could not survive in America."[8] To be black in America was to be forced to live a lie.

But the answer of Jesus to this dilemma was not merely falling back on racial solidarity, searching for a magic recipe for eliminating one's enemies, or thinking that external oppression provided a moral imprimatur to all the acts of the oppressed. Thurman's Jesus was skeptical of all existing institutions and all existing sources of authority and power, Roman and Jewish. Like many young intellectuals in the 1930s, Thurman felt that blacks needed to learn to be skeptical of their own institutions and ask of them deep and searching questions. In a commencement address in April 1931 at Florida Normal and Collegiate Institute in Tallahassee (Thurman's high school alma mater, in the process of transforming itself into a four-year college), he told the graduates that black colleges "must first teach individuals how to think, rather than what to think." Freedom and independent thought go hand in hand. While "no one knows how far thinking will go once started," those in positions of authority have no choice. "We must trust our youth to think." And they must be taught difficult lessons. "Every teacher must be a philosopher, for she is preparing her students to go through a world as hard as flint, and she must prepare them to move through it with relaxation."[9]

Black colleges, all too often, taught their students how to be good Romans in a world in which they will always be viewed and treated as Jews. "When we come out of such institutions of learning, we have the technique of the controlling member of society and not the technique of the controlled member." For those living as part of a minority under a dominant majority, functioning "in society without full participation in its life," religion had a possible answer. "Christianity was started as technique of survival to the underprivileged," Thurman is quoted as saying in Baltimore. "That its saving efficacy might reach the race, you must love without cowardice and fear; you must be wary without hypocrisy, and you must be full of peace without contentment." Back in the days of slavery, when black men and women weren't treated as people but as expendable and disposable automata, "religion came to their rescue. 'You're God's children,' they were told, inspiring into them a hope." This was the message of the religion of Jesus for the underprivileged. Religion could help an individual overcome the feelings of hatred, fear, and deception that denature and distort the oppressed. And when like-minded individuals join together, uncowed, to confront their oppression, the oppressors become afraid.[10]

Thurman's thinking about the religion of Jesus was shaped in the maw of segregation, with black people, about black people, and for black people. But whether by personal design or due to the exigencies of his career, his first publication on the life of Jesus was a version delivered before a white audience at Boston University in early 1935, and was published later that year as "Good News for the Underprivileged" shortly before he left for India. The Boston University lecture advanced his previous work on the life of Jesus, adding the contrast between Jesus and Paul and arguing that the religion of Jesus was the religion of a man without Roman citizenship and therefore subject to the whims of the occupying powers, while Paul could never escape "the consciousness of his [Roman] citizenship, and this would have a profound effect on their respective theological outlooks." The religion of Jesus, "in its social genesis, seems to me to have been a technique of survival for a disinherited minority," while the religion of Paul was an accommodation to the strength of the empowered majority. "Good News for the Underprivileged" contains no appeals to racial solidarity, no discussion of the white Jesus, and very little mention of race at all, save a brief discussion of the Negro spiritual "Alls God's Chillun." However, as all but the most obtuse would have instantly recognized, Thurman had universalized the plight of blacks in mid-twentieth-century America.[11]

Thurman would make frequent recourse to his conception of the religion of Jesus in the years to come. He would mention it often in India, where he told the Ceylonese lawyer who had challenged his right to speak for darker skinned races that he "made a careful distinction between Christianity and the religion of Jesus."[12] He approached the religion of Jesus somewhat differently in the first lecture of The Significance of Jesus series in 1937, not making a contrast with Paul but explaining why Jesus was not satisfied with any of the main Jewish religious options open to him—Pharisee, Sadducee, Zealot, Essene (which he broadly analogized to the Democrats, Republicans, Communists, and the apolitical and otherworldly religious seekers of his own time, respectively). If Jesus was familiar with all the currents of religious and political opinion of his day, he sought his own path.[13] When in the fall of 1938 Eden Theological Seminary invited Thurman to offer a lecture series, he suggested the Message of the Religion of Jesus to the Disinherited before settling on Mysticism and Social Change.[14]

It would be another decade before Thurman was invited to give another sponsored lecture series, five lectures at Samuel Huston College in Austin, Texas, in early 1948. We do not have the actual texts of the lectures as delivered, which he gave extemporaneously. The first lecture was a version of "Good News for the Underprivileged" contrasting the religion of Jesus and Paul. Each of the next three lectures examined one of the triad of torments that plague the life of the underprivileged—fear, deception, and hate. Fear is the product of "violence, precipitate and stark," explicit and implicit, physical and mental, which he likens to a dense fog of the sort very common in San Francisco, a cloud within which one can neither see clearly nor to any great distance. Deception is the most common way those who lack power—little children, women, members of racial minorities—deal with the arbiters of their lives. They withhold, they offer false flattery, they attempt to misdirect their attention. But "the penalty of deception is to *become* a deception," unable to turn off the lying, even to oneself. If hatred is a natural reaction of the disinherited to the powerful, it narrows and restricts, tending to "dry up the springs of creative thought in the life of the creator" so that "the urgent needs of the personality for creative expression are starved to death." Taken together, when the disinherited allow themselves to give in to fear, deception, and hatred, they only reinforce their powerlessness.[15] Speaking to a black audience, he said much about the status of blacks that remained implicit in the 1935 "Good News for the Underprivileged," and how black lives were ruined and stunted from the need to live under such constant, withering pressures. The final lecture was on love and how the religion of Jesus points a way out of the dilemma. At the end of the final lecture, the audience rose and gave him the "kind of ovation I have experienced only once before in my life."[16]

A Methodist publishing house had the rights of first consideration for publishing the lectures, and somewhat to Thurman's surprise and displeasure—he wanted them published by a bigger commercial house and one that was less Southern—they picked up the option. After what Thurman describes as a painful and intrusive editorial process, the manuscript was ready for release. He had originally wanted to call the book, perhaps drawing from black folklore, "The Hounds of Hell," a metaphor that appears frequently in its pages as a description of fear, hate, and deception, and in some ways the hounds of hell are the book's true subject. This was rejected as being too Sherlock Holmesian. He then suggested "The Religion of Jesus and the Disinherited," which would have, unlike the final title, maintained the distinction between the "religion of Jesus" and Christianity. But it was published in early 1949 as *Jesus and the Disinherited*.[17]

In *Jesus and the Disinherited*, as in all of his works, Thurman refused to sentimentalize suffering, as he refused to trivialize the possible benefits of true democracy and fellowship. While he made absolutely clear his abhorrence of segregation and the need for it to be utterly smashed, it was not an overtly political book. As Vincent Harding has noted, while it "is possible to glean elements of a liberation theology from its pages, this richly endowed seminal work can be more accurately and helpfully described as a profound quest for a liberating spirituality, a way of exploring and experiencing those crucial life points where personal and societal transformations are creatively joined."[18] *Jesus and the Disinherited* opens by asking what the significance of Jesus is "to people with their backs against the wall." It closes by answering the same question. They must find answers in their individual suffering, in the suffering of their people, and in the universality and unity of God. They must love their enemies so unsentimentally and so realistically that they become free to dedicate themselves unreservedly to the fight against Jim Crow and all other barriers between races, classes, religions, and denominations, and to find God reflected in the unity of humanity. If the Negro or other representatives of the disinherited can do this, they will be freed from the dominion of fear, deception, and hatred. This is not an easy path, but if the individual "puts at the disposal of the Spirit the needful dedication and passion, he can live effectively in the chaos of the present the high destiny of a son of God."[19]

Jesus and the Disinherited had few initial reviews outside of the black press.[20] But it found its early readers, among them a twenty-year-old divinity student, then in his second year at Crozer Theological Seminary outside Philadelphia. Martin Luther King Jr. had probably known Thurman, at least in passing, since his childhood, and certainly knew of him.[21] He knew of Thurman's work at the Fellowship Church; a copy of a 1949 issue of the *Growing Edge*, the church newsletter, survives in his papers.[22] That fall he was taking a course in systematic theology with George Washington Davis, a 1928 graduate of Rochester Theological Seminary, classmate of Thurman, and an adherent of the Social Gospel. In an assignment completed between the end of November 1949 and mid-February 1950 King included the following passage:

> The Christian view of God as Father immediately gives the Christian a sense of belonging. When the Christian comes to believe that he is a child of an all loving Father he feels that he counts, that he belongs. He senses the confirmation of his roots, and even death becomes a little thing. Let me give an illustration. During the years of slavery in America it is said that after a hard days work the slaves would often hold secret religious meetings. All during the working day they were addressed with unnecessary vituperations and insulting epithets. But as they gathered in these meetings they gained a renewed faith as the old unlettered minister would come to his triumphant climax saying: "you—you are not niggers. You—you are not slaves. You are God's children." This established for them a true ground of personal dignity. The awareness of being a child of God tends to stabilize the ego and bring new courage.[23]

This passage was borrowed, more or less verbatim, from *Jesus and the Disinherited*.[24] It was not the only time during his course with

Davis that King borrowed from Thurman's book.[25] King's now notorious practice of unacknowledged textual appropriations in his student papers and graduate work has been extensively discussed, and there is no need to review this extensive literature, though we should add that the extent of King's borrowings from *Jesus and the Disinherited* have not previously been noted. Imitation, and even plagiarism, can be the sincerest form of flattery and an important way of learning. This was one of the few times in his student papers that King made any reference to African American religion or cited, however obliquely, another African American religious thinker.

As Clayborne Carson has noted, the question of when King became acquainted with pacifism is vexed, since his own autobiographical accounts, primarily written for a white audience, slighted Thurman and other African American religious figures who were major influences on his thinking and probably exaggerated the extent to which King was a thorough student of Gandhi prior to his years in Montgomery. In *Stride Toward Freedom*, King discussed his exposure to pacifism during his years at Crozier: his initial skepticism (despite being "deeply moved") at a pacifist speech by A. J. Muste in late 1949, and then being converted to pacifism in the spring of 1950 after hearing Mordecai Wyatt Johnson preach on Gandhi at the Fellowship House in Philadelphia (the descendant of the same interracial fellowship at which Thurman had frequently preached). He learned that the love-ethic of Jesus was not only about personal interactions but was also "a potential instrument for social and collective transformation." The final chapter of *Jesus and the Disinherited* opens with a call for the love-ethic of Jesus to be extended "across the barriers of class, race, and condition" in order to obliterate segregation, "a complete ethical and moral evil." *Jesus and the Disinherited* is not, explicitly, a pacifist tract. But after he read *Jesus and the Disinherited* in late 1949, King certainly was familiar with the principles of Christian radical nonviolence and their crucial importance for the status of the Negro.[26]

When Thurman became the first tenured black faculty member at Boston University in the fall of 1953, it was King's last year of residence in Boston, and although King did not take any courses with Thurman, the two men were acquainted. In his autobiography Thurman writes of watching the 1953 World Series together (when presumably both men rooted in a losing cause for the Brooklyn Dodgers against the still lily-white New York Yankees). Thurman wrote that his wife (who seems to have been on closer terms with King and his new bride, Coretta Scott King, than her husband) discussed "very seriously" with King the possibility of him assuming the pulpit at Fellowship Church, a discussion that ended when King indicated his decision to go to Montgomery.[27] Evidence that Thurman had yet to take the full measure of King can be found in his response in December 1954 to Albert Dent, president of Dillard University in New Orleans, who wanted to know whether King would be a good candidate for dean of chapel. While Thurman allowed that "he has made a good record here in the university and I understand that he is a good preacher," he went on to recommend someone else.[28]

King was quoting Thurman in his sermons even before the latter arrived in Boston.[29] King certainly heard Thurman preach at Marsh Chapel in Boston. Philip Lenud, King's roommate at Boston University, told Lewis Baldwin that King "loved and respected Thurman":

> I'd take him with me sometimes to hear Thurman speak in chapel when we were students in Boston. He always listened carefully when Thurman was speaking, and would shake his head in amazement at Thurman's deep wisdom. Martin didn't have mystical orientation, and he didn't dwell too much on metaphysics. He was concerned with the pragmatics of existence, and the relationship of people "with God in the valley." But he enjoyed Thurman and he loved him, because he knew that Thurman was saying some great things. The ontological meaning of what Thurman said went right over on many folks, including Martin.[30]

We have heard similar comments before about how Thurman's sermons were at once profoundly moving while going over the heads of listeners, though it seems unlikely that anyone with King's theological sophistication would have had any problem understanding Thurman's message. In any event, over the next several years there are numerous instances of King quoting, borrowing, and paraphrasing Thurman's work.[31] In the summer of 1955 King invited Thurman to be the speaker at the next summer's Men's Day at the Dexter Avenue Baptist Church in Montgomery, but Thurman had to turn down the invitation because of prior commitments.[32]

In time, they would develop a closer friendship, with Thurman in a familiar role as a behind-the-scenes advisor. After King was almost killed in an assassination attempt in September 1958 in Harlem by a deranged black woman, Thurman had a sudden "visitation" and knew he had to come down from Boston to see King immediately, which he did. His advice to King was to get away from the movement for a while. This would "give him time away from the immediate pressure of the movement to reassess himself in relation to the cause, to rest his body and mind with healing detachment, and to take a long look that only solitary brooding can provide." They did not discuss "in depth the progress, success, or failure of the movement itself." Instead they discussed King's relation to the civil rights movement, which had "become an organism with a life of its own to which he must relate in fresh or extraordinary ways or be swallowed up by it."[33] King wrote Thurman shortly thereafter that their meeting had been "a great spiritual lift" and was "of inestimable value in giving me the strength and courage to face the future of that trying period." King told Thurman he was feeling much better and he "was following your advice on the question, "'where do I go from here?'"[34] The months in convalescence after the assassination attempt were, as Taylor Branch writes, "a period of relative stillness unique to his entire adult life" during which he delivered no speeches or sermons away from Montgomery for many weeks.[35] This period culminated with King, following in Thurman's footsteps, taking his own five-week pilgrimage to India in February 1959.

Let us return to the events of a few years before, to the evening of December 5, 1955, the day a group of black civic leaders in Montgomery formed the Montgomery Improvement Association to conduct (initially) a one-day boycott of the local buses to protest the arrest of Rosa Parks. After a testy meeting, the association picked King, a relatively little-known newcomer, to be its head. Having no time to prepare an address, he went to the Holt Street Baptist Church to address the overflow crowd, with a few points and several familiar tropes running through his head. The speech would be the turning point of his life, and perhaps the turning point in the long struggle of blacks for racial justice in America. In it he spoke of the events of the last few days; the arrest of Rosa Parks, the aims of the boycott, the need for nonviolence, and the need for the protests to be informed by "teachings of Jesus." As he moved to his conclusion, he told his audience that they must love their enemies, and that the justice they were demanding was just another form of love. He told the crowd, "We, the disinherited of this land, we who have been oppressed so long, are tired of going through the long night of captivity. And now we are reaching out for the daybreak of freedom and justice and equality."[36] That evening, the words and thoughts of Howard Thurman were with Martin Luther King Jr.

According to Lerone Bennett, King reread *Jesus and the Disinherited* in the months after the boycott began and kept a copy with him on his travels in the years ahead.[37] Perhaps King reread it so frequently his copy fell apart. Unlike some other works by Thurman, such as an inscribed copy of *Deep River* (1955), which can be seen today in the archives of Atlanta University, complete with King's underlining and marginal comments, no copy of *Jesus and the Disinherited* survives in his personal library.[38] But for those of us who have come to admire Thurman and love his words, Lerone Bennett's story evokes a pleasing, romantic image. Martin Luther King Jr.—late at night, weary on his endless journey, his energy flagging—falling into a chair, opening his battered copy of *Jesus and the Disinherited* at random, seeking inspiration and renewal. As Gary Dorrien has suggested, regarding King drawing sustenance from Thurman's words and thoughts, "progressive American Christianity has no greater legacy."[39]

Acknowledgments

THE TWO OF US met in the fall of 1995. We do not remember the subject of our first conversation, but it probably was about Howard Thurman. We had both just moved to Rochester, New York, hired as editors on the Howard Thurman Papers Project. We have both gone on to do a number of different things in the past decade and a half, but despite a few lengthy hiatuses, we are still both editors for the Howard Thurman Papers Project, and we have followed the project in its peregrination from Rochester to Atlanta and now to Boston. By now, Howard Thurman feels like an old friend, a regular part of our lives, and this book is our attempt to provide our sense of why Howard Thurman is important and should be known to a wider audience. This book is not an official product of the Howard Thurman Papers Project, but it is in every way a shoot from its fertile roots. Without it and the people we have worked with on the project, this book would not have been possible. We hope this book can serve as a portal to the documentary edition of Thurman's works that the project has created.

The Howard Thurman Papers Project is the brainchild of Walter Earl Fluker, and he has nurtured it since the beginning with his deep love of Howard Thurman and his identification with Thurman's broader philosophical and theological project. We are both greatly in his debt. We have worked closely with two managing editors. Catherine Tumber, in Rochester, created the intellectual and practical structure for the dense archival foundation on which the project, and this book, stands. In Atlanta, Kai Jackson-Issa has been a constant joy and pleasure to work with, and has gently tolerated our occasional eccentricities and mood swings. And we have worked with a host of other staff members, too numerous to mention (or remember) in full, among them Jamison Collier, Michelle Meggs, Michael Sauter, and Rebecca Edwards. They have all been wonderful colleagues and friends. At Beacon Press, Amy Caldwell and Alex Kapitan have been exemplary editors, collaborators in shaping the manuscript and a pleasure to work with. Doe Coover has been our supportive and always helpful agent. Portions of this manuscript have been presented before the RUSH (Rochester United States Historians) Group.

In the fall of 2009, at the release of *The Papers of Howard Washington Thurman, Volume 1: My People Need Me*, we were privileged to meet a number of members of the Thurman family, including his daughter Olive Thurman Wong. We hope she, and everyone whom we have met and worked with during our association with Howard Thurman, appreciate our book. Our references to primary documents, unless otherwise noted, are from the holdings of the Howard Thurman Papers Project, which are copies of documents from several repositories, primarily the Howard Thurman Papers in the archives of Boston University.

At the core of *Visions of a Better World* is Howard Thurman's time in India and South Asia from 1935 to 1936 and his famous meeting, the first for an African American, with Mahatma Gandhi. More broadly, this is a historical and biographical study of Howard Thurman roughly covering the first half of the twentieth century until the early 1950s. Most of those who have written on Thurman have been theologians and religious writers. We are both historians, and while one, of course, cannot write about Howard Thurman without deeply considering his religious thought, we are most interested in placing Thurman within the broader contours of American and African American history and to make the case, as our subtitle indicates, that he was a critical figure in the development of a distinctive African American understanding of the ideas of radical nonviolence and Gandhian resistance in the 1930s and 1940s.

We have a few personal debts to acknowledge. Peter wants to thank, as always, his beautiful and multitalented wife, Jane DeLuca, who has recently added a doctorate in nursing to her many accomplishments.

Quinton wants to thank his children, John, Jillian, Jacqueline, and James, and his wife, Kimberly.

Howard Thurman closed his autobiography *With Head and Heart* with a short meditation, which we excerpt. It is a reminder of the difficulties that all of us face in trying to understand our own lives and how much greater is the challenge to write about another human being, especially one who lived a life as interiorly as did Howard Thurman:

> No one shares the secret of a life; no one enters into the heart of the mystery. . . . And this is the strangest of all the paradoxes of the human adventure: we live inside all experience, but we are permitted to bear witness only to the outside. Such is the riddle of life and the story of the passing of our days.

Notes

Works and individuals frequently cited have been identified by the following abbreviations:

FOAD   *Footprints of a Dream: The Story of the Church for the Fellowship of All Peoples.* Howard Thurman. New York: Harper, 1959.

HT   Howard Thurman.

HTPP   The Howard Thurman Papers Project, Boston University, Boston, MA.

PHWTV1   *The Papers of Howard Washington Thurman.* Walter Earl Fluker, ed. Vol. 1, *My People Need Me, June 1918–March 1936.* Columbia: University of South Carolina Press, 2009.

PHWTV2   *The Papers of Howard Washington Thurman.* Walter Earl Fluker, ed. Vol. 2. Columbia: University of South Carolina Press, forthcoming.

PHWTV3   *The Papers of Howard Washington Thurman.* Walter Earl Fluker, ed. Vol. 3. Columbia: University of South Carolina Press, forthcoming.

PHWTV4   *The Papers of Howard Washington Thurman.* Walter Earl Fluker, ed. Vol. 4. Columbia: University of South Carolina Press, forthcoming.

PMLKJ   *The Papers of Martin Luther King Jr.* 6 vols. Clayborne Carson, ed. Berkeley: University of California Press, 1992–.

WHAH   *With Head and Heart: The Autobiography of Howard Thurman.* Howard Thurman. New York: Harcourt Brace, 1979.

INTRODUCTION

1. "Pilgrimage of Friendship," *PHWTV*1, 186.

2. Although the Negro Delegation traveled not only to India but also to Ceylon and Burma, the trip was commonly referred to by Thurman and the other delegates as "the India trip," and we will follow this convention. All cities and territorial divisions are referred to by their names current in 1935 and 1936.

3. "Detailed Schedule," *PHWTV*1, 283–99.

4. "With Our Negro Guests," *PHWTV*1, 337.

5. "Committee on the Negro Delegation in India," 10 April 1934, HTPP.

6. "India Report," *PHWTV*2.

7. "Colombo Journal," *PHWTV*1, 300–305.

8. *WHAH*, 112–13.

9. Ibid., 122.

10. "Colombo Journal," 301.

11. *WHAH*, 112–13.

12. "India Report." Thurman noted in his 1938 report that "a Student Movement secretary who was traveling with us up to Masulipatam [on India's east coast] found it impossible to occupy a room in the section reserved for Europeans at the Bezwada Junction" where the delegation was accommodated.

13. "Colombo Journal."

14. *WHAH*, 115.

15. "Colombo Journal."

16. Ibid., 302. We have expanded Thurman's frequent shorthand "X-ianity" in his "Colombo Journal" to the more standard "Christianity."

17. "Colombo Journal."

18. Ibid.

19. *FOAD*, 23.

20. "Christian Ideal: 'Under Privileged' Negroes," *Ceylon Daily News*, 29 October 1935. Thurman evidently opened his talk by discussing the encounter: "Professor Thurman said he had been asked by a student of a Colombo College how it happened that he, an American Negro, was interested in Christianity. Thurman then provided his audience, by means of an answer, a version of his recent paper, 'Good News for the Underprivileged.'"

21. "Colombo Journal."

22. Ibid.

23. Although no record of the precise questions asked about Scottsboro in Colombo survives, the Negro Delegation wrote an article that was published in March 1936 in the *Intercollegian*, a magazine of the American Student Christian Movement. This included a list of some of the questions they had been asked by Indian students, and the questions quoted here are drawn from the article "Our Delegation in India," *Intercollegian*, March 1936.

24. "Colombo Journal"; "Our Delegation in India."

25. In the first published account, appearing in a Colombo newspaper within a week of the encounter, he is merely called (by the reporter) a "student of a Colombo college"; see "Christian Ideal: 'Under Privileged' Negroes." In Thurman's journal of his time in Colombo, the man is called a "young lawyer"; see "Colombo Journal." In the report he submitted to the India Committee, written in early 1938, he is a law student; see "India Report." In Thurman's *Jesus and the Disinherited* (1949; repr., Boston: Beacon Press, 1996), 14, and in *FOAD*, 23, he is elevated to principal of the Law College, and in Thurman's autobiography, the man is the chairman of the law club who had in addition requested the topic for Thurman to discuss. *WHAH*, 113.

26. *FOAD*, 25.

27. This account of the encounter is a composite, derived from several sources: "Christian Ideal: 'Under Privileged' Negroes"; "Colombo Journal"; *FOAD*, 23–24; *Jesus and the Disinherited*, 15; *WHAH*, 113–14.

28. This was somewhat unfair to Newton (1725–1807) who was not a practicing Christian at the time of his involvement in the slave trade, and whose revulsion at the practice eventually helped prompt his conversion. In his later years he was a leader in the antislavery movement that resulted in the abolition of the British slave trade in 1808.

29. Thurman, *Jesus and the Disinherited*, 15.

30. "Colombo Journal"; *WHAH*, 114–15.

31. Christopher H. Evans, *Liberalism without Illusions: Renewing an American Christian Tradition* (Waco, TX: Baylor University Press, 2010), 68–73.

32. See "Man and the World of Nature," *PHWTV*2.

33. Howard Thurman, "Contribution of Baptist Schools to Negro Youth" (1938), *PHWTV*2.

34. "Good News for the Underprivileged," *PHWTV*1, 263–70.

35. Thurman would write in his autobiography about the frequent questioning of Christianity he heard in Asia: "I knew that I would have to admit what they were saying to be true, even as I kept on affirming my own deeply felt religious faith. Challenged as I was in the vastness of Indian life, all the thinking and working out of this problem that I had done over the years on the word of Jesus to the disinherited now came to the fore." *WHAH*, 118.

CHAPTER ONE: SOUTHERN BOY, MOREHOUSE MAN, ROCHESTER SCHOLAR

1. "Colombo Journal," *PHWTV*1, 300.

2. *WHAH*, 8.

3. Ibid., 8.

4. Ibid., 263.

5. For a study of Thurman that sees him as a combination of a rationalist and a "modern shaman," see Mozella Mitchell, *Spiritual Dynamics of Howard Thurman's Theology* (Bristol, IN: Wyndham Hall Press, 1985).

6. W. E. B. Du Bois, "The Souls of Black Folk," in *Writings* (New York: Library of America, 1986), 360, 507.

7. Howard Thurman, *The Luminous Darkness: A Personal Interpretation of the Anatomy of Segregation and the Ground of Hope* (New York: Harper and Row, 1965), x.

8. For evidence that Thurman was born in West Palm Beach, see "Biographical Essay," *PHWTV*1, xxxi, lxxx.

9. Ibid., xxxiii.

10. *WHAH*, 4–6; *FOAD*, 15–16.

11. See "The Fascist Masquerade," *PHWTV*3.

12. *FOAD*, 17.

13. "Biographical Essay," xxxii; *WHAH*, 231–32.

14. Ephesians 6:5. See also Colossians 3:22.

15. Thurman, *Jesus and the Disinherited*, 30–31, 50 (see intro., n. 25); *WHAH*, 20.

16. *WHAH*, 20.

17. Ibid., 17.

18. *FOAD*, 17.

19. *WHAH*, 9; "Biographical Essay," xxxvii–xxxix.

20. Ibid., xxxviii–xxxix.

21. Ibid, xxxviii; Ralph Bunche, *The Political Status of the Negro in the Age of FDR* (Chicago: University of Chicago Press, 1973), 451–54, 480–82.

22. *WHAH*, 23; "Biographical Essay," xxxix. The two would remain close, and often consulted one another on issues of the day. HT would return to Daytona Beach in 1955 to deliver the eulogy at her funeral.

23. *WHAH*, 15, 16.

24. Ibid., 8.

25. Ibid., 9.

26. Ibid., 17.

27. HT to Mordecai Wyatt Johnson, 18 June 1918, *PHWTV*1, 1–4.

28. Ibid.; *WHAH*, 24; "Biographical Essay"; "Academic Transcripts," *PHWTV*1, xl–xli, 342–43; "Florida People Read the Defender," *Chicago Defender*, 19 June 1915.

29. "Biographical Essay," xli. By the time Thurman was a senior his school would have a new name and new location, the Florida Normal and Industrial Institute in St. Augustine.

30. *WHAH*, 24–25.

31. HT to Mordecai Wyatt Johnson, 18 June 1918, *PHWTV*1, 2.

32. He would write in 1951 that God "does not stand apart as some mighty spectator but is in the process and the facts, ever shaping them (in ways that we can understand and in ways beyond our powers to grasp)." Howard Thurman, *Deep is the Hunger: Meditations for Apostles of Sensitiveness* (1951; repr., Richmond, IN: Friends United Press, 1973), 2.

33. *WHAH*, v.

34. Ibid., 28; HT to Ethel Simons, 4 June 1919, *PHWTV*1, 6–7.

35. Mordecai Wyatt Johnson has yet to receive what he so richly deserves, a comprehensive biography, but see Richard I. McKinney, *Mordecai, The Man and His Message: The Story of Mordecai Wyatt Johnson* (Washington, DC: Howard University Press, 1997); Zachery R. Williams, *In Search of the Talented Tenth: Howard University Public Intellectuals and the Dilemmas of Race, 1926–1970* (Columbia: University of Missouri Press, 2009), 40–79.

36. HT to Mordecai Wyatt Johnson, 18 June 1918.

37. Mordecai Wyatt Johnson to HT, 8 July 1918, *PHWTV*1, 4–5.

38. *WHAH*, 35.

39. "Proposal for a Negro Scholarship Fund," *PHWTV*1, 22–24.

40. Leroy Davis, *A Clashing of the Soul: John Hope and the Dilemmas of African American Leadership and Black Higher Education in the Early Twentieth Century* (Athens: University of Georgia Press, 1998), 258–59; *WHAH*.

41. *WHAH*, 40–43.

42. Ibid., 43–44; "Biographical Essay," lvii. The texts for the course were John Dewey, *How We Think* (Boston: Heath, 1910), and Laurence Buermeyer et al., *An Introduction to Reflective Thinking* (New York: Houghton Mifflin, 1923). Thurman's course "An Introduction to Reflective Thinking" was described in the course catalogue as "a study of types of fundamental beliefs, criticism of their bases, and consideration of reason for their modifications." *Catalogue of Spelman College, 1928–1929* (Atlanta, 1928), 39.

43. *WHAH*, 35; "The Torch," *PHWTV*1, 25–30.

44. *WHAH*, 34; "The Athenaeum Writings," *PHWTV*1, 10–16.

45. For the rhetorical traditions that informed Thurman's address, see David Howard-Pitney, *The Afro-American Jeremiad: Appeals for Justice in America* (Philadelphia: Temple University Press, 1990); Kevin Kelly Gaines, *Uplifting the Race: Black Leadership, Politics, and Culture in the Twentieth Century* (Chapel Hill: University of North Carolina Press, 1996).

46. "Our Challenge," *PHWTV*1, 20–22.

47. "The Torch"; "Themes and Variations," Gamewell Valentine, *Atlanta Daily World*, 31 May 1937.

48. For background on blacks in the YMCA and YWCA, see Nina Mjagkij, *Light in the Darkness: African Americans and the YMCA, 1859–1946* (Lexington: University of Kentucky Press, 1994); Judith Weisenfeld, *African American Women and Christian Activism: New York's Black YWCA, 1904–1946* (Cambridge, MA: Harvard University Press, 1997); Nancy Robertson, *Christian Sisterhood, Race Relations, and the YWCA, 1906–1946* (Urbana: University of Illinois Press, 2007).

49. *WHAH*, 36; "'Relaxation' and Race Conflict," *PHWTV*1, 146.

50. *WHAH*, 37.

51. Ibid., 46.

52. Ibid., 47.

53. Ibid., 48.

54. Ibid., 53–54; Howard Thurman, *Mysticism and the Experience of Love* (Wallingford, PA: Pendle Hill, 1961).

55. *WHAH*, 54.

56. Christopher H. Evans, *The Kingdom Is Always But Coming: A Life of Walter Rauschenbusch* (Grand Rapids, MI: William B. Eerdmans, 2004), 255.

57. Cited in Grant Wacker, *Augustus H. Strong and the Dilemma of Historical Consciousness* (Macon, GA: Mercer University Press, 1985), 106. For Strong, Cross's main shortcoming was that he viewed "scripture as only the record of man's gropings after God instead of being primarily God's revelation to man."

58. *WHAH*, 55. For the influence of Cross on HT, see Luther E. Smith Jr., *Howard Thurman: The Mystic as Prophet* (1991; repr., Richmond, IN: Friends United Press, 2007), 22–29.

59. "Virgin Birth," *PHWTV*1, 31–36.

60. "Can It Be Truly Said That the Existence of a Supreme Spirit Is a Scientific Hypothesis?" *PHWTV*1, 54–67.

61. "The White Problem," *PHWTV*3; *WHAH*, 58.

62. Ibid., 51–52. Thurman would discover another informal rule in his senior year, when as class president he was asked to be the pallbearer for the funeral of a member of the RTS maintenance staff. Just before the funeral, the president of the seminary pulled him aside and told him that this just wasn't done.

63. Ibid., 49–51. For the Klan in New York State, see "Ku Klux Klan," in Peter Eisenstadt, ed., *The Encyclopedia of New York State* (Syracuse, NY: Syracuse University Press, 2005).

64. "Biographical Essay," xciv–xcvii.

65. "The Sphere of the Church's Responsibility in Social Reconstruction," *PHWTV*1, 41–43.

66. "The Perils of Immature Piety," *PHWTV*1, 47–52.

67. "College and Color" and "Let Ministers Be Christians!" *PHWTV*1, 36–41, 43–46.

68. "College and Color," 37–38; "Let Ministers Be Christians!" 46.

69. "College and Color," 37. For the earliest recounting of the Nigerian Muslim in Roanoke, see "India Report," *PHWTV*2.

70. "College and Color," 39; Gary Dorrien, *The Making of American Liberal Theology: Idealism, Realism and Modernity, 1900–1950* (Louisville, KY, and London: Westminster John Knox Press, 2003), 558.

71. *WHAH*, 59–60.

72. Ibid., 59. For HT on Schreiner, see Howard Thurman, ed., *A Track to the Water's Edge: The Olive Schreiner Reader* (New York: Harper and Row, 1973), xi–xxxviii. For Schreiner, see Ruth First and Ann Scott, *Olive Schreiner: A Biography* (New Brunswick, NJ: Rutgers University Press, 1990).

73. Thurman, *Track to the Water's Edge*, xi, xxix.

74. Ibid., xviii–xix.

75. Ibid., xxviii.

76. Ibid., xxxii.

77. "The Basis of Sex Morality: An Inquiry into the Attitude toward Premarital Sexual Morality among Various Peoples and an Analysis of Its True Basis," *PHWTV*1, 71–107.

78. *WHAH*, 61–62.

CHAPTER TWO: STARTING A CAREER

1. "Biographical Essay," *PHWTV*1, lxii–lxiii; *WHAH*, 53–54.

2. *WHAH*, 65.

3. "Biographical Essay," lxv HT to Thomas W. Graham, 9 January 1927, *PHWTV*1, 70.

4. "Oberlin College News," *Pittsburgh Courier*, 19 March 1927.

5. *WHAH*, 65–69.

6. Ibid., 71–74.

7. HT to Mordecai Wyatt Johnson, 21 September 1926, *PHWTV*1; Lester Walton, "Negro Minister Fills Pulpit at Vassar," *PHWTV*1, 109–10, 122–24; "Lone Star News," *Chicago Defender*, 3 May 1928; "Ask Equal Chance For All Races," *Pittsburgh Courier*, 22 January 1927; "Y Workers to Meet at Kings Mountain," *Pittsburgh Courier*, 28 May 1927; "At Howard," *Baltimore Afro-American*, 4 February 1928; "Date Announced for Annual Student Confab," *Chicago Defender*, 2 June 1928; "'Y' Workers to Meet July 6–21," *Pittsburgh Courier*, 23 June 1928.

8. For the conference, see Francis P. Miller, ed., *Religion on the Campus: Report of the National Student Conference, Milwaukee, December 28, 1926, to January 1, 1927* (New York: Association Press, 1927).

9. "Finding God," *PHWTV*1, 110–14.

10. HT to Mordecai Wyatt Johnson, 8 April 1927, *PHWTV*1.

11. HT to Mordecai Wyatt Johnson, 20 September 1927, *PHWTV*1, 117–18.

12. "Higher Education and Religion," *PHWTV*1, 118–22.

13. Ibid.

14. "The Task of the Negro Ministry," *PHWTV*1, 139–44.

15. HT to Mordecai Wyatt Johnson, 20 September 1927.

16. "The Task of the Negro Ministry."

17. *WHAH*, 74.

18. Rufus M. Jones, *Finding the Trail of Life* (New York: Macmillan, 1927), 10.

19. Rufus M. Jones, *Social Law in the Spiritual World: Studies in Human and Divine Inter-Relationship* (Philadelphia: John C. Winston, 1904), 9–10.

20. Dorrien, *Making of American Liberal Theology*, 369, 364–71 passim (see ch. 1, n. 70).

21. Ibid., 369–70.

22. Leigh Eric Schmidt, *Restless Souls: The Making of American Spirituality, From Emerson to Oprah* (San Francisco: Harper, 2005), 233.

23. HT to John Hope, July 13, 1926, HTPP.

24. *WHAH*, 76.

25. HT to Mordecai Wyatt Johnson, 21 May 1928, *PHWTV*1, 124; *WHAH*, 76.

26. *WHAH*, 77.

27. HT to Rufus Jones, 4 June 1929, *PHWTV*1, 152–53; *WHAH*, 76–77.

28. For the importance of religious experience in Thurman's student papers, see "Can It Be Truly Said?" 62–63. For Cross's critique of mysticism, see *PHWTV*1, 64.

29. "The Strength of Corporate Worship," sermon delivered 8 April 1951, HTPP.

30. For Thurman and the development of American spirituality, see Schmidt, *Restless Souls*, 266–68.

31. For courses on mysticism at Howard and Morehouse, see "Introduction," *PHWTV*2, and *Morehouse College, Annual Catalogue, 1930–31* (Atlanta, 1930), 91. The latter describes the course "Christian Mysticism," offered a year after Thurman studied with Jones, as "designed to give students a clear conception of the philosophical and practical implications of Christian mysticism." His only publication on mysticism in the mid-1930s was a short review in 1934 of Mary Anita Ewer's *A Survey of Mystical Symbolism*, *PHWTV*1, 203–4.

32. HT to Mordecai Wyatt Johnson, 23 May 1928, *PHWTV*1, 125.

33. Davis, *A Clashing of the Soul*, 292–93, 313–14 (see ch. 1, n. 40).

34. Ibid., 292, 297–302.

35. *WHAH*, 78–80.

36. Ibid., 79.

37. "Biographical Essay," cii.

38. *WHAH*, 82–83.

39. Lucius I. Jones Jr., "Society Slants," *Atlanta Daily World*, 24 February 24 1932; "Ministers' Confab at Shaw Closed by Thurman," *Atlanta Daily World*, 20 August 1932; Milton Randolph, "Holmes to Discuss Demos at 27 Club Sunday," *Atlanta Daily World*, 20 May 1932.

40. Lucius Jones, "Society Slants," *Atlanta Daily World*, 10 April 1932.

41. Lucius Jones, "Society Slants," *Atlanta Daily World*, 7 October 1932.

42. For a discussion of the roots of his most important work, *Jesus and the Disinherited*, in Atlanta in the early 1930s, see the epilogue.

43. Howard Thurman, "General Introduction," *Deep River and the Negro Spiritual Speaks of Life and Death* (Richmond, IN: Friends United Press, 1975), iii–iv.

44. Raymond Wolters, *New Negro on Campus: Black College Rebellions of the 1920s* (Princeton, NJ: Princeton University Press).

45. James Weldon Johnson, "Preface to the Second Book of Negro Spirituals," *Writings* (New York: Library of America, 2004), 737. Disdain of the spirituals among some black intellectuals dates back to at least the turn of the twentieth century. See Doug Seroff, "The Fisk Jubilee Quartet with John Work II," *There Breathes a Hope*, Archeophone Records 5020.

46. "The Message of the Spirituals," *PHWTV*1, 127.

47. See for instance, Alain Locke, "The Negro Spirituals," in Alain Locke, ed., *The New Negro* (1925; repr., New York: Atheneum, 1992), 199–213.

48. "Religious Ideas in Negro Spirituals," *Christendom* 4, no. 4 (Autumn 1939): 515–28.

49. "The Message of the Spirituals," 131–32.

50. "The Sphere of the Church's Responsibility in Social Reconstruction," *PHWTV*I, 41–43. For the history of the Fellowship of Reconciliation, see Joseph Kip Kosek, *Acts of Conscience: Christian Nonviolence and Modern American Democracy* (New York: Columbia University Press, 2009).

51. "Christmas and the Spirit of Survival," sermon delivered 21 December 1952, HTPP.

52. Devere Allen, "Introduction: Pacifism Old and New" and "The New White Man," xviii, 49–64; A. J. Muste, "Pacifism and Class War," 91–102; George L. Collins, "Pacifism and Social Injustice," 103, 114, all in Devere Allen, ed., *Pacifism in the Modern World* (Garden City, NY: Doubleday, 1929).

53. "'Relaxation' and Race Conflict," *PHWTV*1, 144–52.

54. For possible influences from religious psychology and mysticism literature on Thurman's notion of relaxation, especially the work of Union Theological Seminary psychologist George Coe, whom Thurman frequently cited in these years, see *PHWTV*1, 145, 152.

55. *PHWTV*1, lxix–lxxiii.

56. Mordecai Wyatt Johnson to HT, 22 September 1926, *PHWTV*1, 108–9.

57. See "Introduction," *PHWTV*2. On Howard, see Walter Dyson, *Howard University: The Capstone of Negro Education* (Washington, DC: Howard University, 1941); Rayford W. Logan, *Howard University: The First Hundred Years* (New York: New York University Press, 1969).

58. *WHAH*, 87.

59. Logan, *Howard University*, 51.

60. For Thurman's intellectual life in the 1930s, see Jonathan Scott Holloway, *Confronting the Veil: Abram Harris Jr., E. Franklin Frazier, and Ralph Bunche, 1919–1941* (Chapel Hill: University of North Carolina Press, 2002); Williams, *In Search of the Talented Tenth* (see chap. 1, n. 35).

61. "A 'Native Son' Speaks," *PHWTV*2.

CHAPTER THREE: PLANNING THE PILGRIMAGE OF FRIENDSHIP

1. HT to Channing Tobias, 21 February 1938, *PHWTV*2.

2. *WHAH*, 104; "India Report" (see chap. 1, n. 6). Secondary accounts of Thurman's time with the Negro Delegation start with his own autobiographical writings, especially *FOAD*, 22–25, and *WHAH*, 103–36. Other accounts include Sudarshan Kapur, *Raising Up a Prophet: The African American Encounter with Gandhi* (Boston: Beacon Press, 1992), 83–98; and Gerald Horne, *The End of Empires: African Americans and India* (Philadelphia: Temple University, 2008), 96–108.

3. "India Report."

4. *WHAH*, 104.

5. *WHAH*, 104; "India Report."

6. Winnifred Wygal to HT, 16 May 1934, *PHWTV*1, 192–93.

7. Marion Cuthbert, *Juliette Derricotte* (New York: The Woman's Press, 1933), 32.

8. HT to Winnifred Wygal, 24 March 1934, *PHWTV*1, 178–79.

9. Herbert King to HT, 11 October 1934, HTPP. King, who had worked many years as a YMCA national secretary to Negro colleges in the South, and who had tense relations with his higher-ups, knew whereof he spoke.

10. HT to Grace Virginia Imes, 5 December 1934, *PHWTV*1, 225–26.

11. Shelton Hale Bishop to HT, 1 May 1935, HTPP.

12. Paul Hutchinson to Winnifred Wygal, 14 March 1935, *PHWTV*1, 245–46.

13. Horne, *End of Empires*, 88.

14. April meditations by Sue Bailey Thurman in Jean Beaven Abernethy, ed., *Meditations for Women* (New York: Abingdon, 1947), 98.

15. For Thurman's eulogy at Juliette Derricotte's funeral, which unfortunately exists only in a brief excerpt, see the headnote to "Commencement Address Delivered at the A&I State College," *PHWTV*2.

16. For Sue Bailey Thurman's work on the Juliette Derricotte Scholarship in the period 1936 to 1939, see "Biographical Essay," *PHWTV*2.

17. Biographical information is taken from Myra Scovel, *I Must Speak: The Biography of Augustine Ralla Ram* (Allahabad: North India Christian Literature Society, 1961), 8 and passim.

18. "A Great Christian from India," *Spelman Messenger* 48 (October 1931): 24–25.

19. "A Great Christian from India."

20. *Intercollegian*, June 1933.

21. Committee on the Negro Delegation to India, minutes, 13 March 1934, HTPP.

22. Augustine Ralla Ram to Frank Wilson, 28 June 1934, *PHWTV*1, 193–95.

23. One of the most influential works in this vein was Daniel Johnson Fleming's *Whither Bound in Missions?* (New York: Association Press, 1925). Fleming, a prominent professor at Union Theological Seminary who had been a missionary in India for twelve years, quoted an Indian statesman as saying, "Your Jesus is hopelessly handicapped by His connection to the West." For an analysis of this turn in thinking about missionary efforts, see William R. Hutchinson, *Errand to the World: American Protestant Thought and Foreign Missions* (Chicago: University of Chicago Press, 1987), 150.

24. "What We May Learn From India," in Walter Earl Fluker and Catherine Tumber, eds., *A Strange Freedom: The Best of Howard Thurman on Religious Experience and Public Life* (Boston: Beacon Press, 1998), 204.

25. "India Report." In his 1939 lecture series Mysticism and Social Change, see *PHWTV*2, Thurman would write, "It is the attitude of condescension, of arrogance, the 'holier than thou' manifestation much of which I have experienced in missions and observed on the mission field. It says, I am better than you, poor devil, I am really a very different order of being and out of my plenty, out of my advantage over you, I deign to come to your rescue. You ought to be grateful to me. In fact your gratitude must have in it a certain abjectness in order that my own position and ego may be rendered even more immune to attacks of unity."

26. "Biographical Essay," in *PHWTV*1.

27. Scovel, *I Must Speak*, 35–42.

28. Committee on the Negro Delegation to India, minutes, 13 March 1934, HTPP.

29. Frank Wilson (1900–1976) was a graduate of Lincoln University in Pennsylvania, and a national secretary of the YMCA at the time of his service on the India Committee. He would later serve as a dean of religion at both Lincoln and Howard universities.

30. "General Principles to Be Followed in Sending to the Student Christian Movement of India: A Deputation of Negro Representatives by the Student Christian Movement of the United States," April 1934, HTPP; Frank T. Wilson, "Minutes Regarding the Decision of the Personnel of the Proposed Delegation to India," 19 April 1934, HTPP.

31. HT to Elizabeth Harrington, 13 May 1935, *PHWTV*1, 258–60.

32. Ralla Ram to Frank Wilson, 28 June 1934, *PHWTV*1, 193–95.

33. "India Report," *PHWTV*2.

34. Ibid.

35. "What We May Learn From India," 203.

36. *WHAH*, 116–17. See Thurman's similar praise of storefront churches in Northern cities in comparison to mainline black congregations in "A 'Native Son' Speaks," *PHWTV*2.

37. "Colombo Journal," *PHWTV*1.

38. "India Report," citing (and slightly misquoting) Carl Sandburg, "Flying Fish," in *Smoke and Steel* (New York: Harcourt, Brace, and Howe, 1920), 189.

39. Ralla Ram to Frank Wilson, 28 June 1934.

40. E. Stanley Jones, *The Christ of the Indian Road* (New York: Abingdon, 1926).

41. HT to Elizabeth Harrington, 6 September 1934; *WHAH*, 116. Thurman did meet with Jones in Delhi, and it was appropriately bizarre. Because the members of the delegation were under a partial quarantine (Phenola Carroll had contracted a case of scarlet fever), they met on opposite ends of a tennis court, shouting questions and answers back and forth to each other. For Thurman's detestation of Jones, see his letter of 1 October 1936 to Frank Wilson where Thurman writes of Jones agreeing to participate in meetings of the National Preaching Mission in Atlanta despite the insistence of its organizers that no blacks be permitted to attend. HT to Frank Wilson, 1 October 1936, HTPP.

42. For the tour of the Fisk Jubilee Singers in Asia, see Andrew Ward, *Dark Midnight When I Rise: The Story of the Fisk Jubilee Singers* (New York: Amistad, 2000), 389–93.

43. Henrietta Wise to HT, 14 January 1936, *PHWTV*1, 320–21.

44. W. A. Visser't Hooft to Frank Wilson, 5 June 1934, HTPP.

45. Judson College (Rangoon, Burma) to HT, 18 December 1935, HTPP.

46. Winnifred Wygal to Elizabeth Harrington, 14 August 1934, HTPP.

47. Ralla Ram to Frank Wilson, 28 June 1934.

48. "India Report."

49. HT to Mabel Simpson, 14 June 1935, *PHWTV*1, 270–71.

50. Howard Thurman, "Mysticism and Social Change," lecture IV, 1978, Pacific School of Religion, HTPP.

51. Stanley Wolpert, *Gandhi's Passion: The Life and Legacy of Mahatma Gandhi* (New York: Oxford University Press, 2001), 174–81.

52. *WHAH*, 103.

53. W. E. B. Du Bois, "The Clash of Colour: Indians and American Negroes," in Bill V. Mullen and Cathryn Watson, eds., *W. E. B. Du Bois on Asia: Crossing the World Color Line* (Jackson: University of Mississippi, 2005), 68–73; Horne, *End of Empires*, 10.

54. *WHAH*, 121.

55. "Colombo Journal," 301.

56. *WHAH*, 121–22.

57. For more details on the complications of the selection process, see "Pilgrimage of Friendship," HT to members of the India Committee, 20 December 1935, *PHWTV*I, 184–86, 312–18.

58. Committee of the Negro Delegation, minutes, 30 January 1935, HTPP; Lorraine Nelson Spritzer and Jean B. Bergmark, *Grace Towns Hamilton and the Politics of Southern Change* (Athens: University of Georgia, 1997), 63.

59. HT to Elizabeth Harrington, 11 July 1935, *PHWTV*I, 273–74.

60. HT liked Edward Carroll but had expressed some prior doubts about his abilities, writing in confidence prior to the selection of Phenola Carroll that it was "not clear as to the contribution that may be expected" of him. HT to Elizabeth Harrington, 13 May 1935, *PHWTV*I, 258–60.

61. HT to Elizabeth Harrington, 11 July 1935.

62. Frank Wilson to HT, 20 July 1935, *PHWTV*I, 274–75.

63. *WHAH*, 112.

64. "HT to Members of the India Committee," 20 December 1935, HTPP.

65. "Detailed Schedule" *PHWTV*I.

66. *WHAH*, 108–9.

67. HT to Elizabeth Harrington, 11 July 1935.

68. HT to Grace Towns Hamilton, 12 October 1934, HTPP. For another version of the intellectual agenda, see HT to Elizabeth Harrington, 6 September 1934, HTPP.

69. HT to Robert Russa Moton, 30 August 1935, *PHWTV*I, 279.

70. P. Kodanda Rao to HT, 1 May 1935; Thurman to Harrington, 6 September 1934, both HTPP. Rao was the author of many books on India, among them *East Versus West: A Denial of Contrast* (London: G. Allen and Unwin, 1939).

71. For Sue Bailey Thurman's time in Mexico in 1935, and the questions raised about the possible requirement that she like other American blacks post bond before entering the country, see HT to Hubert Herring, 10 November 1934; HT to Sue Bailey Thurman, 12 February 1935; Thomas D. Bowman to William S. Nelson, 25 February 1935, *PHWTV*I, 217–19, 238–40, 242–43. On Mexican immigration

restrictions, see Gerald Horne, *Black and Brown: African Americans and the Mexican Revolution, 1910–1920* (New York: New York University Press, 2005), 183–92.

72. HT to Frank Wilson, 28 May 1935, *PHWTV*1, 261–63.

73. *WHAH*, 109.

74. "Our Delegation in India," *PHWTV*1, 329.

75. "Colombo Journal," *PHWTV*1, 300–305.

CHAPTER FOUR: THE NEGRO DELEGATION IN INDIA

1. "Our Delegation," *PHWTV*1, 328–32. The itinerary is reconstructed from "Detailed Schedule," *PHWTV*1.

2. *WHAH*, 128.

3. "Detailed Schedule," *PHWTV*1, 186–87.

4. "Mysticism and Social Change," Lecture 9, Pacific School of Religion, 1978; "Pilgrimage of Friendship," *PHWTV*1, 187.

5. HT to Ruth Taylor, 12 February 1936, HTPP.

6. "Detailed Schedule."

7. "Mysticism and Social Change," Lecture 9.

8. "Detailed Schedule."

9. Versions of "The Faith of the American Negro" appeared in the *Hindu* (Madras) 19 November 1935 and the *Times of India* (Bombay) 21 February 1936. Sue Bailey Thurman gave a version of the same talk, emphasizing the role of women, in Cochin, "Emancipation of the Negroes: Mrs. Thurman's Address," the *Hindu* (Madras) 28 November 1935, *PHWTV*1, 305–9.

10. "Commencement Address Delivered at the [Tennessee] A&I State College," *PHWTV*2.

11. "One Who Met Them: The Negro Delegation in Madras," *Guardian* (Madras), 12 December 1935.

12. T. J. George to HT, 14 January 1936, HTPP.

13. Ch. John to HT, 21 November 1935, HTPP.

14. *WHAH*, 123–24.

15. Henry W. Luce to HT, 12 February 1936, *PHWTV*1, 325–27; Bettis Aliston Garside, *One Increasing Purpose: The Life of Henry Winters Luce* (New York: F. H. Revell, 1948).

16. "The Perils of Immature Piety," *PHWTV*1, 51. Thurman quoted Tagore's translations of Kabir, a fifteenth-century Indian religious poet, from a Bengali and Hindi edition prepared by Kshiti Mohan Sen. Tagore, *One Hundred Poems of Kabir* (New York: Macmillan, 1915), xliii.

17. For a description of Santiniketan by Amartya Sen (a student there in the late 1930s and early 1940s), see *The Argumentative Indian: Writings on Indian History, Culture, and Identity* (New York: Picador, 2005), 115.

18. Paul Judson Braisted, *Indian Nationalism and the Christian Colleges* (New York: Association Press, 1935), 135.

19. Abernethy, *Meditations for Women*, 113 (see ch. 3, n. 14).

20. *WHAH*, 130.

21. Ibid., 129.

22. Rabindranath Tagore, *The Religion of Man* (London: George Allen and Unwin, 1931), which includes two appendices by Kshiti Mohan Sen.

23. For Sen's biography see Amartya Sen's foreword to the new edition, Kshiti Mohan Sen, *Hinduism* (New York: Penguin, 2005), vii–xxii. (The younger Sen had helped his grandfather translate the original version to English.) Sen came to Santiniketan at Tagore's pleading in 1908.

24. In his letter to philosopher W. E. Hocking of 29 May 1936, Thurman referred to his meeting at "Shantineketan" with "Dr. Sin," *PHWTV*2. In his autobiography he wrote of "Dr. Singh," the "head of the division of Oriental studies," at Shantineketan, *WHAH*, 129.

25. Sen, *Hinduism*, vii.

26. *WHAH*, 129.

27. Kshitimohan Sen, *Medieval Mysticism of India* (1930; repr., New Delhi: Oriental Books Reprint Corporation, 1974), dedication page.

28. Sen, *Medieval Mysticism of India*, xvii–xviii; Sen, *Hinduism*; also Amartya Sen, "Tagore and His India," in *The Argumentative Indian*, 89–120.

29. Sen, *Medieval Mysticism of India*, xvii–xviii and passim. For Sen on the Hindu mystic poet Dadu, see "Dadu and the Mystery of Form," in Rabindranath Tagore, *The Religion of Man* (London: George Allen and Unwin, 1931), 226–30.

30. For a recent account of the literature on the Bauls that emphasizes the importance of Sen and Tagore in creating an interest in the Bauls as a unique religious culture, see Jeanne Openshaw, *Seeking Bāuls of Bengal* (Cambridge, UK: Cambridge University Press, 2003), 32–54. Openshaw faults Sen for his failure to write about the Bauls' extravagantly esoteric sexual and scatological practices, an absence in Sen's writings that his grandson attributes to his natural prudishness. Sen, *Hinduism*, vii–xxii.

31. "India Report" *PHWTV*2.

32. Or so the meeting of Gandhi with the Negro Delegation has been invariably billed. But, as always, beware of claims of superlatives. In his autobiography, Gandhi writes about meeting an "American Negro" in Pretoria in 1893, at the very beginning of his public career as a campaigner for civil rights, who after a racial confrontation on a train helped him find a hotel that would accommodate non-whites. The anonymous Negro was probably a missionary. M. K. Gandhi, *Gandhi's Autobiography: The Story of My Experiments with Truth* (Washington, DC: Public Affairs Press, 1954), 149.

33. Kapur, *Raising Up a Prophet*, 29, 39, 10–71 passim (see chap. 3, n. 2).

34. Ibid., 39.

35. Muriel Lester to HT, 21 January 1935, *PHWTV*1, 231–33.

36. HT to Muriel Lester, 30 January 1935, *PHWTV*1, 236–37.

37. *WHAH*, 105–7; Kapur, *Raising Up a Prophet*, 83–85.

38. *WHAH*, 130–31. For Thurman's extant correspondence with Gandhi, see HT to Mahatma Gandhi, 9 September 1935; Mahatma Gandhi to HT, 6 October 1935, *PHWTV*1, 279–80, 282–83.

39. Gandhi took ill in early December and was diagnosed with high blood pressure; total bed rest was prescribed for a period. M. K. Gandhi, *Collected Works of Mahatma Gandhi*, vol. 62 (Delhi: Publications Division, Ministry of Information and Broadcasting, Government of India, 1975), 171, 173.

40. Mahadev Desai to HT, 26 January 1936, HTPP; Howard Thurman, "Mahatma Gandhi," unpublished 1948 sermon, *PHWTV*3.

41. "Dr. Jazz" to HT, 18 February 1936. For the reasons behind identifying "Dr. Jazz" as Teddy Weatherford, see *PHWTV*1, 327–28.

42. Bardoli, a small town near Bombay, was the site of an experiment in satyagraha and of total noncooperation with the British authorities from 1921 to 1922, and again in 1928. The Congress Party had an encampment, or ashram, in Bardoli that Gandhi frequently used; see Louis Fischer, *The Life of Mahatma Gandhi* (New York: Harper & Brothers, 1950), 197–99, 253–56. Bardoli was in a native state, Dharampur (now in Gujarat). Like other native Indian states, Dharampur was controlled by a prince and had some powers of self-rule. *Indian Year Book, 1935–36* (Bombay and Calcutta: Bennett, Coleman, 1935), 200–201; C. B. Dalal, *Gandhi: 1915–1948, A Detailed Chronology* (New Delhi: Gandhi Peace Foundation, 1971), 115.

43. "With Our Negro Guests," *Harijan*, 14 March 1936, *PHWTV*1, 332–41. This is the only contemporary record of the interview, but it is supplemented by Thurman's accounts of the conversation, which both corroborate and diverge from the account provided by Desai, though Thurman's accounts, unlike Desai's, were recollected from memory long after the interview. "Mahatma Gandhi," *WHAH*, 131–35.

44. Margaret Chatterjee, *Gandhi's Religious Thought* (South Bend, IN: University of Notre Dame Press, 1983), 1–2.

45. *WHAH*, 132. In the *Harijan* article, the length of the interview is given as two hours.

46. Ibid.

47. For a similar argument, see W. E. B. Du Bois, *Black Reconstruction in America* (1935; repr., New York: Athenaeum, 1992), 349–52.

48. For Johnson's support of Gandhi, see Kapur, *Raising Up a Prophet*, 85–86, 146–47.

49. "A 'Native Son' Speaks," *PHWTV*2.

50. For Gandhi's apparent criticism of intermarriage for Hindus and Muslims, see C. F. Andrews, *Mahatma Gandhi's Ideas, Including Selections From His Writings* (New York: Macmillan, 1930), 36–37, 57–59, 128. In a statement in the *Baltimore Afro-American* on 16 June 1934, Gandhi denied that he opposed intermarriage; see Kapur, *Raising Up a Prophet*, 77–79. Gandhi's position on the subject was complex and somewhat contradictory; see "Hinduism," in Homer Jack, ed., *The Gandhi Reader* (Bloomington: Indiana University Press, 1956), 167–72. In the end, Gandhi's commitment to celibacy made him feel that any sort of marriage was a distraction from the goal of ahimsa.

51. Robert A. Huttenback, *Gandhi in South Africa: British Imperialism and the Indian Question, 1869–1914* (Ithaca, NY: Cornell University Press, 1971), 43–44, 138. Certainly the basis of Gandhi's civil rights campaign in South Africa—that Indians had the same rights as white British subjects—would have become immensely more complicated if he had included blacks, and in the end Gandhi believed that national liberation could not imposed from without, even by well-meaning friends.

52. *WHAH*, 132.

53. "India Report."

54. For the appreciation of Islam among black American intellectuals in the early twentieth century, see Richard Brent Turner, *Islam in the African American Experience* (Bloomington: Indiana University Press, 1997), 47–90.

55. "India Report."

56. Ibid.

57. For the influence of Jainism on Gandhi and his notion of ahimsa, see Chatterjee, *Gandhi's Religious Thought*, 52–54.

58. Chatterjee, *Gandhi's Religious Thought*, 51. For Thurman on Paul, see Thurman, *Jesus and the Disinherited* (see intro., n. 25).

59. Whether George Lucas took the term directly from Gandhi or, more likely, secondhand from the Eastern philosophy he was reading at the time, there is a striking similarity between Gandhi's force and "the force" that animates Lucas's *Star Wars* trilogy, an all-pervasive moral and physical reality, one that can be mastered only by those in touch with its power, though Lucas's masters of "the force" did not seem to have much use for ahimsa.

60. "The Cosmic Guarantee" (1944), *PHWTV2*.

61. Judith Brown, *Gandhi: Prisoner of Hope* (New Haven, CT: Yale University Press, 1989), 187–88.

62. "Good News for the Underprivileged," *PHWTV1*, 266.

63. HT to James Farmer, 11 March 1943, *PHWTV2*.

64. Jack, *Gandhi Reader*, 310.

65. Ibid., 319.

66. Americans had tried to lure Gandhi across the Atlantic before. When

Gandhi had been invited to the United States in the mid-1920s, in what would have been a lucrative speaking tour, he told his sponsors, "If I go to America . . . I must go in my strength, and not my weakness, which I feel today. . . . I believe in thought-power more than in the power of the word, whether written or spoken. And if the movement that I seek to represent has vitality and has divine blessing upon it, it will permeate the whole world." "To American Friends" (1925), quoted in Wolpert, *Gandhi's Passion*, 123 (see chap. 3, n. 51).

67. *WHAH*, 134.

68. HT, "Mahatma Gandhi," 1948.

69. "With Our Negro Guests," *PHWTV*1, 337. In a 1958 talk that HT gave to Indian students, he described the end of the meeting as follows: "Just as we were about to take our leave he made one request. He asked that we sing 'Were You There When They Crucified My Lord?' adding that it is in suffering that the full-orbed meaning of Truth stood most utterly revealed. We sang as he and his few companions were in the attitude of prayer. It was after the long silence that the latterly oft-quoted statement was made: 'It may be that through your people and their suffering America may be saved.'" "Talk to Students from India," 1958, HTPP.

70. Chatterjee, *Gandhi's Religious Thought*, 15–16.

71. *WHAH*, 135.

72. Mabel E. Simpson to HT, 24 April 1936, HTPP.

73. "Even in the Face of Death," in *Down the Line: The Collected Writings of Bayard Rustin* (Chicago: Quadrangle Books, 1971), 103. Originally published in *Liberation*, February 1957.

74. "Uprising Quelled on India Frontier," *New York Times*, 28 August 1935. See also "British Bare Plot for Afghan Coup," *New York Times*, 25 June 1938.

75. "India Report."

76. HT, "The Historical Perspective," in *The Fellowship Church of All Peoples* ([San Francisco?]: [1947?]), 3.

77. *FOAD*, 24–25.

78. HT, "The New Heaven and the New Earth," *Journal of Negro Education* 27 (Spring 1958): 115–19.

CHAPTER FIVE: WHAT THURMAN LEARNED FROM INDIA

1. Peter Dana, "Dr. Thurman Speaks on Indian Question," *Pittsburgh Courier*, 29 August 1942.

2. Ibid.

3. Ralph Bunche, *A World View of Race* (Washington, DC: Association for Negro Folk Education, 1936); Holloway, *Confronting the Veil* (see chap. 2, n. 60).

4. "Negro Youth and the Washington Conference," *PHWTV*1, 67–69.

5. HT to Max Yergan, 15 January 1937, *PHWTV*2.

6. HT to Beverly Oaten, 23 March 1937, *PHWTV*2. Thurman had written about Yergan as early as 1925; see "Negro Youth and the Washington Conference," *PHWTV*2, 67–69. For Yergan's turbulent career, which concluded with a sharp turn to the far right and included, shamefully, an endorsement of apartheid, see David Anthony, *Max Yergan: Race Man, Internationalist, Cold Warrior* (New York: New York University Press, 2006).

7. See Lester A. Walton, "Negro Minister Fills Pulpit at Vassar," *PHWTV*1, 122–24.

8. HT purchased a number of books on socialism in 1932; Kirby Page to HT, 25 November 1932, HTPP. He told his friend Ralph Harlow, chaplain at Smith College in Massachusetts, running for Congress as a Socialist, "I only wish I was located in a community where that sort of activity would be possible for me," HT to Ralph Harlow, 6 November 1936, HTPP.

9. For anomalous (and not terribly reliable) evidence of Thurman's support of Communism in the late 1930s, see "Claims Communists [*sic*] Is Help to Church," *Richmond News-Leader*, 10 April 1937. For Thurman and Communism in the 1940s, see *WHAH*, 145.

10. As early as 1926, Thurman and Niebuhr were on the same program at the conference at which Thurman delivered his talk "Finding God." See "Student Group Bans War Aid," *Christian Science Monitor*, December 29, 1926. For Thurman's friendship with Niebuhr, see *PHWTV*1, 174–75, 229–30.

11. Reinhold Niebuhr, *Moral Man and Immoral Society* (New York: Charles Scribner, 1932); "Can We Be Christians Today?" *PHWTV*1, 251–52.

12. Cliff Mackay, "Political Strategy Needed—Neibuhr [*sic*]," *Atlanta Daily World*, 30 May 1932.

13. "The Significance of Jesus II: The Temptations of Jesus," *PHWTV*2.

14. "Mysticism and Social Change IV: Mysticism and Social Change," *PHWTV*2.

15. "The Significance of Jesus III: Love," *PHWTV*2.

16. Ibid.

17. See "The Fascist Masquerade" (1945), *PHWTV*3.

18. "What We May Learn from India," in *A Strange Freedom*, 200–210 (see chap. 3, n. 24).

19. Ibid.

20. "A 'Native Son' Speaks," *PHWTV*2. This was the (not terribly apt) title assigned by the weekly Jewish newspaper that published the lecture. Thurman's own title was "The Negro in the City."

21. Ibid.

22. For Bunche and the promise of interracial unions, see Holloway, *Confronting the Veil.*

23. "The Will to Segregation," *PHWTV2.*

24. "N.C. College Students Hear Howard U Chaplain," *Norfolk Journal and Guide,* 23 May 1942.

25. Dana, "Dr. Thurman Speaks on Indian Question."

26. *FOAD,* 97.

27. See, for example, William L. Savage (of Charles Scribner's Sons) to HT, 21 February 1938, HTPP.

28. Amos N. Wilder, review of *The Greatest of These,* by Howard Thurman, *Journal of Bible and Religion* 13, no. 4 (November 1945): 212.

29. Kosek, *Acts of Conscience,* 57 (see ch. 2. n. 50).

30. For Thurman's failed attempt to learn to drive, see *WHAH,* 56–57.

31. "He [Thurman] has never been known to travel without two things—a volume of detective stories and a book of poems. He is an authority on both types of literature, although he keeps the former as completely absent from his conversation as he most richly interjects the latter into sermons and discussions." Harold B. Ingalls, "Howard Thurman: Being a Few Highlights on an Interesting Life," *Intercollegian,* April 1941, 137–38.

32. Application form, Board of National Mission of the Presbyterian Church in USA, 17 July 1944, HTPP.

33. "Howard Divides Religion Responsibilities," *Norfolk Journal and Guide,* 15 August 1936; "Biographical Introduction," *PHWTV2.*

34. HT to Stella Scurlock, 27 May 1937, HTPP.

35. For the Howard Thurman Club, see *PHWTV1,* 230–31.

36. G. James Fleming, "Preacher at Large to Universities," *Crisis,* August 1939, 233, 251, 289.

37. Ibid.

38. For analysis of King speaking before white and black audiences, with Thurman's role as a forerunner, see Jonathan Rieder, *The Word of the Lord Is Upon Me: The Righteous Performance of Martin Luther King, Jr.* (Cambridge, MA: Harvard University Press, 2008).

39. Marshall Talley to HT, 3 March 1941, HTPP.

40. Fleming, "Preacher at Large to Universities." Another description of Thurman's speaking style from the same time comes from the National Urban League's Lester Granger: "He is a very intelligent person, with a great deal of 'audience charm'—but he does not rely on charming his audience; he also makes them think. I have found him to be in great demand by student groups of both races. His delivery is felt by some people to be a little on the flowery side, and his expressions frequently smack of mysticism. But every now and then he throws his mysticism

away and delivers his audience a hard sock on its intellectual solar plexus." Lester
Granger to Virgil Louder, 23 December 1941, HTPP.

41. Lucius L. Jones, "Society Slants," *Atlanta Daily World*, 24 February 1932.

42. James Farmer, *Lay Bare the Heart* (New York: Arbor House, 1985), 135.

43. "Commencement Address Delivered at the A&I State College," *PHWTV*2.

44. "Lauds Gandhi in Stirring Chapel Talk," *Atlanta Daily World*, 4 November
1936.

45. HT to J. Bernard Walton, Haverford College, 28 December 1934, HTPP.

46. William M. Ashby to HT, 2 February 1938; HT to William M. Ashby, 8
February 1938, *PHWTV*2.

47. *FOAD*, 47.

48. HT to B. F. Lamb, 18 August 1940, HTPP.

49. HT to Ruth Cunningham, 18 January 1937, HTPP.

50. "Kingdom of God," *PHWTV*2.

51. *WHAH*, 44–45.

52. HT to Lewis Douglass, 10 April 1940, HTPP.

53. Ibid.

54. Fleming, "Preacher at Large to Universities."

55. James Earl Massey, "Thurman's Preaching: Substance and Style," ed. Henry
James Young, *God and Human Freedom: A Festschrift in Honor of Howard Thurman*
(Richmond, IN: Friends United Press, 1983), 118–19. Beethoven was Thurman's
favorite composer and is a key to understanding him. Thurman wrote in his autobiography of his love for the late string quartets, and that "if he could share the
mystery of the lonely giant Beethoven I would have the clue to my own solitari-
ness." *WHAH*, 248.

56. Evilio Grillo, *Black Cuban, Black American: A Memoir* (Houston, TX: Arte
Público, 2000), 75.

57. Farmer, *Lay Bare the Heart*.

58. Ingalls, "Howard Thurman."

59. Ibid.

60. For details of Thurman's arrangements for the conferences, see the annota-
tions for "The Sources of Power for Christian Action" and "Christian, Who Calls
Me Christian?" *PHWTV*2. (In 1938, when the Methodist merger was completed,
black Methodists were relegated to a segregated Central Jurisdiction, separate and
not quite equal, where they would remain for the next three decades.)

61. *WHAH*, 165–67.

62. "The Sources of Power for Christian Action."

63. Ibid.

64. "Christian, Who Calls Me Christian?"

65. Ibid.

66. "The Sources of Power for Christian Action"; "Christian, Who Calls Me Christian?"

67. Niebuhr, *Moral Man and Immoral Society*, 241; Kosek, *Acts of Conscience*, 189–90.

68. "Mysticism and Social Change."

69. "Christian, Who Calls Me Christian?"

70. "The Significance of Jesus V: Jesus' Cross," *PHWTV*2.

71. Ibid.; "The Sources of Power for Christian Action,"

72. "The Sources of Power for Christian Action."

73. Kosek, *Acts of Conscience*, 163, 185 (see ch. 2, n. 50).

74. "The Sources of Power for Christian Action," "The Significance of Jesus IV: The Prayer Life of Jesus," *PHWTV*2. For the roots of Thurman's non-Trinitarianism in nineteenth- and early twentieth-century Protestant thought, see Evans, *Liberalism without Illusions*, 33–55 (see intro., n. 31).

75. *WHAH*, 165–67; HT to H. D. Bollinger, 19 January 1938, *PHWTV*2.

76. *New Directions for Campus Action* (New York: National Intercollegiate Christian Council, 1938), 7.

77. HT to A. Roland Elliott, 11 January 1938, HTPP.

78. "Man and the World of Nature," *PHWTV*2. Thurman is conspicuously absent from the otherwise excellent Kimberly A. Smith, *African American Environmental Thought: Foundations* (Lawrence: University of Kansas, 2007).

79. Thurman delivered a talk with the title "Christian, Who Calls Me Christian?" in Rochester as early as 1927. See *PHWTV*1, xcix.

80. "Christian, Who Calls Me Christian?"

81. Ingalls, "Howard Thurman."

82. Ruth Harris to HT, 3 January 1938, HTPP.

83. Robert Adams to HT, 5 January 1938, HTPP. Another letter stated that "your talk and reading on December 31 was so inspiring to me that I want to ask you for a copy, personally autographed." Richard Nutt to HT, 7 January 1938, HTPP.

84. Kenneth I. Brown to HT, 11 January 1938, HTPP.

85. George Collins to HT, 18 January 1938, HTPP.

86. Allan Hunter to HT, 28 January 1935, HTPP. The book was eventually published in 1939 without the chapters on Thurman and Lester. See Allan A. Hunter, *Three Trumpets Sound: Kagawa, Gandhi, Schweitzer* (New York: Association Press, 1939).

87. Hortense Powdermaker, *After Freedom: A Cultural Study in the Deep South* (New York: Viking, 1939), cited in Barbara Dianne Savage, *Your Spirits Walk Beside Us: The Politics of Black Religion* (Cambridge, MA: Harvard University Press, 2008), 87.

CHAPTER SIX: THURMAN'S WAR AND THE CREATION OF
THE FELLOWSHIP CHURCH

1. HT to Muriel Lester, 9 September 1935, *PHWTV*1, 280–81.

2. "Keep Awake," *PHWTV*2.

3. "Kingdom of God," *PHWTV*2.

4. HT to Juanita I. Harris, 10 August 1937, *PHWTV*2.

5. HT and Frank Wilson, "To the Fellowship of Religious Workers," September 1940, *PHWTV*2.

6. Allan A. Hunter to HT, 27 March 1939, *PHWTV*2. Once the war came to America, Thurman would continue to express his pacifism to friends like Hunter, writing that the "times are certainly crucial for all of us who believe that there is a better way to solve the problems of the world than by the destruction of life." HT to Allan A. Hunter, 21 August 1942, HTPP.

7. A. J. Muste to HT, 10 September 1940, HTPP; HT to A. J. Muste, 20 September 1940, *PHWTV*2.

8. A. J. Muste to HT, 14 March 1941, *PHWTV*2.

9. HT to Russell C. Barbour, 18 March 1940; HT to Russell C. Barbour, 31 May 1940, *PHWTV*2.

10. HT to William Stuart Nelson, 19 August 1942, *PHWTV*2. As far as we know, Thurman suffered no adverse consequences as a result of his conscientious objector status.

11. Kosek, *Acts of Conscience*, 189–90 (see ch. 2, n. 50).

12. HT to A. J. Muste, 20 September 1940, *PHWTV*2.

13. HT to John Nevin Sayre, 29 December 1941, *PHWTV*2.

14. "Religion in a Time of Crisis," *PHWTV*2.

15. "Annual Report of Dean of Chapel of Howard University, 1942–43," HTPP.

16. HT to M. C. Merriweather, 9 February 1943, HTPP.

17. HT to Florence Cate, 1 May 1943, HTPP.

18. HT to Patricia Van Blarcom, 17 April 1942, *PHWTV*2.

19. "The Will to Segregation," *PHWTV*2.

20. Greg Robinson, *A Tragedy of Democracy: Japanese Confinement in North America* (New York: Columbia University Press, 2009). For Thurman's visit to a California (probably Santa Anita) racetrack used as temporary housing for Japanese internees, see HT to Raymond Harvey, 29 July 1942, *PHWTV*2. For his visit to the Amache Relocation Center in Colorado, see Emiko Hinoki to HT, 4 April 1943, and HT to Emiko Hinoki, 31 May 1943, HTPP.

21. Thurman, *The Luminous Darkness*, 2 (see ch. 1, n. 7).

22. "The Will to Segregation."

23. HT to Kay H. Beach, 4 September 1942, HTPP.

24. Other black pacifists had similar concerns. James Farmer told A. J. Muste in

1942 that "the masses of Negroes will not become pacifists. Being Negro for them is tough enough." Farmer, *Lay Bare the Heart*, 111 (see ch. 5, n. 42).

25. Kay H. Beach, 4 September 1942, *PHWTV*2. The previous year, speaking of the reluctance of blacks to trust in nonviolent protests, he wrote that blacks had "been exploited in so many ways that it is hard for them to believe in anybody under any circumstances. . . . So much education has to be done to overcome this handicap." HT to A. J. Muste, 19 March 1941, *PHWTV*2.

26. HT to Kay H. Beach, 4 September 1942.

27. Kosek, *Acts of Conscience*, 146.

28. "The Will to Segregation."

29. Ibid.

30. HT to Sherwood Eddy, 26 May 1937, HTPP.

31. Risa L. Goluboff, *The Lost Promise of Civil Rights* (Cambridge, MA: Harvard University Press, 2007), 183–84.

32. Prentice Thomas to HT, 15 October 1937, HTPP.

33. William Sutherland to HT, 1 June 1941, HTPP. For Sutherland's career in Africa, see Gaines, *African Americans in Ghana* (see ch. 1, n. 45).

34. Glenda Elizabeth Gilmore, *Defying Dixie: The Radical Roots of Civil Rights, 1919–1950* (New York: W. W. Norton, 2008), 327, 315–47 passim; *Pauli Murray: The Autobiography of a Black Activist, Feminist, Lawyer, Priest, and Poet* (Knoxville: University of Tennessee Press, 1989), 228.

35. Farmer, *Lay Bare the Heart*, 135–36.

36. Ibid., 142, 143.

37. Ibid., 142.

38. James Farmer, "The Race Logic of Pacifism," *Fellowship* 8, no. 2 (February 1942): 24–25.

39. Kosek, *Acts of Conscience*, 178.

40. Farmer, *Lay Bare the Heart*, 89–116.

41. HT to James Farmer, 11 March 1943, *PHWTV*2.

42. "The Apostles of Sensitiveness," *PHWTV*3.

43. "The Cultural and Spiritual Prospect for a Nation Emerging from Total War," *PHWTV*3.

44. "The Will to Segregation."

45. HT to Lois Wendell, 4 June 1946, HTPP.

46. *FOAD*, 24.

47. Howard Thurman, "The Church of the Fellowship of All Peoples," *Common Ground* (Spring 1945): 29–31.

48. Howard Thurman, "The Historical Perspective," in *The Fellowship Church of All Peoples* ([San Francisco?]: [1947?]).

49. Thurman, "Historical Perspective," 3; Marjorie Penney to HT, 22 October

1942. HT evidently first spoke at the Fellowship Church in 1938. Marjorie Penney to HT, 25 April 1940, HTPP.

50. For interracial congregations in Detroit, Pasadena, and Los Angeles, see, respectively, Cedric Belfrage, *A Faith to Free the People* (Hinsdale, IL: Dryden Press, 1944); Jones, *The Christ of the American Road*, 97 (see ch. 3, n. 40); Dan Genung, *A Street Called Love: The Story of All Peoples Christian Church and Center, Los Angeles, CA* (Pasadena, CA: Hope Publishing House, 2000).

51. For the Harlem Ashram, see Kosek, *Acts of Conscience*, 186. For Farmer's wry account of his time in the Harlem Ashram, see *Lay Bare the Heart*, 149–50. For the Newark Ashram, see Andrew E. Hunt, *David Dellinger: The Life and Times of a Nonviolent Revolutionary* (New York: New York University Press, 2006), 41–42, 68–69, 72, 79. Farmer discusses a similar arrangement in Chicago in *Lay Bare the Heart*, 90–92.

52. Thurman, *FOAD*, 29–30. For San Francisco during the war, see Albert S. Broussard, *Black San Francisco: The Struggle for Racial Equality in the West, 1900–1954* (Lawrence: University of Kansas Press, 1993), 133–92.

53. Alfred Fisk to HT, 15 October 1943, *PHWTV*3.

54. HT to Alfred G. Fisk, 25 October 1943, in *PHWTV*3.

55. For Thurman's other vocational opportunities, see *PHWTV*3.

56. *FOAD*, 31.

57. Broussard, *Black San Francisco*, 185; *FOAD*, 31–32.

58. *FOAD*, 31–32.

59. HT to Alfred Fisk, 2 March 1944, *PHWTV*3.

60. HT to Alfred Fisk 11 April 1944, *PHWTV*3.

61. HT to Alfred G. Fisk, 3 January 1944, *PHWTV*3. Thurman was earning $4,100 at Howard and would earn only $2,400 at the Fellowship Church.

62. Alfred Fisk to A. L. Roberts, 24 December 1943, HTPP.

63. Thurman's two books about it: *FOAD* and *The First Footprints: The Dawn of the Idea of the Church for the Fellowship of All Peoples, Letters between Alfred Fisk and Howard Thurman, 1943–1944* (San Francisco, 1975).

64. See Alfred Fisk to HT, 28 December 1943, HTPP; Alfred Fisk to HT, 17 April 1944; Alfred Fisk to HT, 16 May 1944; HT to Paul Robeson, 21 April 1944, all *PHWTV*3; *FOAD*, 45–46.

65. The Cleage-Fisk contretemps is discussed at greater length in Angelo Herndon to HT, 12 May 1944, *PHWTV*3.

66. *WHAH*, 145.

67. Thurman, "The Historical Perspective."

68. HT to Alfred Fisk, 12 November 1943, *PHWTV*3.

69. *FOAD*, 37.

70. For the three versions of the Commitment, see *FOAD*, 37–39, 51–52, 158.

71. George Haynes to HT, 15 September 1945, *PHWTV*3.

72. John Haynes Holmes to HT, 16 March 1946, *PHWTV*3.

73. *FOAD*, 69–70.

74. Alfred Fisk to HT, 15 October 1943, *PHWTV*3.

75. Thurman, "The Historical Perspective."

76. *FOAD*, 47.

77. Ibid., 46–50.

78. Thurman, "The Historical Perspective."

79. Ibid.

80. Ibid.

81. Jacob A. Long to HT, 10 August 1945, HTPP.

82. *FOAD*, 46–50.

83. Benjamin Mays to HT, 22 October 1946, *PHWTV*3.

84. HT to Emily Crosby, 16 May 1946, *PHWTV*3.

85. HT to William Stuart Nelson, 16 May 1946, *PHWTV*3.

86. Alfred Fisk to HT, 27 August 1946, *PHWTV*3.

87. HT to Adelbert Lindley, 14 March 1945, HTPP.

88. *FOAD*, 71–72.

89. HT to Ann Perry, 6 May 1948, HTPP.

90. HT to Alfred Fisk, 19 May 1944, *PHWTV*3.

91. Alfred Fisk to Charles Moffat, 2 August 1945, HTPP.

92. For instances of Thurman's advice to other potential interracial congregations, see "Introduction," *PHWTV*3.

93. HT to Frank T. Wilson, 16 May 1946, *PHWTV*3.

94. HT to Edmund Gordon, 5 June 1946, HTPP.

95. Homer A. Jack, "The Emergence of the Interracial Church," *Social Action* 13, no. 1 (January 1947): 31–38; George Edmund Haynes, "Along the Interracial Front: An Interracial Experiment Station," Department of Race Relations, Federal Council of Churches, October 5, 1945, HTPP.

96. *FOAD*, 53.

97. *WHAH*, 162.

98. Langston Hughes, "Dixie in the Golden Gate," *Chicago Defender*, May 6, 1944.

99. Cited in Savage, *Your Spirits Walk Beside Us*, 217 (see ch. 5, n. 87). Martin Luther King Jr. makes much the same point in "A Knock at Midnight," *Strength to Love* (New York: Harper and Row, 1963), 57.

100. *FOAD*, 157.

101. Broussard, *Black San Francisco*, 189.

102. W. E. B. Du Bois, "The Winds of Time," *Chicago Defender*, 8 June 1946.

103. Broussard, *Black San Francisco*, 189.

104. *WHAH,* 168. In 1946 Thurman was offered a professorship at the University of Iowa but turned it down because of his commitments at the Fellowship Church. See "Biographical Essay," *PHWTV*4.

EPILOGUE: MARTIN LUTHER KING JR. AND
JESUS AND THE DISINHERITED

1. Rieder, *The Word of the Lord Is Upon Me,* 277 (see ch. 5, n. 38).

2. Davis, *A Clashing of the Soul,* 313–14 (see ch. 1, n. 40).

3. The course "The Life of Christ," which Thurman taught three or four times during his years at Spelman, was described as "a course designed to introduce the students to a scientifically historical and spiritual appreciation of the life of Jesus, based primarily on the materials found in the four Gospels." *Catalogue of Spelman College, 1928–29* (Atlanta, 1928), 27.

4. *WHAH,* 79.

5. For Thurman's knowledge and reliance on Case, see "The Significance of Jesus I: Jesus the Man of Insight," *PHWTV*2.

6. Jesse O. Thomas, "Urban League Weekly Bulletin," *Atlanta Constitution,* 28 February 1932.

7. "Tired of Being Underdog, Says Forum Speaker," *Baltimore Afro-American,* 19 December 1932.

8. "Sincerity Will Not Work, Thurman Tells N.A.A.C.P.," *Baltimore Afro-American,* 4 April 1932.

9. "Hold Founders Day at Florida Normal," *Chicago Defender,* 25 April 1931.

10. "Sincerity Will Not Work."

11. "Good News for the Underprivileged," *PHWTV*1, 263–70.

12. "Colombo Journal," *PHWTV*1, 303.

13. "The Significance of Jesus I."

14. Harold Pflug to HT, 28 October 1938, HTPP.

15. Thurman, *Jesus and the Disinherited,* 36–37, 65, 88 (see intro, n. 25).

16. HT to Aubrey and Marigold Burns, 23 April 1948; Nolan B. Harmon to HT, 29 May 1948, *PHWTV*3.

17. Pat Beaird to HT, 1 November 1948, *PHWTV*3.

18. Vincent Harding, foreword to *Jesus and the Disinherited,* ii (see intro., n. 25).

19. Ibid., 109.

20. Gertrude Martin, "Thurman's Book Treats Problems of Oppressed," *Chicago Defender,* 11 June 1949. It did, however, receive generally positive, if brief, reviews in academic religious journals. By far the most touching response to *Jesus and the Disinherited* was from Thurman's mother, then in failing health, who wrote him in her rough-hewn prose, "My dear Son I thank you for the book It A great

book. . . . I wonder where you got so much knowledge from God only could give it to You I am verry thankful to God for permitting me to be your mother." Alice Sams to HT, 4 May 1949, *PHWTV*3.

21. Thurman certainly knew King's father, Martin Luther King Sr., a 1930 Morehouse graduate, and the two would occasional appear together, as in 1942 when Thurman gave the seventy-fifth anniversary sermon at Morehouse, while the elder King offered the benediction. William A. Fowlkes Jr., "Overflow Crowd Hears Dr. Thurman," *Atlanta Daily World*, 16 February 1942.

22. Howard Thurman, "The Commitment," March 1949, from *The Growing Edge*, *PMLKJ*, 6:661.

23. *PMLKJ*, 1:281.

24. Thurman, *Jesus and the Disinherited*, 49–50 (see intro., n. 25).

25. In an earlier paper for the same course, prepared from mid-September to late November 1949, "Six Talks in Outline," beginning a section entitled "Who Was Jesus of Nazareth?" King borrowed largely verbatim from *Jesus and the Disinherited*, 15–16, in *PMLKJ*, 1:245.

26. Martin Luther King Jr., *Stride Toward Freedom: The Montgomery Story*, introduction by Clayborne Carson (1958; repr., Boston: Beacon Press, 2010), xv–xvii, 83–86.

27. *WHAH*, 254–55.

28. HT to A. W. Dent, 14 December 1954, *PHWTV*4.

29. In 1959, the Baptist minister and future politician Walter E. Fauntroy reminded King that, in the summer of 1953, at an interseminary conference at Virginia Union University in Richmond, King had quoted "Howard Thurman's treatment of the story of Elijah at Mt. Horeb." See *PMKLJ*, 5:469–70.

30. Lewis V. Baldwin, *There Is a Balm in Gilead: The Cultural Roots of Martin Luther King Jr.* (Minneapolis: Fortress Press, 1991), 300–301; Thomas F. Jackson, *From Civil Rights to Human Rights: Martin Luther King, Jr., and the Struggle for Economic Justice* (Philadelphia: University of Pennsylvania, 2007), 25.

31. For Thurman's influence on King's early sermons, all preached at Dexter Avenue Baptist Church, see "A Religion of Doing," 4 July 1954, *PMLKJ*, 6:170–74; notes to "God's Love," preached 5 September 1954, *PMLKJ*, 6:179–80; "Worship," 7 August 1955; "Redirecting our Missionary Zeal," 22 January 1956, *PMLKJ*, 6:249–50; "Overcoming an Inferiority Complex," 14 July 1957, *PMLKJ*, 6:303–16; "Living Under the Tensions of Modern Life," September 1956, *PMLKJ*, 6:262–70; "Unfulfilled Hopes," 5 April 1959, *PMLKJ*, 6:357–67. For Thurman references and allusions in King's first sermon collection, see "A Knock at Midnight," "The Death of Evil Upon the Seashore," and "Shattered Dreams," in *Strength to Love*, 59, 80, 92 (see ch. 6, n. 99).

32. For details of Thurman's relation to King after 1954, see *PHWTV*4.

33. *WHAH*, 253–54.

34. Martin Luther King Jr. to HT, 8 November 1958, cited in Walter Earl Fluker, *Ethical Leadership: The Quest for Character, Civility and Community* (Minneapolis: Fortress Press, 2009), 29.

35. Taylor Branch, *Parting the Waters: America in the King Years, 1954–63* (New York: Simon & Schuster, 1988), 245.

36. *PMKLJ*, 3:73.

37. Lerone Bennett Jr., *What Manner of Man: A Biography of Martin Luther King, Jr., 1929–1968* (New York: Pocket Books, 1968), 57–58.

38. King also had copies of *FOAD* and *The Growing Edge*. See *PMLKJ*, 6:652.

39. Dorrien, *The Making of American Liberal Theology*, 566, 558 (see ch. 1, n. 70).

Index

Adams, Robert, 220n83
ahimsa: kingdom of heaven and, 108–9; marriage and, 215n50; satyagraha vs., 103–4; self-immolation and, 109–11; soul force as, 104–6, 107, 108–11, 113, 215n59; vitality and, 107–8. *See also* nonviolent resistance
Allen, Devere, 60
"Amazing Grace" (Newton), xix
Ambrose, Nancy (grandmother), xx, 2, 4, 5–6, 8–9, 10–11, 37, 61
American Baptist Home Mission Society, 12
American Fascisti Order of the Black Shirts, 184
"Apostles of Sensitiveness" (Thurman–sermons), 127, 163–64
Athenaeum (literary magazine), 18
Atlanta Baptist College, 14. *See also* Morehouse College

Bailey, Sue, 63. *See also* Thurman, Sue Bailey (spouse)
Baldwin, Lewis, 192
Baptist faith: and doctrine of the virgin birth, 28; and HT membership in Mount Bethel Baptist Church, 6–7; National Baptist Convention, 131, 153; ordination of HT into, 28. *See also* Rochester Theological Seminary

Barbour, Russell C., 221n9
Bardoli (Dharampur), 99, 214n42
"Basis of Sex Morality" (Thurman–student work), 37–40, 101
Bauls of Bengal, 95, 213n30
Beach, Kay H., 156–57, 221n23, 222n25, 222n26
Beaird, Pat, 225n17
Bennett, Lerone, 194
Bethune, Mary McLeod, 8, 202n22
Bethune-Cookman College, 8, 55
Black, Hugh, 135
Black Reconstruction (Du Bois), 100
Boston University, 146, 180, 187, 191–92
Branch, Taylor, 191, 193–94
Broussard, Alfred, 179
Brown, Judith, 106
Brown, Kenneth I., 220n84
Buddhism, xv–xvi, xxi, 91, 102
Bunche, Ralph, 64, 119
Burns, Aubrey and Marigold, 225n16

"Can It Be Truly Said That the Existence of a Supreme Spirit Is a Scientific Hypothesis?" (Thurman–student work), 29
Carroll, Edward: on miscegenation laws, 101; Negro spirituals and, 112; participation in Negro Delegation, xii, 86, 87, 99; selection for Negro Delegation, xii, 80, 81, 211n60; United Methodist career, 80

229

vitality, 107–8
Voss, Dave, 30

war. *See* Civil War; Italo-Ethiopian
War (1935); World War I; World
War II
Washington, Booker T., 16, 100
"What We Learn from India"
(Thurman–lectures and talks),
123–24
White, Walter, 160
"Will to Segregation" (Thurman–
articles, essays, and papers),
157–59, 164–65, 177–78
Wilson, Frank T.: antiwar stance
of, 152; correspondence with
Vissert' Hooft, 76, 210n44; correspondence with HT, 210n41,
211n62, 212n72, 224n93; correspondence with Ralla Ram, 75,
209n22, 210n32, 210n39, 210n47;
and membership on India Com-
mittee, 72–73, 75, 76, 209n29
Wise, Henrietta, 210n43
With Head and Heart (Thurman–
books), 180, 197
women: feminism, 35, 37–40, 101;
HT on marginalization of women,
39; interracial relations and, 101,
215n50; marriage and, 37–39, 101,
215n50; Muslim women in India,
103; Sakai group, 16, 166, 167, 169;
Sue Bailey Thurman on, 87–88
Women and Labor (Schreiner), 35, 38
Workers Defense League, 160
World Student Christian Federation
(WSCF), 69, 71–72
World Student Federation Confer-
ence (Mysore), 66

World War I, 31, 35, 59, 70–71, 125–26,
126–27, 151
World War II: and antidiscrimination
legislation, 154; anti-imperialism
vs. pacifism, 117, 152–53; conscientious objectors, 152–53; impact on
black soldiers, 153–57; interracial
church movement and, 166; interracial relations during, 126, 151,
155–59; Japanese internments, 155–
56; moral equivalence argument of
pacifists, 158; Nazi persecution of
Jewish people, 109–10, 152
Wygal, Winnifred, 66, 67, 68, 77,
208n6, 208n8, 210n46

Yergan, Max, 21, 119–20, 217n6
YMCA (Young Men's Christian
Association): Sue Bailey and,
63; black colleges and, 21, 208n9;
Juliette Derricotte and, 66–67,
68–69; HT involvement with, 21,
22, 31, 45, 55; India Committee
and, 72; Mordecai Wyatt Johnson
and, 14; Herbert King and, 208n9;
Kings Mountain, NC, confer-
ence, 14, 21, 45, 130; racial relations
and, 21–22, 66–67, 72, 208n9; St.
Antoine Street YMCA, 55, 130;
Student Christian Movement and,
xii, 65; Frank Wilson and, 209n29;
YMCA conferences, 14, 21. *See also*
Student Christian Movement
YWCA (Young Women's Christian
Association), xii, 21, 63, 65, 66, 68,
72, 86. *See also* Derricotte, Juliette;
Student Christian Movement;
YMCA (Young Men's Christian
Association)

DATE DUE

GAYLORD   #3523PI   Printed in USA